Affirmative Action, Ethnicity, and Conflict

This book deals with two crucial questions that policy-makers have long debated. First, should a government adopt policies that are targeted at specific communities or those that are universal in nature when dealing with serious social inequalities that could lead to conflict between ethnic groups? Second, would a race-based orientation to policy planning inevitably lead to the essentializing of the identities of ethnic groups, fostering in the long run the idea of insurmountable or unalterable differences between these communities that could lead to conflict?

To examine if targeting ethnic groups to resolve socio-economic inequalities is the best mechanism to resolve or reduce inter-racial disputes, the methodology adopted here examines the implementation of a progressive though controversial policy – affirmative action. This study involves a comparative study of selected multi-ethnic and multi-religious countries that have adopted affirmative action to target particular communities as a means to resolve social and economic inequalities. This pioneering study reviews affirmative action in developed and developing countries, including the United States of America, India, Malaysia, Fiji, South Africa, Northern Ireland and Brazil.

Edmund Terence Gomez is a Professor of Political Economy in the Faculty of Economics & Administration at the University of Malaya.

Ralph Premdas is Professor of Public Policy at the University of the West Indies.

Routledge Malaysian studies series
Published in association with Malaysian Social Science Association (MSSA)
Series Editors:
Mohammed Hazim Shah
University of Malaya
A.B. Shamsul
University Kebangsaan Malaysia
Terence Gomez
University of Malaya

The Routledge Malaysian Studies Series publishes high quality scholarship that provides important new contributions to knowledge on Malaysia. It also signals research that spans comparative studies, involving the Malaysian experience with that of other nations.

This series, initiated by the Malaysian Social Science Association (MSSA) to promote study of contemporary and historical issues in Malaysia, and designed to respond to the growing need to publish important research, also serves as a forum for debate on key issues in Malaysian society. As an academic series, it will be used to generate new theoretical debates in the social sciences and on processes of change in this society.

The Routledge Malaysian Studies Series will cover a broad range of subjects including history, politics, economics, sociology, international relations, geography, business, education, religion, literature, culture, and ethnicity. The series will encourage work adopting an interdisciplinary approach.

1 **The State of Malaysia**
   Ethnicity, equity and reform
   Edited by Edmund Terence Gomez

2 **Feminism and the Women's Movement in Malaysia**
   An unsung (r)evolution
   Cecilia Ng, Maznah Mohamad and Tan Beng Hui

3 **Governments and Markets in East Asia**
   The politics of economic crises
   Jungug Choi

4 **Health Care in Malaysia**
   The dynamics of provision, financing and access
   Edited by Chee Heng Leng and Simon Barraclough

5 **Politics in Malaysia**
The Malay dimension
Edited by Edmund Terence Gomez

6 **Privatization in Malaysia**
Regulation, rent-seeking and policy failure
Jeff Tan

7 **The State, Development and Identity in Multi-Ethnic Societies**
Ethnicity, equity and the Nation
Edited by Nicholas Tarling and Edmund Terence Gomez

8 **Race and Multiculturalism in Malaysia and Singapore**
Edited by Daniel P.S. Goh, Matilda Gabrielpillai, Philip Holden and Gaik Cheng Khoo

9 **Media, Culture & Society in Malaysia**
Edited by Yeoh Seng Guan

10 **Islam and Politics in Southeast Asia**
Edited by Johan Saravanamuttu

11 **Malaysia's Development Challenges**
Graduating from the middle
Edited by Hal Hill, Tham Siew Yean and Ragayah Haji Mat Zin

12 **Ethnicization and Identity Construction in Malaysia**
Frederik Holst

13 **Malaysia and the Developing World**
The Asian Tiger on the Cinnamon Road
Jan Stark

14 **Affirmative Action, Ethnicity, and Conflict**
Edited by Edmund Terence Gomez and Ralph Premdas

Affirmative Action, Ethnicity, and Conflict

Edited by Edmund Terence Gomez and
Ralph Premdas

LONDON AND NEW YORK

First published 2013
by Routledge

2 Park Square, Milton Park, Abingdon, Oxon OX14 4RN
711 Third Avenue, New York, NY 10017, USA

Routledge is an imprint of the Taylor & Francis Group, an informa business

First issued in paperback 2016

Copyright © 2013 selection and editorial material, Edmund Terence Gomez and Ralph Premdas; individual chapters, the contributors

The right of Edmund Terence Gomez and Ralph Premdas to be identified as the authors of the editorial material, and of the authors for their individual chapters, has been asserted in accordance with sections 77 and 78 of the Copyright, Designs and Patents Act 1988.

All rights reserved. No part of this book may be reprinted or reproduced or utilised in any form or by any electronic, mechanical, or other means, now known or hereafter invented, including photocopying and recording, or in any information storage or retrieval system, without permission in writing from the publishers.

Notice:
Product or corporate names may be trademarks or registered trademarks, and are used only for identification and explanation without intent to infringe.

British Library Cataloguing in Publication Data
A catalogue record for this book is available from the British Library

Library of Congress Cataloging in Publication Data
Affirmative action, ethnicity, and conflict / edited by Edmund Terence Gomez and Ralph Premdas.
  p. cm. – (Routledge Malaysian studies series ; 14)
  Includes bibliographical references and index.
  1. Affirmative action programs. 2. Ethnicity. 3. Social conflict.
  4. Equality. I. Gomez, Edmund Terence. II. Premdas, Ralph R.
  HF5549.5.A34A4633 2013
  331.13′3–dc23
                                                                    2012021780

ISBN: 978-0-415-62768-9 (hbk)
ISBN: 978-1-138-20558-1 (pbk)

Typeset in Times New Roman
by Wearset Ltd, Boldon, Tyne and Wear

Contents

List of tables ix
Notes on the contributors x
Acknowledgements and preface xi
Abbreviations and acronyms xiii

Introduction: affirmative action, horizontal inequalities, and equitable development 1
EDMUND TERENCE GOMEZ AND RALPH PREMDAS

1 **Poverty, equality, and affirmative action in India** 27
SUNITA PARIKH

2 **The struggle for equality and justice: affirmative action in the United States of America** 43
RALPH PREMDAS

3 **Ethnicity, economy, and affirmative action in Malaysia** 67
HWOK-AUN LEE, EDMUND TERENCE GOMEZ, AND SHAKILA YACOB

4 **Coerced preferences: affirmative action and horizontal inequality in Fiji** 95
STEVEN RATUVA

5 **Affirmative action in South Africa: disadvantaging the many for the benefit of the few** 126
ANTHEA JEFFERY

6 **Power-sharing, communal contestation, and equality: affirmative action, identity, and conflict in Northern Ireland** 154
COLIN HARVEY

7 **Appraising affirmative action in Brazil** 183
   JOAZE BERNARDINO-COSTA AND FERNANDO ROSA

   Index 204

Tables

1.1	Percentage of SCs in central government posts by category: 1965, 1995, and 2001	33
1.2	Percentage below the poverty line (BPL), 1983, 1993–4, 2004–5	34
3.1	Share capital ownership (at par value) by ethnic group, 1970–2008 (%) (Malaysia)	74
3.2	Summary of affirmative action programmes and notable features	79
3.3	Percentage of labour force with tertiary education, by race group	80
3.4	Unemployment rates within ethnic group, by highest education attained, 1995 and 2007	80
3.5	Ethnic representation in occupation groups (percentage of Malaysian employed population), 1970–2000	83
3.6	Ethnic representation in occupation groups (percentage of Malaysian employed population), 2000–2005	84
3.7	Teachers and nurses as percentage of total professionals and technicians, within race, 2000–2005	85
3.8	Registered professionals by race, percentage of total	85
4.1	Civil service staff turnover, 1987–1994	105
4.2	Occupational categories of economically active population by ethnicity (Indians and Fijians only), 1986	108
4.3	Equity index for selected different professions	116
4.4	Allocations towards rural and outer island development programmes: 2009 budget	118
7.1	Modality of affirmative action in federal and state public universities in Brazil	189
7.2	Beneficiaries of affirmative action in federal and state public universities in Brazil	190

Contributors

Joaze Bernardino-Costa is Professor of Sociology at the University of Brasilia, Brazil.

Edmund Terence Gomez is Professor of Political Economy at the University of Malaya, Malaysia.

Colin Harvey is Professor of Human Rights Law at Queen's University, Belfast, Northern Ireland.

Anthea Jeffery is Head of Special Research, Muriell Horrell Research Fellow, and Dick Gawith Fellow at the South African Institute of Race Relations in Johannesburg, South Africa.

Hwok-Aun Lee is Senior Lecturer at the Faculty of Economics & Administration, University of Malaya, Malaysia.

Sunita Parikh is Associate Professor of Political Science at the Washington University in St. Louis, USA.

Ralph Premdas is Professor in the Sir Arthur Institute of Social and Economic Research (SALISES) at the University of the West Indies, St. Augustine, Trinidad and Tobago.

Steven Ratuva is a political sociologist at the Center for Pacific Studies, University of Auckland, New Zealand.

Fernando Rosa, an anthropologist and historian, is Senior Research Fellow at University of Malaya, Malaysia.

Shakila Yacob is Associate Professor of History at the University of Malaya, Malaysia.

Acknowledgements and preface

When this research project was conceived at the University of Malaya, our primary concern was to understand why affirmative action, an extremely progressive social policy implemented to redress serious social and economic inequities in multi-ethnic and multi-religious countries, has been the subject of much controversy. We well understood that the rise of ethnic inequalities, including those that had led to serious conflicts, was due to a range of social, economic, and political inequities that had emerged because of the mode of development as well as the form of political governance.

While discussing these issues our attention was drawn to the manner in which public policies were conceived and implemented. It was evident that the governments of multi-ethnic countries have adopted different strategies to deal with inequality and the issues of exclusion and marginalization. Of particular concern to us was whether policy mechanisms to resolve structural inequalities in societies should be universal in orientation or targeted at disadvantaged groups. As we delved more into this debate we were compelled to deal with the burgeoning literature on horizontal inequalities. Proponents of a horizontal inequality perspective have argued that ethnic conflict and inter-ethnic social and economic differences can be better resolved by targeting ethnic groups that are in most need of help. Our primary concern, however, given the case of Malaysia, was whether the employment of race-based policies was a viable method to help resolve social inequities and help promote cohesion in a multi-ethnic context.

To determine if targeting ethnic groups to resolve horizontal inequalities is the best mechanism to help resolve or reduce inter-racial conflict, we felt that one insightful methodology we could adopt would be an examination of the implementation of the policy of affirmative action. Affirmative action-based initiatives had been implemented in a number of countries from a perspective that was horizontal in orientation. It was then proposed we conceive a project involving a comparative study of selected multi-ethnic or multi-religious countries that have adopted affirmative action targeting particular communities as a means to resolve social and economic inequalities.

We invited Ralph Premdas, Professor of Public Policy from the University of the West Indies, who has published extensively on the issue of ethnic conflict, to join the University of Malaya to help us implement this project. A series of debates ensued regarding the policy of affirmative action in different countries, after an extensive review of the literature was carried out. We then identified a number of countries for joint assessment. A workshop was convened in April 2010 in Kuala Lumpur where we gathered academics from eight countries to deliver preliminary ideas on the working paper that we had prepared. The scope of the research to be done was determined at this workshop. In November 2010 we gathered again at a conference convened in Kuala Lumpur, attended also by guests from the Malaysian government and academics from a few countries who were called on to comment on the papers that were tabled for discussion. The countries assessed in this conference included Malaysia, South Africa, Fiji, Northern Ireland, India, the United States, and Brazil.

I am grateful to a number of people who helped us implement this project. Wilhelm Hofmeister of the Konrad-Adenauer Stiftung (KAS), who was approached to fund this study, was most supportive of the need to undertake comparative research that would help inform the nature of social policies that promote ethnic cohesion. I am deeply indebted to the academics and administrative staff at the University of Malaya's International Institute of Public Policy and Management (INPUMA), which hosted the workshop and conference. I wish to mention in particular the support of Khadijah Khalid and Sharifah Mariam Alhabshi, Director and Deputy Director respectively of INPUMA, who ensured that this project ran smoothly. Ralph Premdas devoted a year to this project as Visiting Professor at INPUMA. Ralph also spent much time and effort discussing research ideas with academics and post-graduate students at various faculties at the University of Malaya. A number of academics commented on the papers at the workshop and conference. These academics include Gregor Benton, Michaeline Crichlow, Stephen Small, Siri Hettige, Lily Zubaidah Rahim, Hazim Shah, Hussein Ahmad, and Sulaiman Mahbob. I acknowledge the generous support I received from the academics who prepared articles for this volume. All of them, Joaze Bernardino-Costa, Colin Harvey, Anthea Jeffery, Hwok-Aun Lee, Sunita Parikh, Steven Ratuva, Fernando Rosa, and Shakila Yacob, graciously accepted the invitation to join this project and invested much time in it by attending two meetings, preparing articles, and responding promptly to our numerous requests for revisions. I am very grateful that Peter Sowden, Commissioning Editor at Routledge, recognized the value of the study and agreed to have this book published. While all of them have contributed enormously to this venture, I remain responsible for any shortcomings in this volume.

Terence Gomez,
University of Malaya,
February 2012

Abbreviations and acronyms

AMPS	All Media and Products Surveys
ANC	African National Congress
APNI	Alliance Party of Northern Ireland
BEE	Black Economic Empowerment
BEECom	Black Economic Empowerment Commission
BJP	Bharatiya Janata Party
CEE	Commission for Employment Equity
CLFS	Commercial Loans to Fijians Scheme
CSI	Corporate Social Investment
CSS	Compulsory Savings Scheme
CUT	Unified Workers' Central
DMR	Department of Mineral Resources
DP8	Development Plan 8
DP9	Development Plan 9
DR	Distribution Ratio
DTI	Department of Trade and Industry
DUP	Democratic Unionist Party
ECNI	Equality Commission for Northern Ireland
EDO	Economic Development Officers
EEOC	Equal Employment Opportunity Commission
EI	Equity Index
EIMCOL	Equity Investment Management Company Limited
EPF	Employees Provident Fund
ESCAP	Economic and Social Commission for Asia and the Pacific
FAB	Fijian Affairs Board
FBV	The Fijian Banan Venture
FDF	Fijian Development Fund
FDI	Foreign Direct Investment
FEC	Fair Employment Commission
FET	Fair Employment Tribunal
FETO	Fair Employment and Treatment Order
FHC	Fijian Holdings Company
FHL	Fijian Holdings Limited

FICAC	Fiji Islands Commission Against Corruption
FICAC	Fiji Independent Commission Against Corruption
FIG	Fijian Initiative Group
FNPF	The Fiji National Provident Fund
FTL	Fiji Television Limited
GAO	Government Accountability Office
GDP	Gross Domestic Product
GICL	Gaunavou Investments Company Limited
GLCs	Government-linked Companies
GSP	Global Supplier Programme
GTDEO	Task Force for the Elimination of Discrimination in Employment and Occupation
GTI	Inter-ministerial Task Force
GTP	Government Transformation Programme
HICOM	Heavy Industries Corporation of Malaysia
IBGE	Brazilian Institute of Geography and Statistics
IJR	Institute of Justice and Reconciliation
ILO	International Labour Organization
ILP	Industrial Linkage Programme
JSE	Johannesburg Stock Exchange
MABA	Majority-based affirmative action
MAS	Malaysia Airlines
MASD	Management Advisory Services Department
MIBA	Minority-based affirmative action
MNCs	Multinational Companies
MPRDA	Mineral and Petroleum Resources Development Act
NAACP	National Association for the Advancement of Colored People
Nail	New Africa Investments Ltd
NBF	National Bank of Fiji
NCBBF	National Council for Building a Better Fiji
NEM	New Economic Model
NEP	New Economic Policy
OBCs	Other backward classes
OBE	Outcomes-based education
OFCCP	Office of Federal Contract Compliance Programs
PCEEO	President's Committee on Equal Employment Opportunity
Petronas	Petroliam Nasional
PNB	Permodalan National Berhad
ProUni	The program University for All
PSC	Public Service Commission
PSNI	Police Service of Northern Ireland
RSS	Rashtriya Swayamsevak Sangh
RUC	Royal Ulster Constabulary
SACHR	Standing Advisory Commission on Human Rights
Sanas	South African National Accreditation System

Abbreviations and acronyms xv

SAP	Structural adjustment policies
SBA	Small Business Administration
SC	Scheduled Castes
SDL	Soqosoqo Duavata ni Lewenivanua
SDLP	Social Democratic and Labour Party
SEDCs	State Economic Development Corporations
SEPPIR	Special Secretariat for Policies Promoting Racial Equality
SF	Sinn Féin
SMEs	Small and medium-sized enterprises
ST	Scheduled Tribes
SVT	Soqosoqo ni Vakavulewa ni Taukei
TER	Target Equity Ratio
TFZ	Tax Free Zones
TPEP	The Ten Point Economic Plan
TUV	Traditional Unionist Voice
TVNZ	Television New Zealand
UERJ	Universidade Estadual do Rio de Janeiro/Rio de Janeiro State University
UMNO	United Malays' National Organization
UNB	Universidade de Brasília
Uneb	Bahia State University
UUP	Ulster Unionist Party
VDP	Vendor Development Programme
VHP	Vishva Hindu Parishad
VHS	Village Housing Scheme
YHL	Yasana Holdings Limited

Introduction
Affirmative action, horizontal inequalities, and equitable development

Edmund Terence Gomez and Ralph Premdas

Why study affirmative action?

In recent years a number of countries have introduced affirmative action in order to address historical injustices and economic inequalities involving ethno-cultural communities. The adoption of affirmative action policies has occurred most frequently in heterogeneous societies marked by deep ethno-cultural divisions in which one ethnic community tended to dominate the rest. By implementing affirmative action to rectify old wrongs, eradicate injustices, extend benefits, and provide special preferences, governments aspired to establish a new, just, and equal society. This would prove to be no mean undertaking. To overcome inequalities and ingrained segmental prejudices in multi-ethnic countries that had witnessed over the years the cementing of advantages and privileges among certain economically or politically dominant ethnic groups would prove a daunting redistributive challenge. In this sense, affirmative action suggests a radical and revolutionary transformative experiment in social engineering. In this experiment, the meaning of justice and equality becomes mired in controversy, especially in multi-ethnic countries under the cultural hegemonic control of one ethnic community.

In the evolution of these plural societies, most of which were created by colonialism, a coercively institutionalized order was established so that the distribution of economic, social, and political advantages was concentrated unevenly in favour of and against certain communities (Gurr 1993; Premdas 2010). In most cases, a defining moment or event triggered the inauguration of affirmative action. In an inflamed environment of rising expectations and growing frustrations, mobilization by the disadvantaged had threatened the entire social fabric and in particular the property and lives of those more privileged in the country. In extending remedy and hope to the disadvantaged, affirmative action was introduced to promote stability and regulate discontent stemming from unjust discriminatory practices. Prominent cases include South Africa where the indigenous African population, after Nelson Mandela led them to power, initiated policies to achieve equality and justice, primarily between the white and black populations. While this has been the most conspicuous recent case of the introduction of affirmative action, several other countries, including Northern Ireland and Brazil, were adopting and actively implementing the policy. In other countries with a longer history of adoption of this policy, such as India, the United States of America (US), Malaysia, and Fiji, affirmative action involved similar experiments in social, economic, and political engineering; in all four countries affirmative action has also been subject to review and intense debate.

This volume provides an assessment of the implementation of affirmative action in seven countries: India, the US, Malaysia, Fiji, South Africa, Northern Ireland, and Brazil. In this review, what became evident was the fact that several of the countries that have adopted affirmative action claimed that they were inspired by the example of another country. Fiji, for instance, had gone the farthest in trying to replicate the experience of Malaysia. South Africa was inspired in part by Malaysia and the US. Brazil and Northern Ireland imported aspects of the discourse and conduct of affirmative action from the US. India and the US were the first to implement affirmative action, but they have not shown the capacity to draw lessons from the experience of its execution in other countries, in spite of animated debates about this policy by their citizens. Although the US case has generated the most attention, many observers espouse the view that whatever its achievements it was won at a heavy cost of persistent controversy, contentiousness, and divisiveness. On the other hand, the Malaysian case is often described as a success story. Many of these observations are based on assumptions, outright poor information, and unsystematic analysis.

What is true is that the experiences of affirmative action around the world have been very controversial and continue to generate new problems when adopted. In spite of this, the number of countries that have been introducing affirmative action has been growing, and the results have been diverse and require tracking. The outcomes of affirmative action in these countries have differed even as they have utilized a common vocabulary to describe their programmes. The historical experiences in the life of affirmative action have left in their wake setbacks and achievements; as well as unanticipated dilemmas and solutions. They have attested to changes in institutions and societal practices; to deviation from the original aims; to winners and losers; distortions and deviations; and economic gains and losses.

However, one pertinent question has emerged: does prolonged affirmative action sustain, even encourage, ethno-cultural divisions in society? That is, does it establish identity politics as a norm of political life so that divisions and mutual antipathy and systemic inter-ethnic discontent (and even hate and bigotry) become routinized as part of citizen life? Is affirmative action a sound framework of conflict management and a remedy for resolving group discrimination, or is it very different from country to country? Is it covert class warfare that communal elites jointly cultivate and mobilize to manipulate ethnic group divisions for their own benefit?

A more systematic analysis is required of the performance of affirmative action where it has been implemented. If there is a problem of incommensurability that argues that each affirmative action policy is culture specific, then clearly no comparisons can be validly made and policy lessons across borders are futile. We do not share this view. We argue that these experiments in social engineering have much in common, and from them much can be leant and shared; for instance, when dealing with the issue of whether justice has been served on behalf of the original victims. We also argue that there are discernible patterns from which lessons can be adduced and policy transfers recommended to create a more equitable society through affirmative action. We do not claim that there are universal principles of affirmative action as a mode of distributive justice that can create a new society based on shared beliefs. Nor do we contend that there are guaranteed outcomes. But, we affirm that the experience from one case to the next is not so unique that it inhibits comparative insights, even though these must be deduced with utmost caution and plenty of qualifications. What then can be attempted? More limited range explanations are quite possible with a potential for beneficial policy transfers across countries.

In this volume we have revisited the issues thrown up by affirmative action in seven countries by utilizing an approach that focuses on the concepts of horizontal versus vertical equality. We have offered in both this Introduction and in the separate country studies that follow insights into the nature of affirmative action and the sorts of issues and controversies that tend to arise. With the theoretical discussion on affirmative action, the case histories, and the concepts of horizontal and vertical inequality, we offer new insights into the problems and opportunities that are likely to arise in the numerous cases of affirmative action that are evident in the world today.

Targeting horizontal inequalities

The origins of socio-economic inequalities between ethnic groups, and the corresponding increase in the powerlessness felt by disaffected groups, is the result of a number of cross-cutting factors, including colonial histories, differing paths of development, economic growth strategies, changes in migratory and settlement patterns, and the nature of the political system and form of governance. The nature of inequalities is complex and multi-dimensional, with causes and indicators including access to education, availability and standard of healthcare, opportunities for employment, and quality of infrastructure (Rawls 1971; Nozick 1972; Walzer 1983; Dworkin 1985; Westen 1985; Sen 1992; Phillips 1996; Pojman and Westmoreland 1997; Campbell 2000). Problems emerging from ethnic-based inequalities have led to conflict in both developed and developing countries, including Afghanistan, Lebanon, Sri Lanka, India, Guyana, Trinidad and Tobago, Fiji, Indonesia, Malaysia, Rwanda, Sudan, Ethiopia, South Africa, Zimbabwe, Australia, Yugoslavia, France, Britain, and the US (Geertz 1963; Gellner 1983; Young 1993; Premdas 1995; Stavenhagen 1996). The key matters that have contributed to ethnic cleavages in these countries include colonialism and conquest, the pattern of political mobilization, the nature of government policies, and manner of economic development (Horowitz 1985; Gurr 1992; McGarry and O'Leary 1993; Pfaff-Czarnecka *et al.* 1999; Varshney 2002; Brubaker 2004; Premdas 2010). Important studies also indicate that contact between different ethnic communities inevitably leads to an assertion of difference (Barth 1967; Tajfel 1970; Young 1990; Premdas 1993; Taylor and Moghaddam 1994;

Mahajan 1998). At the centre of this issue of difference are the important themes of identity, belonging, migration, citizenship, separatism, and nation building, factors that have contributed to strife in countries with developed as well as developing economies (Anderson 1983; Brubaker 1992; Premdas 1996; Kymlicka 1996; Carnegie Commission 1997; Brubaker and Cooper 2000; Fenton and May 2002; Castles and Davidson 2004; Bangura 2006).

Governments of multi-ethnic nations have adopted different strategies to deal with inequality and the issues of exclusion and marginalization (Bangura 2006). In the literature on policy mechanisms aimed at resolving structural inequalities within societies, there are broadly two schools of thought that can be seen to have emerged. The first major school of thought argues that the nature of the implementation of social policies should be universal in orientation. The other school of thought contends that to help overcome social inequalities it is more viable to develop policies that target disadvantaged groups, for example those that are lagging behind economically along class or ethnic lines. The implementation of policies based on either of these schools of thought has enormous implications in the context of multi-ethnic countries, as the outcome of these policies can lead to ethno-political tensions or add to already existing grievances, erupting into conflict. On the issue of policy implementation and ethnic conflict, scholars have more recently argued that one reason for the persistence of ethno-cultural strife in multi-ethnic societies is that policies have been viewed from a perspective that is vertical in orientation; that is, broadly speaking, one that addresses social inequities from a universal perspective. Vertically-based policies address the plight of individuals in economic need, regardless of their ethnic background. This socio-economic argument, which stresses basic need and economic well-being, has often been identified from a class perspective (Despres 1975; Gellner 1983; Hobsbawm 1990). The counter argument is that ethnic conflict and inter-ethnic difference, which tend to encompass economic as well as cultural differences and claims, can be better resolved by adopting a horizontal perspective; that is by targeting ethnic groups as culturally autonomous communities that are in most need of help. This is often described as an ethno-cultural perspective which engages the collective group interests of rival communities in the state (Geertz 1963; Loury 1987; Connor 1994; Kymlika 1995).

The concept of horizontal inequality is said to provide a means of assessing the level of inter-group inequality. Horizontal inequalities, it is argued, impact negatively on social stability in a way that is different from the consequences of vertical inequality, particularly in cases where distinct ethnic and cultural differences coincide with economic and political inequalities, a situation which can then result in violent conflict (Rabuska and Shepsle 1972; Stewart 2002, 2008; Stewart *et al.* 2008; Brown 2005, 2008; Østby 2008). This perspective is increasingly used to explain the causes of conflict.

The horizontal perspective rests on an understanding of societal organization that revolves around the group dimension. The argument in favour of attaching significant weight to the idea of horizontal inequality is that a purely vertical view of inequality provides no social or cultural perspective regarding the organization of society and the existing group hierarchies and structures that may be in place. An examination of horizontal inequality highlights these existing forms of organization by focusing on the socio-cultural or group dimension within a society. This focus on 'groups' may be relevant in certain contexts, particularly when clearly defined groups such as castes, tribes, or new migrants can be identified. However, the group dimension is not necessarily applicable in all social contexts, and contemporary societal conflict is not solely group-based. Groups within society are defined by both their members and those outside the group. And, over different time periods and in different contexts, groups can range from the easily identifiable to those whose membership is more nebulous. Importantly too, it has been argued that policies directed at reducing inequalities between groups benefit primarily those with the best mobilization capacity, creating new and distinct identities and inequalities, such as intra-ethnic wealth and income disparities, therefore, inhibiting social cohesion.

However, a key problem with the theory of horizontal inequality is that group construction is dynamic, and group boundaries are rarely static, as individual and societal perceptions and preferences shift over time (Barth 1967; Young 1993; Brubaker 2004; Tarling and Gomez 2008; Premdas 2010). A horizontal cross-section of the structure of society does not appear to take into account the fluidity of individual identity and group membership, nor does it allow for the spaces where boundaries and identities overlap and transform. The horizontal perspective also tends to compartmentalize individuals into groups lacking real significance in contemporary contexts. This construct of horizontal organization leans towards a homogenous view of group members, neglecting multiple individual allegiances and identities, the high degree of heterogeneity within groups, intra-ethnic changes and class, and other socio-economic shifts and divisions.

To examine if the targeting of ethnic groups to resolve horizontal inequalities is the best mechanism to help resolve or reduce communal and inter-ethnic conflict, this study entails an examination of the implementation of the policy of affirmative action. Direct measures to combat socio-economic horizontal inequalities can be taken as roughly coterminous with the policy of affirmative action. Countries in the developed and developing world have employed affirmative action (Oberst 1986; Nevitte and Kennedy 1986; Bennell and Strachan 1992; Castle 1995; Parikh 1997, 2001; Lindsay 1998; Gomez and Jomo 1999; Htun 2004; Bailey 2004; Sowell 2004; Weisskopf 2004). And, unlike universal and group-neutral policies, affirmative action explicitly targets individuals and groups on the basis of ascriptive characteristics such as race and ethnicity.

Introducing affirmative action

Key features and issues

Affirmative action, in essence, is a form of justice that seeks to establish equality by using compensatory benefits to rectify past discrimination (Nagel 1973; Fullinwider 1975; Glaser 1975; Goldman 1976; Rosenfeldl 1991; Skrentny 1996;

Kellough 2006). It aims to reorganize, usually over a short duration, the distribution of the benefits and burdens of society by facilitating the participation of the previously disadvantaged through special policy preferences and programmes. Proponents of affirmative action argue that this policy is not a dismissal, disavowal, negation, or denial of the egalitarian principle, merely a temporary suspension and diversion of it to restore a level playing field (Sterba 2003; Rachels 1978; Sher 1979; Young 1990; Lawrence and Matsuda 1997). The policy seeks to promote unity through wider inclusion, by compensating for past injustices and discrimination that created inequality and systemic deprivation for entire classes, castes, and groups. Affirmative action strives to end exclusion and facilitate access for the disadvantaged by socially engineering the institutions of a society (Castle 1995; Curry 1996; Fryer and Loury 2005; Parikh 1997; Skrentny 2001; Weisskopf 2004).

There are normally two types of affirmative action programmes: hard and soft. Hard programmes explicitly prescribe set-asides, quotas, and timetables, while the latter provides for outreach and training facilities. Some disadvantaged groups may benefit from the soft variant of affirmative action programmes involving outreach opportunities through training and education. However, these soft programmes often tend to be too slow and gradual in achieving their outcomes in relation to the urgency of the demand for change. Furthermore training programmes depend on voluntary compliance by employers. Consequently, more compulsory measures have been required that include timetables, quotas, and reviews (Skrentny 1996; 2001). In most countries affirmative action programmes that have been introduced to assign preferences to the historically disadvantaged have built on other preferences that were being practiced in favour of disadvantaged groups, such as veterans, senior citizens, and the disabled. Affirmative action is therefore not new. The policy has been pervasive in practically all democratic egalitarian, merit-based, societies where such practices have been institutionalized for many years without resistance and with near universal consent (Skrentny 1996). In the new order of affirmative action involving castes, classes, and historically disadvantaged and marginalized ethno-cultural communities, since much larger sections of a society require accommodation, such programmes tend to be more costly and impact more radically on the social structure in rectifying systemic inequalities. In extending remedy and hope to the disadvantaged, affirmative action was introduced to promote stability and regulate discontent stemming from unjust discriminatory practices. Affirmative action can therefore be seen as a conflict management policy.

In making the case for affirmative action the key arguments point to the need for compensation, rectification, and the temporary suspension of egalitarian principles to create a level playing field for all in the long term (Goldman 1979). Affirmative action tends to occur in states where social advantages and disadvantages coincide with the ethnic or cultural fault lines that reputedly divide that country. To establish a more just and inclusive society, a distinct need exists to recognize all ethno-cultural communities (Taylor 1994; Premdas 2003). Affirmative action, in principle, recognizes differences, racial, cultural, and gender alike, in a multi-ethnic society, instead of forcing assimilation and cultural hegemony of a particular group's values and practices. Cultural recognition bestows dignity and space for a separate identity. The policy is anti-hegemonic in conferring equal recognition of cultural symbols and practices of ethnic groups, rather than just the dominant one. In this way affirmative action promotes equal citizenship in a divided state.

In particular, when individual rights are pitted against group rights, and procedures for adjudicating differ according to religious faith, the claims of justice for one community often run contrary to those of others (Glazer 1983; Loury 1987; Kymlika 1995). In each multi-ethnic country then, where affirmative action is proposed as a form of compensatory justice, different and rival assumptions of justice cause bitter and irreconcilable arguments and can trigger deeper divisions that border on civil war and the disintegration of that country (Dworkin 1985; Sher 1997; Cohen 1995, 1998; Pojman 1992, 1998; Cohen and Sterba 2003). Affirmative action could then become a critically contentious issue in some countries, a reason why when the policy is introduced caveats are attached, such as a fixed duration for the implementation of the policy while its objectives are clearly delineated.

The seven country studies in this volume reflect the range of affirmative action policies that have arisen across diverse historical, political, and economic contexts. India began experimenting with affirmative action policies in the early twentieth century, whereas Brazil has only recently introduced the policy after years of societal opposition to such programmes. Early policy efforts in the US and India focused on social groups who comprised a minority of the total population and who had experienced discrimination, oppression, and exclusion (Graham 1990; Parikh 1997; Weisskopf 2004). Affirmative action policies were initially developed to offer accelerated guaranteed opportunities for members of ethnic groups who had endured discrimination and exclusion. When these groups formed a minority of the population (as in the US, India, and Brazil), the preferences embedded in the policies were justified on the grounds that abolition of discrimination was insufficient to advance the community. When the groups comprised a majority of a society's population (as in Malaysia, Fiji, and South Africa), the preferences were justified as providing a return to a more appropriate status quo.

In all seven countries affirmative action was justified, first and foremost, in terms of compensation for past wrongs. In practice, however, and in some cases, the aim of affirmative action was subsequently extended beyond compensation to more diffuse social goals such as diversity of representation. In the US and India affirmative action was also eventually expanded to include groups who collectively constituted a majority of the population (Graham 1990; Skrentny, 1996; Sheth 1998; Dipankar 1998).

Importantly too, since affirmative action involves redistribution of limited and scarce resources within a society, it tends to lead to zero-sum contests and struggles between the privileged and underprivileged, usually resulting in winners and losers among individuals and groups (Despres 1975; Banton 1983; Depres and Premdas 1993). Typically, this competition is manifested in such material areas as employment (in the public and private sectors) and access to educational and business opportunities including government procurement, contracts, and licences (Horowitz 1985; Premdas 1989; Gurr 1992; McGarry and O'Leary 1993). This type of inter-ethnic competition prevails in symbolic areas such as political representation, recognition of cultural symbols of identity, for example, religion and language, as well as in relation to access to important services such as medical, water, and transportation. Where the contests and competition become group-based and communalized, as they often do, they tend to evoke strong irrational passions that are difficult to reconcile and easy to manipulate by political entrepreneurs aspiring to secure control of government or to ascend the hierarchy of a party (Isaacs 1975; Anderson 1983; Connor 1994; Mamdani 2001; Premdas 2007).

In South Africa and Northern Ireland the nature of politics deteriorated into open protracted communal violence. In both cases external intervention played an indispensable role in halting the conflict and setting in motion negotiations towards a solution. In both cases consociational relationships were introduced so that, along with power-sharing, a system of affirmative action was instituted that sought to reduce inequality between communities through proportional allocation of resources or redistribution from one group to the other via the budget (Lijphart 1977).

Of the seven country cases, four in particular – Northern Ireland, Fiji, Malaysia, and South Africa – undertook a thorough and multi-faceted radical overhaul of their societies in the spheres of employment, education, and equity ownership in order to promote equality and justice. The others had more limited spheres of activity, such as Brazil in higher education, the US in employment and higher education, and India in employment, higher education, and political representation. In all seven cases resort was made to impose quotas, goals, and timetables with the threat of sanctions. In every instance the experiment in social engineering through affirmative action was explicit in its intent both as a measure of conflict management and promoting equality on behalf of the previously discriminated against communities.

In all seven countries the programmes were intended to reduce poverty and develop an educated and thriving elite that could assume leadership of their communities. Programmes were developed in three areas: electoral representation, in which targeted groups were guaranteed a proportion of legislative seats; access to positions in government employment and institutions of higher education; and enterprise development, in which targeted groups received preferences in capital accumulation, investment, and ownership. In several cases many of the stated goals were met. Malaysia, the US, and India have experienced a reduction in poverty among the beneficiaries of affirmative action, and members of targeted groups have become politically influential at the national and sub-national levels (Parikh 1997; Gomez and Jomo 1999; Weisskopf 2004). In each case a prosperous middle class has emerged. South Africa's experience with affirmative action is of a shorter duration, but similar trajectories in economics and politics are obvious.

Meritocracy, duration, and access

Affirmative action policies seek to abridge the merit principle even though they often claim that in doing so they practice a form of justice that is quite consistent with standard egalitarian procedures associated with justice (Daniels 1978). In effect, affirmative action is not disavowal of equality or the merit principle, but a justifiable detour that is essential to lay the foundations in which fair and equal competition is facilitated. A clear proviso in this justification is that the setting aside of merit is a temporary but necessary short-term tactic to achieve the larger long-term goal of establishing a level playing field where there is fair competition in employment and in business that can help sustain economic growth.

Arguments against affirmative action are numerous and incisive but they tend to pivot around the dogma of merit, which is an integral part of the edifice of egalitarian justice (Curry 1996; Beckwith and Jones 1997; Cohen *et al.* 2003). Opponents of affirmative action tend to articulate an uncompromising argument that underscores the essential role of merit in maintaining a society based on democratic rights and equality. They vehemently inveigh against affirmative action as detrimental to equal citizenship, because it destroys the relationship between equal work and equal reward. The merit principle, however, is vulnerable to attack, with opponents arguing that the criteria applied are not normatively and culturally neutral (Young 1990; Lukes and Campodonica 1996; Guinier and Sturm 2001; Lichtenberg and Luban 2002).

Another feature associated with the performance of affirmative action relates to its breach of its original promise of short duration, evolving instead as a permanent structure that becomes locked into local partisan interests that promote its continued existence. Rebuttals against this phenomenon rest on the counter claim that affirmative action programmes can only come to an end when the needs of the disadvantaged community have been served or when other objectives such as the elimination of poverty and the integration of all communities in society have been attained. These arguments and patterns are evident in cases around the world, including in the country studies in this volume such as Fiji, Malaysia, and South Africa.

In these countries, the history of affirmative action is one replete with resistance, in what was deemed as a zero-sum struggle of apportioning benefits and rewards outside the rigorous application of the principles of merit. The aim of achieving societal integration was rarely achieved, and in most cases a more divided society was fashioned, characterized by persistent acrimony and resistance. Affirmative action programmes based on patronage have delivered benefits to the aggrieved community, specifically by creating a middle stratum, but have also nurtured entrenched dependence on the state, primarily because the policy has been extended beyond the stipulated time limit. In many cases a core critique of affirmative action is that members of the targeted disadvantaged community, usually those mired in poverty, did not emerge as the main beneficiary, while an elite of this group garnered much of the benefits.

It does seem, however, that the acrimony and divisiveness that have come to be associated with affirmative action are amplified in the context of a majority ethnic community which controls the government. There is a persistent pattern in affirmative action cases of the wrong people or groups benefiting, with the better off within these groups enjoying a disproportionate share of sanctioned privileges and becoming a new parasitic elite. While this observation is often made, it is often simultaneously asserted that affirmative action programmes have succeeded in creating a new middle class out of the beneficiaries. This means that intra-ethnic inequality is an inevitable outcome of affirmative action projects and programmes, an argument borne out in the country studies.

Apart from some of the undeniable successes of affirmative action, there appear to be a number of clear patterns which attest to negative aspects of the policy. It is claimed that these programmes inculcate a dependency syndrome such that the disadvantaged group, instead of integrating in the wider community, becomes permanently ghettoized. This is accompanied by a psychology of defeatism which contributes to an ideology of victimology in which the disadvantaged accuse the dominant and more well off members of the society of being exploitative and that the social institutions are arranged to perpetuate their subordinate condition. All this tends to exacerbate division and maintain a riven social fabric that appears beyond repair and chronically lacking in cohesion.

The rise of intra-ethnic inequalities can be attributed to the way affirmative action programmes are defined and implemented. In every case under consideration, access to and utilization of affirmative action incentives have been distributed unequally among members of eligible groups. When the beneficiaries are members of a numerical majority, a subset of the targeted group almost always has utilized preferential access – and their large numbers (in the case such of South Africa, Malaysia, and Fiji) – to achieve political prominence and to enrich themselves through government-controlled economic opportunities. By contrast, where the targeted groups comprise a minority of the population, economic gains are not always matched by political gains. In the US, African-Americans, Native Americans, and Latinos have experienced uneven economic and social improvements without gaining political dominance, as have minority social groups in India (Weisskopf 2004; Sowell 2004). Such outcomes suggest the need for institutional reforms to ensure more transparency and equity in the way incentives created are deployed among targeted groups.

One key lesson emerging from the country studies is that institutions matter. Since institutions of governance remain in place following a regime change, the decision-making framework permits the continued implementation of affirmative action policies (though the types of incentives offered may vary). An issue of related importance is that of institutional capacity. In South Africa, Fiji, and Malaysia, a factor contributing to spatial and ethnic inequities was the quality of institutional capacity at the local level to deliver policies, a factor that can hinder access by those who are most in need to the privileges offered through affirmative action programmes. Moreover, even if, for example, decentralization is introduced to help devolve power to ensure more equitable access, inefficiencies in the policy delivery system will impair implementation of redistribution policies.

In most of the countries analysed here, programmes are targeted at the highest levels of education, adult employment, and enterprise development. During the implementation of affirmative action, policy planners assume that the beneficiaries have the requisite human capital that allows them to employ these concessions productively. If these beneficiaries do not have the requisite human capital, there are no provisions within the programmes to overcome this deficiency. This is because affirmative action seldom includes programmes that build educational – and financial – skills before adulthood. Inevitably, those without these skills, predominantly the poor within targeted groups, are seldom able to take advantage of affirmative action, a factor contributing to the rise in intra-ethnic inequality. In India social groups have received both preferential access to universities and subsidies towards tuition and housing. But many of the benefits go unclaimed because the beneficiaries have not received the sort of primary and secondary level of schooling necessary to meet the relaxed requirements. Inadequate primary education, and an over-emphasis on tertiary education, benefited the middle class, exacerbating intra-ethnic class inequalities in India. In Malaysia, where implementation of affirmative action is reputed to have had extremely favourable outcomes, one important lesson was that the young of the targeted group were plucked out of rural areas, sent to well-equipped residential schools, and then provided preferential access to tertiary education. Beneficiaries privy to such quality education from an early stage of their lives have now emerged as the new middle class and have established a growing presence as a community with entrepreneurial capacity.

The impact of affirmative action on enterprise development is especially noteworthy in so far as it raises a crucial question about this policy: has affirmative action helped nurture a new domestic entrepreneurial community which encouraged inter-ethnic wealth distribution parity, or does it merely foster unproductive rent-seeking while suppressing a dynamic domestic entrepreneurial base that could have helped generate growth? In countries where this dimension of affirmative action has been actively pursued (South Africa, Fiji, and Malaysia) redistribution of corporate equity has led to serious intra-ethnic class inequalities. In South Africa and Malaysia the promotion of the Black Economic Empowerment (BEE) policy and the New Economic Policy (NEP) has contributed to close ties between politics and business along ethnic lines, contributing to the rise of a new elite signifying fresh class configurations. The implementation of the BEE and NEP has led to the bypassing of entrepreneurial non-black capital, undermining economic development. The NEP's promotion of ethnic Malay capital has involved intra-ethnic selective patronage, ostensibly in an attempt to identify, pick, and groom 'winners' (Gomez and Jomo 1999: 24–74). This non-transparent mechanism of 'picking winners' has diminished the capacity of ethnic Chinese entrepreneurs to move up the technology ladder because of the latter's reluctance to invest in research and development for fear of losing ownership and control of their firms during equity redistribution exercises. Targeting in business, through affirmative action (in Malaysia and South Africa) has therefore been to the detriment of the industrial development of these emerging economies. Moreover, in these two countries, where there is a concerted attempt by the state to promote ethnic capital as a redistributive mechanism, this has not led to the deracialization of society. The policy has contributed to a merger of indigenous business and state elites, with such capital still highly dependent on the state for survival.

In addition to intra-group inequality, spatial inequities frequently persist or worsen after affirmative action policies are implemented. Preferences designed to encourage entrepreneurship and investment will be disproportionately utilized by members of targeted groups in urban and prosperous rural areas because they assume a level of infrastructural support that many regions do not have. Affirmative action in South Africa, Malaysia, and India has not helped develop rural enterprises, even though this was one objective of the policy in some countries. And even where there are programmes that recognize important differences at the sub-national level, affirmative action will be unevenly distributed unless disparities within regions are acknowledged and accounted for in the implementation process.

Spatial differences have also been exacerbated by the limited ability of the rural poor to take advantage of access to higher education, an issue conditioned on primary and secondary education success. In India, when reserved seats were introduced at the prestigious and highly competitive Indian institutes of technology, many students from targeted social groups were unable to take advantage of a relaxation of the entrance requirements because their secondary school training had usually been gained at inferior public schools. Prosperous group members who can afford private schools and personalized tutoring are the predictable beneficiaries of these reservations.

Country studies: mixed outcomes

In all case studies the outcomes of the implementation of affirmative action have been mixed. Aimed in part at promoting societal unity by rectifying historical discriminatory wrongs and ameliorating inequality, these policies and programmes have left in their wake an assortment of setbacks and achievements.

India has the longest record of affirmative action having established reservations for scheduled castes (SC) and scheduled tribes (ST) constitutionally in 1950. Sunita Parikh's study of India discusses affirmative action in both a majority and a minority context. At the national level it was a majority group that devised the affirmative action programme and at the state level in the Indian southern states, it was the majority community. In both cases there were successes and failures in attaining the objectives of the policy. The goals of affirmative action, implemented through employment practices and university admissions, have been met, most evidently in increased economic and political opportunities for members of the targeted groups. Affirmative action did have some success in alleviating poverty, but exceeded its term limit of ten years and became embedded in partisan politics and locked into patronage and political dependency. The policy did succeed in creating a middle class among the impoverished castes and other groups, but it was a minority who benefited, contributing to greater intra-caste inequality. Parikh stresses that since the basis of the formulation of the policy is ethnic identity, ethnicity continues to be a highly salient category. In every state within India's federal system that she analysed, ethnic identities were reinforced and solidified. Her conclusion is that although the explicitly stated goals of affirmative action are 'to reduce the importance of ethnicity in explaining life chances, there are no cases in which affirmative action policies have led to an overall decline in ethnic identification by either beneficiaries or non-targeted groups'.

In the US, Ralph Premdas stresses the importance of the issues of equality and justice associated with the policy of affirmative action. First initiated in the mid-1960s, affirmative action in the US was in part justified as a temporary preparatory measure on behalf of African-Americans for equal access to jobs and opportunities. Equity and justice were well served in the case of creating a segment of middle income minorities. However, implementation was in practice a protracted and often painful experimental process with constant revisions and redesigns, with unending legal and constitutional challenges. Having started off as a policy involving mainly African-Americans, in a chequered career it has metamorphosized into a different creature with new recipients, accumulated interests and aims, and has come to be rooted almost permanently in the governmental administrative apparatus. Assuming the form of 'diversity', the new affirmative action policies, especially in the area of access to higher education, continue to draw public controversy even as extensive poverty and inequality remains mainly among the non-whites. As the policy has morphed, it has drawn ardent supporters and opponents into a heated controversy, and this has evolved into a tidal wave of mass partisan mobilization both for and against the policy – splitting American society right down the middle. Today, affirmative action practices are found in a variety of inter-related bodies of law that include the US Constitution, federal statutes, federal executive orders, state constitutional provisions, state statutes, state executive orders, self-imposed restrictions by state bodies, and local ordinances. This list also includes judicial decisions interpreting these laws (Malamud 2001: 314).

In Malaysia, Hwok-Aun Lee, Edmund Terence Gomez, and Shakila Yacob note that the affirmative action experiment succeeded as much as it had failed. It was a Malay-fashioned policy implemented for the benefit of this ethnic group, and even though it was argued that the better-off Chinese would not be left behind as the economy grew, the experiment had the flavour of coercion. Affirmative action, after 20 years, had important outcomes, specifically a major reduction in poverty while a vibrant new middle class has emerged among the targeted group, primarily through a focus on providing high quality education from an early stage to poor students in rural areas. Although the primary objective of affirmative action was to ultimately achieve national unity, since implementation of the policy has continued indefinitely after its original duration of 20 years lapsed in 1990, ethnic Chinese and Indians have complained bitterly of reverse discrimination. The ramifications of affirmative action have been noted in terms of the quality of the public delivery system and in terms of 'institutional decline', manifested particularly in the loss of faith in education-based public institutions such as universities as a result of racial quotas. These issues have contributed to numerous debates about the racialization of the bureaucracy and the decline of meritocracy, a reason why large numbers of highly educated Malaysians are migrating abroad to work, and an indication also of their high level of dissatisfaction with the opportunities available to them. Official sources estimate, relatively modestly, that 350,000 Malaysians are working abroad, over half of whom have tertiary-level qualifications.

South Africa's affirmative action endeavours were largely based on emulating the policy as implemented in Malaysia. Anthea Jeffery notes that the government's comprehensive programme of affirmative action was introduced to achieve equality and justice for the grossly discriminated against African peoples under Apartheid. When first introduced it was understood that affirmative action was going to be voluntary, involving no quotas or timetables implying compulsion. The Employment Equity Act of 1998 required employers (of 50 people or more) to attain demographic representivity, and it also provided for substantial fines for failure to achieve this. The Act did, however, initially allow employers to set their own targets, albeit in consultation with employees and trade unions. Meanwhile, the Black Economic Empowerment (BEE) policy, introduced to promote black capital, has contributed to the bypassing of entrepreneurial non-black capital, undermining economic development. Under BEE rules, employment equity targets have effectively been set for private sector employers, at 60 per cent for senior managers and 80 per cent for junior managers by 2017. These policies did help create a new middle class, but the more well off elite became the primary beneficiaries of the resources and business opportunities that came with affirmative action, contributing to new intra-ethnic wealth and income inequities, while corruption has emerged on a grand scale and the quality of services provided by public institutions has declined appreciably. As for poverty, Jeffery notes that it is still unclear if affirmative action has reduced poverty. Poverty has been alleviated through social grants, that is cash payments, along with free houses and other forms of social welfare. By 2013, expenditure on social protection will have increased by 1,500 per cent since 1994. The number of beneficiaries of social grants (mainly child support grants) has increased from around two million in 1994 to close on 15 million in 2010. However, with government debt rising and more than a quarter of the population on social grants, the sustainability of the grant system is questionable, especially as the country has only about 5.9 million income tax payers.

Fiji, like South Africa, adopted and implemented affirmative action based on a study of Malaysia. For this reason, Fiji falls into the category of what Steven Ratuva calls 'majority-based' affirmative action, initiated as it was by majority indigenous Fijians who, in control of the military, dictated the redistributive policy. Ratuva notes that Fiji had experienced six coups since independence, or one every four-and-a-half years. Nearly all these coups directly or indirectly concerned the claims by indigenous Fijians for a more just and equal order, through special preferential access to resources and benefits in relation to the seeming superior well-being of other non-native immigrant communities, in particular the Indians. Ratuva argues that one of the consequences of such policies has been the worsening of inter-ethnic relations between Fijians and Indians, and further affirmative action programmes have tended to benefit an elite within the Fijian community. The promulgation of affirmative action programmes for the benefit of creating a more equal order faltered, substantially because in the modern competitive individualistic profit-oriented commercial sector, Fijians were ill prepared for the concessions they received, which contributed to a rather unproductive deployment of these benefits.

In countries where affirmative action has been introduced more recently, the outcomes have so far been favourable, drawing further attention to the issue of duration. The Northern Ireland case is a story of the entrenchment of discrimination and inequality in favour of the Protestants and against the Catholics; one that has bred deep distrust and fear between these communities. The distribution of resources as well as power was heavily tilted against the Catholics, providing the incendiary materials for the outbreak of The Troubles in 1968. Affirmative action emerged in this context as a crisis management tool 'to tackle discrimination and to advance fair employment effectively', as Colin Harvey notes in this country study. Resolution of the conflict required new institutions and legislation, assumed in the form of an Equality Commission and the Fair Employment and Treatment Order of 1998. The fair employment regime has resulted in significant change, in terms of access to employment opportunities on the basis of equality, though Northern Ireland remains a deeply divided society and levels of communal segregation (particularly in areas of socio-economic disadvantage) remains high. The improvements on fair participation that have taken place occurred during and throughout a sustained period of economic growth. What affirmative action did succeed in doing, even when it had to disclaim its overt use of quotas and timetables, was address the problem of inequality and discrimination.

Multi-ethnic Brazil, regarded for a long time as a model of inter-racial harmony and 'racial democracy', is the most recent country to have adopted affirmative action. Possessing a wide kaleidoscope of colours created from extensive inter-ethnic marriages during colonial times, non-racially-defined distribution of society's values was not contested. However, when a link was made between poverty and colour, evidence abounded that the darker the colour, the greater likelihood of poverty and disadvantage. It took two events to trigger a fundamental shift in consciousness and the abandonment of the myth of racial harmony. First was the centenary observation of the abolition of slavery in 1988, and second was the Third World Conference Against Racism, Racial Discrimination, Xenophobia and Related Intolerance in 2001. Joaze Bernardino and Fernando Rosa argue that it was the Durban conference that mobilized black Brazilian activists for a number of state, regional, and national preparatory conferences. The target of activist pressure was focused on university admissions. In

2001, for the first time among state universities, Rio de Janeiro State University adopted affirmative action through the implementation of a quota system in undergraduate admissions for black, mixed, and indigent students. In 2003 the University of Brasilia followed suit. Of Brazil's 230 institutions of higher education, 130 eventually adopted affirmative action. The problem to be solved derived from the fact that only 24.4 per cent of Brazil's college and university graduates were black.

Conclusion: lessons learnt

There is sufficient evidence in this seven country study that horizontal-type initiatives have helped to reduce poverty. Affirmative action programmes have succeeded on their own terms in some contexts, but have had dismal, even perilous, outcomes in other cases such as Fiji. In South Africa the experiment continues with bleak reports of failures, but also counterclaims that symbolic gratification has been achieved in channelling political office, jobs, and education to a community that had been grossly discriminated against in these areas for decades.

Where affirmative action has had favourable outcomes, previously under-represented groups have increased their representation in politics, seen particularly in India and Brazil, and their presence in the economy as in Malaysia and Northern Ireland. In terms of employment, previously excluded minority and majority populations have been integrated into a wide range of positions in mainstream society. The size of the middle class involving members of the targeted groups has grown appreciably, reflecting much of what has been argued in the literature on affirmative action (Fullwider 1975; Oberst 1986; Bennell and Strachan 1992; Castle 1995; Parikh 1997, 2001; Lawrence and Matsuda 1997; Lindsay 1998; Sterba 2003; Bailey 2004; Sowell 2004; Weisskopf 2004).

In all seven cases, with the possible exception of Northern Ireland where affirmative action is still a fairly recent phenomenon, this policy's programmes have attracted substantial criticism – particularly as a result of the new inequities it has created. The emergence of these inequities indicates that in spite of the positive outcomes of affirmative action, the goals of the policy have been achieved in part rather than in their entirety. Although inter-group measures of inequality have decreased, in every case intra-group inequality has increased, even when overall poverty has fallen. Affirmative action policies do not take into account spatial inequality, but it is evident that disparities between beneficiaries in different regions, or between those in urban and rural areas, have continued or increased (Ferguson and Gupta 2002). Spatial differences have also been exacerbated by the limited ability of the rural poor to take advantage of access to higher education, an issue conditioned on primary and secondary education success. These new inequities have not been resolved in these countries through improvements in affirmative action programmes at all levels, rendering even the most generous higher education preferences ineffective.

Preferences designed to nurture entrepreneurship have similarly been disproportionately utilized by members of targeted groups in urban and prosperous rural areas because they assume a level of infrastructural support that many regions do not have. Affirmative action in South Africa, Malaysia, and India has not helped develop rural enterprises, even though this was one objective of the policy. Where redistribution of corporate equity through affirmative action has been actively pursued, specifically in South Africa, Fiji, and Malaysia, selective patronage has led to serious intra-ethnic class inequalities. Targeting and preferential treatment in business have led to serious wastage of government-created concessions to generate growth and industrialization, while gross inefficiencies and acute corruption have emerged in the public and private sectors. Targeting and selective patronage in business, without transparency, has hindered domestic enterprise development, because of capital flight and a reluctance by minorities to invest in research and development for fear of appropriation of their firms during redistributive exercises. In some countries the state's desire to ensure minorities did not expand their ownership and control of the corporate sector undermined the principle of inclusion, universally advocated as the ultimate goal of affirmative action.

For these reasons affirmative action policies have been challenged in all seven countries, formally through legal and political channels, and informally through social protest. These challenges emanate primarily from non-targeted groups who argue that they are unfairly disadvantaged by such programmes, though opposition by individuals and groups from within the targeted population is mounting rapidly. These conflicts have repercussions for society as a whole and for political and social relations between and within groups, especially when affirmative action leads to increased heterogeneity of economic outcomes among beneficiaries.

This increased heterogeneity is a consequence of the second common factor: horizontal inequality-based policies such as affirmative action treat targeted groups as homogeneous, but members' abilities to take advantage of these programmes are not equal. If incentives are extended without accompanying programmes that ensure similar chances for all members, then the programme shifts the competition from one between members of different ethnic groups to one between members of a single ethnic group. Over time, class cleavages among targeted groups become increasingly pronounced, with the best off in these communities more privy to affirmative action while those with fewer resources are left behind. While intra-group solidarity may help mitigate the potential conflicts that arise from growing wealth and income inequalities between ethnic communities, policies that aggregate a variety of ethnic or other identities within one category can create or exacerbate tensions across sub-groups.

Crucially, too, the history of Fiji indicates that horizontal inequality-based policies can play an incendiary role in the emergence of violent conflict between ethnic groups. This is particularly so when horizontal inequalities are consistent across political and economic dimensions. This suggests the need for the careful design of context-specific policies to ensure their effectiveness. As the country studies indicate, group-based affirmative action has critical ramifications in the political arena. First, for many voters from the targeted group, the support of politicians for affirmative action becomes a litmus test of their support; candidates risk losing votes if they criticize the policies, let alone advocate their abolition (Parikh 1997, 2001). Second, the existence of affirmative action affects how individuals and groups identify themselves in politics. If the policies are perceived to be a path to greater economic and social opportunity, then voters are more likely to consider their ethnicity salient and coalesce around affirmative action and other ethnically specific political issues.

Countries experiencing severe horizontal inequalities are therefore faced with a dilemma. Horizontal inequalities constitute a potential problem for peaceful development, but attempting to correct such inequalities can be the spark that transforms a 'potential' problem into an 'actual' problem. Since there are trade-offs during the implementation of affirmative action, such as the creation of new inequities, the legitimacy of the policy among the entire population is diminished. The pattern of policy planning and implementation, involving the way policies target different sections of the intra-group distribution curve, therefore require careful consideration. Policies that target the higher end of the distribution curve are likely to be less costly for the government, but are also probably much less effective in achieving reductions in horizontal inequalities.

A number of these anomalies in affirmative action can, however, be explained in terms of the issue of the persistence of policies across time, its inability to ensure equal access for targeted groups, and its focus on ascriptive identity. Determining the length of affirmative action and abiding by this stipulation appears imperative because the short-term impact of the policy appears positive while its long-term consequence has serious drawbacks, including serving to reinforce ethnic identity in a manner that hinders social cohesion. A major point emerging from the country studies is that long-term implementation of affirmative action has led to the creation of claimed identities as a means of securing the incentives that come with the policy. Importantly too, even in cases where policies have time limits or were implemented with the expectation that they would be temporary, few governments have scaled back these policies, much less abandoned them.

This suggests that much contemplation is required of the type of institutions that are created through which such policies are implemented. A democratic electoral system that allows for a change of government, and encourages moderation and accommodates difference, appears imperative. Federal arrangements that serve to accommodate a plurality of ethnic communities have proven important (Horowitz 1985; Bakke and Wibbels 2006; Lijphart 1977, 2004). In Asia, India's federal system has given previously marginalized groups access to political power and regional elites the chance to influence policy-making at the national level. Decentralization is necessary, though if such devolution of power is uneven or centred on institutions with limited capacity to deliver, it will lead to inefficiencies in policy implementation. Decentralization is also important because institutions with power at the local level can better respond and craft incentives to suit the well-being of recipients. Local level civic institutions that transcend ethnic divisions as well as curb political practices and forms of mobilization fostering ideas that exclude communities from mainstream society have proven crucial to help curb ethnic – and religious – conflict (Varshney 2002; Brubaker 2004).

The country studies indicate, however, that debates about affirmative action may have little to do with their success or failure, and more to do with the political interests of ruling parties benefiting from the constituency that has been created and become mutually dependent on each other. In Northern Ireland, Malaysia, and the US, affirmative action programmes have substantially met their intended goals even though arguments persist that the time is not yet ripe to terminate them. In the US, justification on the basis of compensation has been supplanted by arguments about the usefulness of affirmative action in expanding diversity in employment and education. In Malaysia the policy was recast, though its primary objectives remained unchanged. And targeted group members' support for affirmative action is so widely assumed that if beneficiaries advocate major changes in policy or the complete abolition of affirmative action, they are seen as aberrations. Despite the conflict that affirmative action engenders, it appears to be politically unfeasible for elected actors to change the essential aspects of the policies.

The three most important lessons from these countries are, first, that affirmative action is a sound policy for rectifying historical social injustices. However, after a short duration, this horizontal inequality-based policy must expand the range of targeted groups and individuals to include not only ethnicity, but also class position, in determining eligibility status. This change would enhance the ability of disadvantaged members of society to have access to programmes, since they would no longer have to compete with more privileged members of their own ethnic group. This is imperative as long-term implementation of horizontal inequality-based policies indicates that their programmes are divisive, prevent social cohesion, and perpetuate a notion of the importance of ethnic identity over national identity. Continued discrimination on the basis of ethnicity leads to protest that can be articulated in various forms, more so as minorities identify themselves with the country of their birth and see themselves as 'indigenous'. The negation of rights as citizens can lead to massive outward migration among those with class resources, such as education and investment funds, as evident in Fiji, Malaysia, Northern Ireland, and South Africa. Since long-term implementation of affirmative action reinforces ethnic identity as a basis for continued access to privileges, the policy has emerged as a highly divisive issue. While the beneficiaries, usually the majority community, are disinclined to end it, minorities argue that by being denied these privileges, this raises the notion of their status as second class citizens. In most of the country studies affirmative action has failed to create a more inclusive environment, suggesting a credibility gap between state rhetoric on equity and justice and the exigent realities in social interactions between communities.

Second, developmental type affirmative action incentives appear to be the most persuasive mechanism to help alleviate horizontal inequalities, created and promoted within a viable and transparent institutional framework, though also instituted within a specific time limit. It is evident that policy modifications to exclude the most privileged members of targeted groups – and to target members earlier so that access is more widely available – are crucial to help deal with the limitations of affirmative action. This contention draws attention to the important need to make a distinction between preferential and developmental affirmative action (Fryer and Loury 2005). Developmental affirmative action involves the need to provide incentives to recipients at an early age, based for example on education, to equip the young with skills. This would increase the viability of this policy to overcome social inequities. In the countries analysed here, affirmative action programmes are targeted at the highest levels of education, adult employment, and enterprise development. Beneficiaries are expected to have the human capital and entrepreneurial skills that would allow them to utilize affirmative action provisions productively. However, if the beneficiaries do not have these skills, affirmative action programmes seldom have mechanisms to help them overcome this deficiency. For this reason, an emphasis on providing quality primary education to targeted groups is imperative, though costly, with incentives for the poor to keep their children in schools.

Third, given the rise of serious conflicts among members of the targeted group, this suggests the need for caution when adopting a horizontal inequality-based perspective to policy planning. Two core issues stand out when horizontal inequality-based policies are introduced: duration of the policy, and equitable access. Horizontal inequality-based policies must adhere to a strict time limit. This review of affirmative action indicates that the outcomes of this policy have been most beneficial during the first decade of implementation. Indefinite continuation of the policy has had serious repercussions. Equitable access is imperative as the country studies also indicate that those most in need have little avenue to the opportunities created for them.

The country studies also indicate a clear need to combine both horizontal and vertical aspects within policy planning, to provide innovative and context-specific policy recommendations. In the long term, however, the nature of policy planning must be based on those that adopt a vertical, or class, perspective. This is because long-term race-based policies feed communal politics. This point is now acknowledged in the country studies.

References

Anderson, Benedict. 1983. *Imagined Communities: Reflections on the Origin and Spread of Nationalism*. London: Verso.

Bailey, S.R. 2004. 'Group Dominance and the Myth of Racial Democracy: Antiracism Attitudes in Brazil' in *American Sociological Review*, 69 (5): 728–47.

Bakke, K.M. and E. Wibbels. 2006. 'Diversity, disparity, and civil conflict in federal states' in *World Politics*, 59 (1): 1–50.

Bangura, Yusuf (ed.). 2006. *Ethnic Inequalities and Public Sector Governance*. London, Palgrave.

Banton, Michael. 1983. *Racial and Ethnic Competition*. Cambridge: Cambridge University Press.

Barth, Karl (ed.). 1967. *Ethnic Groups and Boundaries*. Boston: Little and Brown.
Beckwith, Francis J. and Todd E. Jones (eds.). 1997. *Affirmative Action: Social Justice or Reverse Discrimination?* Amherst, New York: Prometheus Books.
Bennell, P. and B. Strachan. 1992. 'The Zimbabwean Experience: Black Occupational Advancement' in P. Hugo (ed.), *Redistribution and Affirmative Action*, Southern Book Publishers, Halfway House.
Brown, G.K. 2005. 'Horizontal inequalities, ethnic separatism, and violent conflict: The case of Aceh, Indonesia' in *Human Development Report Office Occasional Paper 2005/28*, New York: United Nations Development Programme.
Brown, G.K. 2008. 'Horizontal inequalities and separatism in Southeast Asia: A comparative perspective' in F. Stewart (ed.), *Horizontal Inequalities and Conflict: Understanding Group Violence in Multiethnic Societies*, Basingstoke: Palgrave-Macmillan.
Brown, G.K. and A. Langer. 2005. 'Horizontal inequality or polarization?: Inter-group economic disparity and its relationship with conflict'. Paper presented to the IGCC Conference on Disaggregating the Study of Civil War and Transnational Violence, San Diego, CA.
Brubaker, R. 1992. *Citizenship and Nationhood in France and Germany*, Cambridge, MA: Harvard University Press.
Brubaker, R. 2004. *Ethnicity Without Groups*. Cambridge, MA: Harvard University Press.
Brubaker, R. and F. Cooper. 2000. 'Beyond "identity"' in *Theory and Society*, 29 (1): 1–47.
Campbell, Tom. 2000. *Justice*. London: Macmillan.
Carnegie Commission. 1997. *Preventing Deadly Conflict: Final Report*. Washington DC: Carnegie Commission on Deadly Conflict.
Castle, J. 1995. 'Affirmative Action in Three Developing Countries: Lessons from Zimbabwe, Namibia, and Malaysia' in *South African Journal of Labor Relations*, 19 (1): 6–33.
Castles, Stephen and Alistair Davidson. 2004. *Citizenship and Migration: Globalization and the Politics of Belonging*. London: Routledge.
Christie, Kenneth (ed.). 1998. *Ethnic Conflict, Tribal Politics: A Global Perspective*, Richmond: Curzon.
Cohen, Carl. 1995. *Naked Racial Preference*. Lanham, Maryland: Madison Books.
Cohen, Carl. 1998. 'The Corruption That is Group Preference' in *Academic Questions*, 11 (Summer): 14–22.
Cohen, Carl, and James Sterba. 2003. *Affirmative Action and Racial Preferences: A Debate*, New York: Oxford University Press.
Collier, P., V.L. Elliott, H. Hegre, A. Hoeffler, M. Reynal-Querol and N. Sambani. 2003. *Breaking the Conflict Trap: Civil war and development policy*. Washington DC: World Bank.
Collier, P. and A. Hoeffler. 2004. 'Greed and grievance in civil war' in *Oxford Economic Papers*, 56 (4): 563–95.
Connor, Walker. 1994. *Ethnonationalism: The Quest For Understanding*. Princeton, New Jersey: Princeton University Press.
Curry, George E. (ed.). 1996. *The Affirmative Action Debate*. Reading, Massachusetts: Addison-Wesley Publishing Company.
Daniels, Norman. 1978. 'Meritocracy' in John Arthur and William Shaw (eds.), *Justice and Economic Distribution*. Prentice-Hall, Englewood Cliffs, NJ.
Depres, Leo (ed.). 1975. *Ethnicity and Resource Competition*. Hague: Houghton.

Depres, Leo and Ralph Premdas. 2000. 'Theories of Ethnic Contestation and Their Relationship to Economic Development' in Ralph Premdas (ed.), *Identity, Ethnicity and Culture in the Caribbean*. St.Augustine, Trinidad: School of Continuing Studies, University of the West Indies.

Dipankar, Gupta. 1998. 'Recasting Reservations in the Language of Rights' in Gurpreet Mahajan (ed.), *Democracy, Difference, and Social Justice*. Oxford: Mumbai.

Dworkin, Ronald, 1985. *A Matter of Principle*. Cambridge, Massachusetts: Harvard University Press.

Fearon, J.D., 2004. 'Separatist wars, partition, and world order' in *Security Studies*, 13 (4): 394–415.

Fearon, J.D. and D.D. Laitin. 2003. 'Ethnicity, insurgency and civil war' in *The American Political Science Review*, 97 (1): 75–90.

Fenton, Steven and Stephen May (eds.). 2002. *Ethnonational Identities*. Basingstoke: Palgrave.

Ferguson, J. and A. Gupta. 2002. 'Spatializing States: Toward an Ethnography of Neoliberal Governmentality' in *American Ethnologist*, 29 (4): 981–1002.

Fryer Jr., R.G. and G.C. Loury. 2005. 'Affirmative Action and its Mythology' in *Journal of Economic Perspectives*, 19 (3), Summer: 147–162.

Fullinwider, Robert K. 1975. 'Preferential Hiring and Compensation' in *Social Theory and Practice*, (Spring): 307–320.

Fullinwider, Robert K. 1980. *The Reverse Discrimination Controversy: A Moral and Legal Analysis*. Totowa, New Jersey: Rowman and Littlefield.

Gilroy, P. 2000. *Between Camps: Nations, Cultures and the Allure of Race*. London: Routledge.

Glazer, Nathan. 1975. *Affirmative Discrimination: Ethnic Inequality and Public Policy*. New York: Basic Books.

Glazer, Nathan. 1983. 'Individual Rights and Group Rights' in N. Glazer, *Ethnic Dilemmas*. Cambridge: Harvard University Press 1983.

Goldman, Alan. 1976. 'Affirmative Action' in *Philosophy & Public Affairs*, 5 (Winter): 178–95.

Goldman, Alan. 1979. *Justice and Reverse Discrimination*. Princeton, New Jersey: Princeton University Press.

Gomez, E.T. and K.S. Jomo 1999. *Malaysia's Political Economy: Politics, Patronage and Profits*. Cambridge: Cambridge University Press.

Geertz, Clifford. 1963. 'The Integrative Revolution: Primordial Sentiments and Civil Politics in the New States' in C. Geertz (ed.), *Old Societies and New States*. New York: Free Press.

Gellner, Ernest. 1983. *Nations and Nationalism*. London: Blackwell Publishers.

Graham, Hugh Davis. 1990. *The Civil Rights Era: Origins and Development of National Policy 1960–1972*. New York: Oxford University Press.

Green, E.D. 2004. 'The (mis)use of ethnicity in current political economy literature: Conceptual and data issues' in *WIDER Conference on Making Peace Work*, 4–5 June, Helsinki: World Institute of Development Economics Research, United Nations University.

Guinier, Lani and Sturm, Susan. 2001. *Who's Qualified?* Boston: Beacon Press.

Gurr, T.D. 1992. *Minorities at Risk: A Global View of Ethnopolitical Conflicts*, Washington DC: Institute of Peace Press.

Hale, C.R. 2005. 'Neoliberal Multiculturalism: The Remaking of Cultural Rights and Racial Dominance in Central America' in *Political and Legal Anthropology Review*, 289 (1): 10–28.

Harvey, D. 2005. *A Brief History of Neoliberalism*. Oxford: Oxford University Press.
Hechter, M. 1992. 'The dynamics of secession' in *Acta Sociologica*, 35: 267–83.
Hegre, H. and N. Sambanis. 2006. 'Sensitivity analysis of empirical results on civil war onset' in *Journal of Conflict Resolution*, 50 (4): 508–35.
Hobsbawm, Eric. 1990. *Nations and Nationalism Since 1780*. Cambridge: Cambridge University Press.
Horowitz, D.L. 1981. 'Patterns of ethnic separatism' in *Comparative Studies in Society and History*, 23 (2): 165–95.
Horowitz, D.L. 1985. *Ethnic Groups in Conflict*. Berkeley: University of California Press.
Htun, M. 2004. 'From "Racial Democracy" to Affirmative Action: Changing State Policy on Race in Brazil' in *Latin American Research Review*, 39 (1): 60–89.
Isaacs, Harold R. 1975. *Idols of the Tribe: Group Identity and Political Change*. New York: Harper and Row.
Kanbur, R. and A.J. Venables (eds.). 2005. *Spatial Inequality and Development*. Oxford: Oxford University Press.
Kellough, J. Edward. 2006. *Understanding Affirmative Action: Politics, Discrimination, and the Search for Justice*. Washington DC: Georgetown University Press.
Kelly, E. and F. Dobbin. 2001. 'How Affirmative Action Became Diversity Management: Employer Response to Anti-Discrimination Law, 1961–1996' in John D. Skrentny (ed.), *Color Lines: Affirmative Action, Immigration, and Civil Rights Options for America*. Chicago: University of Chicago Press.
Kymlicka, Will. 1996. *Multicultural Citizenship*. Oxford: Clarendon Press.
Lawrence, Charles R. III and Mari J. Matsuda. 1997. *We Won't Go Back: Making the Case for Affirmative Action*. Boston: Hougton Mifflin Company.
Lichtenberg, Judith and David Luban. 2002. 'The Merits of Merit' in Verna V. Gehring and William A. Galston (eds.), *Philosophical Dimensions of Public Policy*. New Brunswick, New Jersey: Transaction Publishers, pp. 101–113.
Lijphart, A. 1977. *Democracy in Plural Societies: A Comparative Exploration*. New Haven: Yale University Press.
Lijphart, A. 1986. 'Proportionality by non-PR methods: Ethnic representation in Belgium, Cyprus, Lebanon, New Zealand, West Germany, and Zimbabwe' in A. Lijphart and B. Grofman (eds.), *Electoral Laws and Their Political Consequences*. New York: Agathon Press.
Lijphart, A. 2004. 'Constitutional design for divided societies' in *Journal of Democracy*, 15 (2): 96–109.
Lindsay, B. 1998. 'Toward Conceptual, Policy, and Programmmatic Frameworks of Affirmative Action in South African Universities' in *Journal of Negro Education*, 66 (4): 522–38.
Loury, Glen. 1987. 'Why Should We Care About Group Inequality' in Paul Miller and Ahrens (eds.), *Equal Opportunity*. Oxford.
Mahajan, Gurpreet (ed.). 1998. *Democracy, Difference and Social Justice*. New Delhi: Oxford University Press.
Mamdani, Mahmood. 2001. *When Victims Become Killers*. New Jersey: Princeton University Press.
Marx, A.W. 2000. *Making Race and Nation: A Comparison of the United States, South Africa and Brazil*. Cambridge: Cambridge University Press.
McGarry, J. and B. O'Leary (eds.). 1993. *The Politics of Ethnic Conflict Regulation: Case Studies of Protracted Ethnic Conflicts*. London: Routledge.

Murdoch, J.C. and T. Sandler. 2002. 'Civil wars and economic growth: A regional comparison' in *Defence and Peace Economics*, 13 (6): 451–64.
Nozick, Robert. 1972. *Anarchy, State, and Utopia*. London: Blackwell.
Nagel, Thomas. 1973. 'Equal Treatment and Compensatory Discrimination' in *Philosophy & Public Affairs*, 2 (Summer): 348–63.
Nevitte, Neil and Paul Kennedy (eds.). 1986. *Ethnic Preference and Public Policy in Developing States*. Boulder, Colorado: Lynne Rienner.
Oberst, R. 1986. 'Policies of Ethnic Preference in Sri Lanka' in N. Nevitte and C.H. Kennedy (eds.), *Ethnic Preference and Public Policy in Developing States*. Boulder: Lynne Rienner.
Østby, G. 2008. 'Horizontal inequalities, political environment and civil conflict: Evidence from 55 developing countries' in F. Stewart (ed.), *Horizontal Inequalities and Conflict: Understanding Group Violence in Multiethnic Societies*. Basingstoke: Palgrave-Macmillan.
Parikh, Sunita. 1997. *The Politics of Preference: Democratic Institutions and Affirmative Action in the United States and India*. Ann Arbor: University of Michigan Press.
Parikh, Sunita. 2001. 'Affirmative Action, Caste, and Party Politics in Contemporary India' in John David Skrentny (ed.), *Color Lines: Affirmative Action, Immigration, and Civil Rights Options for America*. University of Chicago Press, Chicago.
Phillips, Ann. 1996. *Which Equalities Matter?* London: Polity Press.
Pojman, Louis. 1992. 'The Moral Status of Affirmative Action' in *Public Affairs Quarterly*, 6 (April): 181–206.
Pojman, Louis. 1998. 'The Case against Affirmative Action' in *International Journal of Applied Philosophy*, 12 (Spring): 97–115.
Pojman, Louis P. and R. Westmoreland (eds.). 1997. *Equality: Selected Readings*. London: Oxford University Press.
Premdas, Ralph. 1986. 'The Politics of Preference in the Caribbean: The Case of Guyana' in Neil Nevitte and Paul Kennedy (eds.), *Ethnic Preference and Public Policy in Developing States*. Boulder, Colorado: Lynne Rienner.
Premdas, Ralph. 1989. 'The Political Economy of Ethnic Strife' in *Ethnic Studies Report* (Fall).
Premdas, Ralph. 1993. 'The Anatomy of Ethnic Conflict' in R. Premdas (ed.), *The Enigma of Ethnicity: An Analysis of Race and Ethnicity in the Caribbean and the World*. St. Augustine, Trinidad: University of the West Indies Press.
Premdas, Ralph. 1995 *Ethnicity and Development: The Case of Guyana*. London: Avebury Press.
Premdas, Ralph. 1996. *Public Policy and Ethnic Conflict*. Paris: UNESCO. Management of Social Transformation Programme, Working paper No. 12.
Premdas, Ralph. 2003. 'Multi-Ethnic Divisions and Governance: The Problem of Institutional Reform and Adaptation' in Denis Benn and Kenneth Hall (eds.), *Governance in the Age of Globalisation: Caribbean Perspectives*. Jamaica, Mona: Ian Randle Press.
Premdas, Ralph. 2007. *Ethnic Conflict, Inequality and Public Sector Governance*. Basingstoke: Palgrave.
Premdas, Ralph. 2010. 'Ethnic Conflict' in Patricia H. Collins and John Solomos (eds.), *The Sage Handbook of Race and Ethnic Studies*. London: Sage.
Rabuska, A. and K. Shepsle. 1972. *Politics in Plural Societies*. Ohio: Merrill Lynch.
Rachels, James. 1978. 'What People Deserve' in John Arthur and William Shaw (eds.), *Justice and Economic Distribution*. Englewood Cliffs, New Jersey: Prentice-Hall: 150–63.

Rawls, John. 1971. *A Theory of Justice*. Cambridge, Massachusetts: Harvard University Press.
Rosenfeld, Michel. 1991. *Affirmative Action and Justice: A Philosophical and Constitutional Inquiry*. New Haven, Connecticut: Yale University Press.
Sen, Amartya. 1992. *Inequality Examined*. London: Sage.
Sheth, D.L. 1998. 'Reservations Policy Revisited' in Gurpreet Mahajan (ed.), *Democracy, Difference, and Social Justice*. Mumbai: Oxford University Press.
Sher, George. 1979. 'Reverse Discrimination, the Future, and the Past' in *Ethics*, 90 (October): 81–7.
Sher, George. 1997. *Approximate Justice: Studies in Non-Ideal Theory*. Lanham, Maryland: Rowman & Littlefield.
Sowell, T. 2004. *Affirmative Action around the World: An Empirical Study*. New Haven, CT: Yale University Press.
Sterba, James P. 2003. 'Defending Affirmative Action, Defending Preferences' in *Journal of Social Philosophy*, 34 (June): 285–300.
Stewart, F. 2002. 'Horizontal inequalities: A neglected dimension of development', Queen Elizabeth House Working Paper Series 81.
Stewart, F. (ed.). 2008. *Horizontal Inequalities and Conflict: Understanding Group Violence in Multiethnic Societies*. Basingstoke: Palgrave-Macmillan.
Stewart, F. and G. Brown. 2007. 'Motivations for conflict: Groups and individuals' in C. Crocker *et al.* (eds.), *Leashing the Dogs of War: Conflict management in a divided world*. Vols. 217–39, Washington, DC: United States Institute of Peace.
Stewart, F., G.K. Brown and A. Langer. 2008. 'Policies towards horizontal inequalities' in F. Stewart (ed.), *Horizontal Inequalities and Conflict: Understanding Group Violence in Multiethnic Countries*. Basingstoke: Palgrave-Macmillan.
Skrentny. John David. 1996. *The Ironies of Affirmative Action: Politics, Culture, and Justice in America*. Chicago: University of Chicago Press.
Skrentny. John David. (ed.). 2001. *Color Lines: Affirmative Action, Immigration, and Civil Rights Options for America*. Chicago: University of Chicago Press.
Stavenhagen, Rodolfo. 1996. *Ethnic Conflicts and the Nation-State*. New York: St. Martin's Press.
Tarling, Nicholas and Edmund Terence Gomez (eds.). 2008. *The State, Development and Identity in Multi-Ethnic Societies: Ethnicity, Equity and the Nation*. London: Routledge.
Taylor, Charles. 1994. 'The Politics of Recognition' in A. Guttman (ed.), *Multiculturalism*. Princeton NJ: Princeton University Press.
Tajfel, Henry. 1970. 'Experiments in Intergroup Discrimination' in *Scientific American*, 223: 96–102.
Taylor Donald M. and F.M. Moghaddam. 1994. *Theories of Inter-Group Relations*. New York: Praeger.
Tong C.K. and Chan K.B. (eds.). 2001. *Alternate Identities: The Chinese of Contemporary Thailand*. Singapore: Times Academic Press.
Varshney, A. 2002. *Ethnic Conflict and Civic Life: Hindus and Muslims in India*. New Haven: Yale University Press.
Walzer, Michael. 1983. *Spheres of Justice: A Defence of Pluralism and Equality*. New York: Basic Books.
Weisskopf, T.E. 2004. *Affirmative Action in the United States and India: A Comparative Perspective*. London: Routledge.
Westen, Peter. 1985. 'The Concept of Equality' in *Ethics*, 95: 830–50.

Young, Crawford. 1985. 'Ethnicity and the colonial and post-colonial state in Africa' in P. Brass (ed.), *Ethnic Groups and the State*. London and Sydney: Croon Helm.

Young, Crawford. 1993. 'The Dialectics of Cultural Pluralism: Concept and Reality' in Crawford Young (ed.), *The Rising Tide of Cultural Pluralism: The Nation-State At Bay?* Madison: University of Wisconsin Press.

Young, Crawford. 2003. 'Explaining the conflict potential of ethnicity' in J. Darby and R. MacGinty (eds.), *Contemporary Peacemaking: Conflict, Violence and Peace Processes*. Basingstoke: Palgrave-Macmillan.

Young, Iris Marion. 1990. *Justice and the Politics of Difference*. Princeton, New Jersey: Princeton University Press.

1 Poverty, equality, and affirmative action in India

Sunita Parikh

Introduction

Among the sets of policies that countries develop and implement to combat poverty, affirmative action occupies a singular place. While poverty reduction is a stated goal of almost all affirmative action programmes, not all emerged as a direct response to poverty. Unlike universal and group-neutral policies, affirmative action is explicitly targeted at individuals and/or groups on the basis of ascriptive characteristics such as race, ethnicity, and gender. Early policy efforts in the United States and India focused on social groups who comprised a minority of the total population and who had experienced discrimination, oppression, and exclusion. These policies were justified first and foremost in terms of compensation for past wrongs. Increasingly, however, affirmative action has been expanded to include groups who are a majority of the population, and the rationale for the policies has extended beyond compensation to more diffuse social goals such as diversity of representation. While affirmative action has never been completely free of controversy, the expanding scope and range of policies have led to increased opposition and given rise to considerable social conflict. Given the social and political capital that is often expended to defend affirmative action, it is especially important to understand the benefits and drawbacks of these policies across a variety of contexts.

India began experimenting with affirmative action policies at the state level in the early twentieth century and defined eligibility through combinations of characteristics such as caste, national origin, and language. Affirmative action policies have been challenged formally through legal and political channels and informally through social protest. While many of these challenges have come from non-targeted groups who argue they are unfairly disadvantaged by these programmes, opposition has also arisen from individuals and groups within the targeted population. These conflicts have repercussions for society as a whole and for political and social relations within groups, especially when affirmative action leads to increased heterogeneity of economic and political status among beneficiaries.

This increased heterogeneity is a consequence of the second common factor: most affirmative action policies treat targeted groups as homogeneous, but members' abilities to take advantage of these programmes are not equal. Over time, therefore, most targeted groups become increasingly heterogeneous, and in most cases the best off within the targeted group utilize affirmative action while those with fewer resources are left behind. While intra-group solidarity can mitigate the potential conflicts that arise from this inequality, policies that aggregate a variety of ethnic or other identities within one category can create or exacerbate tensions across sub-groups.

This chapter reviews the historical context and specific policies through which affirmative action was formulated and introduced in India, as well as how it was subsequently expanded or constrained. The chapter examines the conditions under which affirmative action policies were adopted, variations in types of policies chosen, and variations in outcomes, with particular attention paid to variations in the ability of groups to make use of the opportunities afforded by the programmes. The effects of affirmative action on the targeted groups as well as between targeted and non-targeted groups in both the short and the long run are also considered. This study determines the capacity of different affirmative action programmes to reduce ethnic and spatial inequalities and considers the trade-offs between negative and positive consequences of policy implementation. The interaction of affirmative action and other social processes, in particular immigration and the influence of immigration on affirmative action implementation, is examined. This study concludes with a more detailed assessment of affirmative action's effects on intra-group and inter-group relations.

Scope and range of reservation policies

India can be considered the earliest adopter of policies which fall under the definition of affirmative action. Independent India established reservations for Scheduled Castes (SCs) and Scheduled Tribes (STs) in the new Constitution of India in 1950. The development of affirmative action policies occurred almost entirely as a result of domestic conditions, and to the extent that there are similarities between policies in India and other countries, such as the United States, they are due to similarities of social and political contexts rather than to any conscious learning and adoption by one country from the other. By contrast, the other countries examined in this study were aware of and influenced by policies in the United States and India.

Early affirmative action policies focused on historically oppressed groups and were intended to provide opportunities beyond those offered by the removal of legal barriers to equality. These policies encompassed political representation and access to positions in government employment and higher education, and their implementation ranged from non-specific "goals and timetables" for representation of targeted groups to precisely enumerated quotas that were required to be filled. The initial groups of beneficiaries comprised a minority of the population at the time: SCs and STs comprised about 22 per cent of Indian society. Over time, affirmative action was expanded to other groups, who raised the targeted population to a majority.

Reservation policy development

In the early twentieth century the British colonial government introduced limited political participation for Indians. Participation was structured according to group identities, which encouraged indigenous demands for group-based preferences as political participation increased. However, the first affirmative action policies were initiated in a princely state that was not in the direct control of British India. In 1922 the Maharajah of Mysore initiated reserved places for low castes in government employment and public higher education. Simultaneously, in the British Indian province of Madras, low caste Hindus demanded and received reservations in provincial elections. Thus, by the time that M.K. Gandhi and B.R. Ambedkar negotiated their famous compromise over Scheduled Caste electoral reservations in the Poona Pact of 1932, the principle of creating quotas on the basis of caste status had already been established. Reservations for SC and STs in the national and state legislatures were institutionalized in the Constitution of India (1950), while reservations for low caste Hindus (Other Backward Classes, or OBCs) in government employment and public higher education continued in the southern states of Madras and Mysore in independent India (Galanter 1984; Parikh 1997). Legislative reservations were envisioned as a transitional policy: they were fixed for a ten-year period and Parliament was responsible for revisiting the issue and renewing the provisions if necessary at the expiration of the decade. To date, reservations have never been made permanent, but Parliament has renewed them every ten years.

Although it is somewhat surprising that reservations were continued and expanded in independent India, these programmes represented a retreat from the colonial policies of separate electorates in representation. Abolition of electoral reservations for SC and STs and the prohibition of state-level reservations in education and employment in southern states of the country would have constituted a departure from the established status quo and created dissent within the Congress Party. Even Jawaharlal Nehru, India's first Prime Minister, who was opposed to ethnically-based policies, grudgingly accepted reservations as "helping backward groups in the country", although he also noted, "I am glad that this reservation also will be limited to ten years" (quoted in Parikh 1997: 158).The dismal conditions in which SC and ST groups lived provided justification for reservation policies, but these conditions also ensured that few members of the groups would be able to utilize the access they were granted. The goals of the policies were fairly vague, especially compared to those put forth later by adopters of affirmative action in other countries. Leaders may have assumed that political access would improve SC and ST conditions over time, and given the daunting political and economic challenges they faced at independence, they were more concerned with increasing economic development for the many impoverished members of Indian society.

In the 1950s and 1960s, Indian politics and society maintained an unstable equilibrium with regard to reservations. The national and state reservations for SCs and STs were expanded to include reservations in government employment and higher education, with little public opposition. The relatively small number of seats involved (a number that shrank further if one considered only the seats that were actually utilized), the very public support of SC issues by Gandhi and his Congress Party, and the clear history of oppression and exclusion suffered by the targeted groups, combined to solidify political support for the policy. There was a political consensus with respect to national and state-level reservations in legislatures, public employment, and public higher education for SCs and STs. In addition, state-level reservations in employment and education for OBCs were accepted for the unusual social conditions in South India. Nevertheless, in the 1950s the debate over the Kalelkar's Commission's recommendations to expand national reservations to OBCs revealed the shaky foundations of this consensus (Parikh 1997).

The adoption of reservation policies for OBCs in South India had led political activists in other parts of India to demand similar benefits at the national level. In response, a commission was formed to explore the feasibility of OBC reservations; it was chaired by a retired judge, Kaka Kalelkar, and it was comprised of other highly regarded judges and academics. The Commission understood its terms of reference as privileging caste status over other identities. But it soon became evident that there could be substantial variation in the relative status positions of castes with similar or identical names and occupations. This led to considerable disagreement over how group qualifications for benefits might be determined. The Commission issued a report to Parliament, but its effectiveness was undercut by the number of commissioners who opposed part or all of the report's findings and recommendations. Kalelkar himself repudiated many of its recommendations, and the report was quickly tabled after a brief, almost perfunctory, discussion in Parliament (Galanter 1984).

There was no disagreement over including OBC groups within the targeted category in South India, where a skewed caste structure had resulted in centuries of social and economic dominance by a tiny Brahmin elite, and low castes were willing to allow prosperous lower castes to monopolize reservations as long as Brahmin privilege was eroded. Unlike SC and ST reservations, OBC quotas were more often fully utilized, but there were so many low castes in the population (in most areas, non-Brahmin high castes and middle castes were few or absent in number) that nearly all of the population was eligible to be part of the targeted group.

The Supreme Court repeatedly attempted to prevent reservations in south Indian states from approaching the same percentages as the total SC/ST/OBC population (which reached nearly 90 per cent in some states). The most important case was *Balaji* v. *Mysore*, in which the Supreme Court restricted the total percentage of reserved seats to 50 per cent, regardless of the population size of the targeted group. But this limitation was politically untenable for south Indian political actors, and implementation of reservations frequently exceeded the Supreme Court's limit.

In the 1970s the then Prime Minister, Indira Gandhi, expanded her electoral base by appealing directly to low caste and SC and ST voters, and a major plank of her platform was the expansion of state-level reservation policies to OBC groups in northern and western India. Despite quota percentages that were set at levels well below the OBC proportion of the population, conflicts erupted in states from impoverished Bihar to prosperous Gujarat. Opposition to reservations reached a climax in 1990, when the central government announced that it would adopt the recommendations of the second national commission on reservations, chaired by B.P. Mandal.

The reintroduction of the Mandal Commission report came as a shock to both supporters and opponents of reservation policies. The Commission had been appointed early in the tenure of the post-Emergency Janata coalition. Janata leaders knew that even though they had handily defeated Indira Gandhi in the 1977 Parliamentary elections, they needed to attract OBC voters, and the consideration of national reservations was part of that strategy. By the time the Commission reported back to Parliament, however, Indira Gandhi had been returned to power, and she quietly shelved the Commission report rather than contend with the controversy it was bound to engender. The report was consigned to bureaucratic oblivion, to the point that in the late 1980s it was impossible to purchase a copy from the government publications offices.

V.P. Singh's tenuous coalition government revived the dormant question of national OBC reservations because, like the Janata coalition before it, it was unsure of their appeal to low caste voters, and reservations were a highly salient electoral issue (Parikh 1997). But the violent backlash that greeted the announcement made it clear that any electoral gains would be offset by the loss of high caste support and widespread social unrest. After weeks of rioting, the government asked the Supreme Court for a fast-track consideration of the constitutionality of the Mandal Commission's recommendations.

The Supreme Court issued its decision in *Indira Sawhney v. Union of India*. It upheld a modified version of the Commission's recommendations in 1992, affirming the constitutionality of reservations but requiring that the "creamy layer" of the OBCs, i.e., the best off within the targeted groups, be excluded from consideration. While many observers expected riots in response to the decision, they did not materialize, and the issue was almost immediately eclipsed by the worst Hindu–Muslim riots since the partition of British India (Parikh 1998).

Reservation policies in India today have essentially the same scope as when they were adopted at independence, but they incorporate more groups. Reservations in the national and provincial legislatures are still limited to SC and ST groups, but reservations in higher education and employment are now provided at the national level in addition to many state-level programmes (Jaffrelot 2003). The Supreme Court's 1992 *Indira Sawhney* decision has extended reserved seats for OBCs to national colleges and universities, including the Indian Institutes of Technology, and to the national services such as the Administrative, Police, and Statistical Services. The decision reiterated the Court's earlier directive that no more than 50 per cent of seats could be reserved in total, and it added the proviso that the wealthiest members of targeted groups, the "creamy layer", should be excluded. Nonetheless, some states continue to implement policies in which more than 50 per cent of seats are reserved, and litigation is ongoing (Jaffrelot 2003).

Despite the apparent acceptance of national reservations for both the SC/ST and OBC populations, it is doubtful that this equilibrium is more stable than the national and regional compacts negotiated in the 1950s. The coalescence of voters into "forward" and "backward" categories obscures the growing heterogeneity within the "backward" bloc, and the growth of economic inequality as a by-product of economic reforms suggests that both OBCs and non-targeted middle castes who are excluded from the benefits of increased growth may decide to challenge the current policies from a variety of perspectives (Parikh 2001). Implementation of quotas has been softened for non-targeted groups by returning unused seats to the general pool, but if greater numbers of OBCs are able to take advantage of the policies this option will diminish.

Reservation policies have contributed to increased political and economic achievement for the targeted groups, but the outcomes have varied. OBCs were best placed to take advantage of increased access, and many OBC groups have gained political and economic power, especially in South India. For the SCs and STs, however, the outcomes have been mixed. Certain SC castes were able to take advantage of reservations because they were in a strategic economic position: for example, Vankars in Gujarat became urban textile workers in the late colonial period, and their increased economic and educational capital enabled them to utilize a disproportionate share of reserved seats in government employment and education. And since the 1990s some SC-dominated political parties have become successful in capturing vote and seat shares in state and national elections in northern states (Chandra 2004). However, because these benefits have been unevenly distributed within the targeted groups, heterogeneity among them has increased and with it internal dissent, as less advantaged targeted groups are left behind.

Outcomes and consequences of reservation policies

This section analyses the intended and unintended consequences of affirmative action policies in order to identify patterns that recur across time and groups. First, whether the stated goals of the policies have been achieved is determined. Then, the effect of affirmative action policies and their outcomes on spatial and ethnic inequality is considered. Next, the effects of the policies on inter-group and intra-group relations are assessed, paying special attention to the ways in which ethnic identities have been shaped or changed. Particular focus is given to examining one of the most distressing, unintended, and widespread consequences of affirmative action; that is the extent to which affirmative action has resulted in a backlash against the policies and their beneficiaries and the occurrence of non-violent and violent conflict.

Affirmative action goals versus outcomes in India

To what extent have the stated goals of affirmative action policies been achieved? In their original formulation reservations were intended to reduce poverty, increase political power, and develop an educated and prosperous elite that could assume leadership of their communities. Programmes were developed in two key areas: electoral representation, in which targeted groups were guaranteed a proportion of legislative seats, and access to positions in government employment and institutions of higher education. India has experienced a reduction in poverty among at least some of the beneficiaries of affirmative action, members of targeted groups have become politically influential at the national and sub-national levels, and in each case a prosperous middle class has emerged.

However, it is important to note that even in the relatively successful cases, these goals have not been fully achieved. In all regions of India, and across all policies, access to and utilization of affirmative action programmes have been distributed unequally across the range of eligible groups. When the beneficiaries are members of a numerical majority, a sub-set of the targeted group almost always becomes politically dominant and frequently becomes economically powerful as well. In South India, for example, majority-group beneficiaries have utilized their preferential access and their large numbers to achieve political prominence and to enrich themselves through government-controlled economic opportunities. By contrast, for the SCs and STs, where the targeted groups comprise a minority of the population, economic gains are not always matched by political gains. Table 1.1 shows SC representation in the prestigious and politically influential Indian Administrative Services employment category. It is worth noting that while there were major increases between 1965 and 1995, especially in the lower ranks, the representation in the highest grade has increased more slowly, and even declined after 1995.

Despite genuine positive outcomes, intra-group inequality has increased even when overall poverty has fallen, and the most prosperous members have made substantial economic gains. And since affirmative action policies also do not take into account spatial inequality, disparities between beneficiaries in different regions, or between urban and rural beneficiaries, have continued or increased. Table 1.2 shows the rural–urban difference in poverty rates for SCs and non-SCs.

These increases in intra-ethnic inequality can be explained at least in part by the way in which affirmative action programmes are defined. Although preferences can in theory be awarded on the basis of a number of different criteria, they are almost always based on ethnic identity, and their access comes at a late

Table 1.1 Percentage of SCs in central government posts by category: 1965, 1995, and 2001

Category	I	II	III	IV	All
1965	1.64	2.82	8.88	17.8	13.2
1995	10.1	12.7	16.2	21.3	17.4
2001	11.4	12.8	16.3	17.9	16.4

Sources: NCSCST 1998; Planning Commission 2005.

Table 1.2 Percentage below the poverty line (BPL): 1983, 1993–4, 2004–5

	Rural			Urban		
	SC	Non-SC/ST	Total	SC	Non-SC/ST	Total
1983	59.0	40.5	46.4	56.1	39.6	42.1
1993–4	48.3	31.4	37.2	49.8	29.4	32.6
2004–5	36.8	22.7	28.3	39.8	22.6	25.6

Source: NSS 1983, (2001, 2007.

stage of human capital development. For example, SCs and STs receive both preferential access to universities, and subsidies in tuition and housing, to enable them to take advantage of that access. But even with these support programmes, many SC and ST reservations go unclaimed because the beneficiaries have not received the adequate primary and secondary schooling to meet the relaxed requirements. Critics have pressed repeatedly for policy modifications to exclude the most privileged members of targeted groups and to target members earlier so that access is more widely used, but the political influence of current beneficiaries makes politicians loath to change the status quo.

Finally, a consistent outcome of affirmative action is the persistence of policies across time. In India, decennial renewal of electoral reservations has brought about regular discussions about whether affirmative action should be continued, but any decision to abolish SC and ST reservations would be difficult to implement without also reducing or abolishing OBC reservations, and no major political party can afford to support such a move.

Ethnic and spatial inequality

The designation of beneficiaries according to racial and ethnic categories flows from the assumption that the ethnic identities of individuals and groups are the primary cause of political and economic inequality. While this assumption is justified at the aggregate level, it obscures at least two other critical variations: intra-ethnic variation (both in inequality and in capital endowment) and spatial variation. In India, reservation policies in southern states such as Tamil Nadu and Karnataka have essentially excluded only Brahmins, who comprise less than 5 per cent of the population. Within the vast OBC population the most privileged "dominant castes" have been best placed to take advantage of reservations, while less advantaged beneficiaries have seen little improvement in their conditions (Srinivas 1962). Recent studies have consistently found that intra-caste inequality is persistent for OBC and ST caste groups (see, e.g. Ajit Zacharias's research on intra-caste inequality).

In addition to intra-group inequality, spatial inequality frequently persists or worsens after affirmative action policies are implemented. Rural–urban differences can be exacerbated by affirmative action because the opportunities provided by the policies are unevenly taken up. For example, the ability to take advantage of access to higher education is conditioned on primary and secondary education success. An analysis of the 2005 Indian Human Development Survey finds that "educational disparities (sometimes called 'premarket inequalities') account for about 50 per cent of the intercaste disparities in earnings" (Desai and Dubey 2011: 46).

If affirmative action programmes do not include improvements at all levels, then even the most generous higher education preferences will be ineffective. In India, reserved seats have recently been introduced at the prestigious and highly competitive Indian Institutes of Technology. But even with a slight relaxation of the entrance requirements, many OBC and most SC and ST students would not be able to take advantage of them because their secondary school training has usually been gained at inferior public schools. Prosperous group members who can afford private schools and personalized tutoring are the predictable beneficiaries of these reservations. Similarly, preferences designed to encourage entrepreneurship and investment will be disproportionately utilized by members of targeted groups in urban and prosperous rural areas, because they assume a level of infrastructural support that many regions do not have. And even programmes that recognize difference at the sub-national level, such as state-level affirmative action, will be unevenly distributed unless disparities within regions are acknowledged and accounted for in the implementation process. Finally, intergroup measures of inequality can show decreases even as intra-group inequality grows.

Affirmative action and ethnic identity

Given the emphasis that affirmative action policies place on ethnicity and ethnic identity, it is not surprising that ethnicity continues to be a highly salient category. Despite explicitly stated goals to reduce the importance of ethnicity in explaining life chances, there is little evidence that affirmative action policies have led to an overall decline in ethnic identification by either beneficiaries or non-targeted groups. The programmes' foci on ethnicity has critical ramifications in the political arena. First, for many targeted group voters, politicians' support for affirmative action becomes a litmus test of support for the group itself, and candidates risk losing votes if they criticize the policies, let alone advocate their abolition. Second, the existence of affirmative action affects how individuals and groups identify themselves in politics. If the policies are perceived to be a path to greater economic and social opportunity then voters are more likely to consider their ethnicity salient and coalesce around affirmative action and other ethnically specific political issues; inevitably, ethnic identities are reinforced and solidified.

However, while ethnicity remains salient, it does not remain unchanged by preference policy development and implementation, and identities are frequently shaped by the way affirmative action eligibility is specified. In India the emergence of the dichotomous categories of "forward" and "backward" in politics, which represent targeted and non-targeted groups, have provided a basis for political alliances that can increase OBC and SC power (Parikh 2001; Jaffrelot 2003). For example, Mayawati, leader of the Bahujan Samaj Party, has served four terms as Chief Minister of Uttar Pradesh.

But while political power may be increased for disadvantaged groups in the aggregate, both political and economic power tends to be concentrated in the hands of the best off within each category. Thus, the Supreme Court's efforts to exclude the "creamy layer" from reservations, fails at the political level, where this creamy layer is able to dominate the distribution of political and economic resources. Ironically, the emergence of this forward/backward electoral polarization makes the empowerment of the less privileged groups within each category even more difficult.

Most recently, the central government has made the decision to include caste identity in the next census enumeration, which will take place in 2011. This is a remarkable turnaround for the ruling Congress Party, which under Nehru was committed to the abolition of caste and declared caste illegal in the Constitution of India. There has been no reliable caste data at the all-India level since the Census of 1931 that was conducted by the British Indian government during the penultimate decade of colonial rule. There have been intermittent efforts by scholars and reservation policy commissions to enumerate caste at local and regional levels. But the controversies created by the efforts of both the Kalelkar and Mandal Commissions have discouraged the creation of an all-India caste ranking. Castes tend to be regionally defined, and castes with the same name or occupation can have different rankings in different regions. From a political point of view, it is extremely problematic to designate a caste as reservation-eligible in one region and not another. Rather than taking such a politically difficult stance, governments and parties have avoided the issue at the national level.

Thus, the decision to enumerate caste categories represents a victory of political pressure over the practical difficulties of the exercise, and it illustrates the salience which caste and the forward/backward distinction have achieved in Indian politics. It is clear that caste has not only failed to become less relevant in Indian society and politics, but that its importance has become institutionalized, albeit in a new and unexpected form.

Reservations and political violence

Given the economic and political stakes that affirmative action policies create, the presence of violent and non-violent backlashes against them is almost inevitable. However, the scale and intensity of conflict in some cases is extremely troubling, and the effects on inter-group relations in particular pose challenges for long-term social and political conditions.

There are at least three important aspects to the production of violence that originates in affirmative action policy formulation and implementation. First, and least surprisingly, affirmative action has led to increased inter-group conflict among historically competitive communities. In northern India, for example, violence between the upper groups within the backward category and the lower groups within the former category has increased as reservation policies have become more entrenched.

Second, the objects of violence have included both the beneficiaries of affirmative action and groups who are not directly implicated in the initial clash. In the state of Gujarat in India in the 1980s, the triggering event was the proposed expansion of OBC policies in employment and education. But the targets of middle and upper caste violence spread from OBC groups to SCs and STs, whose benefits were not being changed, and to Muslims, who were not part of the targeted group. Finally, the violent conflict that has accompanied affirmative action is often exacerbated by political parties, who use their policy positions to attempt to increase their vote shares. Scholars have demonstrated that political parties have played important roles in fomenting and sustaining violent conflict around the reservation issue (Jaffrelot 2003; Wilkinson 2004; Parikh *et al.* 2006). While political parties inherently seek issues around which they can mobilize supporters, the conflictual nature of affirmative action fosters an environment in which organized political groups, and by extension the political process more generally, can employ violence as a strategic and organizational tool.

The widespread conflict over reservations that erupted regularly in northern and western India from the 1970s through the 1980s has been well documented and analysed. The connection between reservation and communal, that is Hindu–Muslim, violence, is less well known. But the Hindutva strategy of the Bharatiya Janata Party (BJP) and its allies, the Rashtriya Swayamsevak Sangh (RSS) and the Vishva Hindu Parishad (VHP), can be directly traced to the 1990 decision to implement the Mandal Commission's recommendations taken by V.P. Singh's National Front government.

The RSS describes itself a socio-cultural organization that promotes the concept of the "Hindu Rashtra", which defines the Indian nation as essentially Hindu. It has formed the organizational backbone of the BJP, providing the party with grass-roots volunteers, organizational infrastructure, and an overarching political ideology. The VHP adheres to the same philosophy from the perspective of a religious organization that aims to unite disparate strands of Hinduism under the Hindutva banner. For these organizations, caste-based policies run counter to their ideological and practical goals by dividing the Hindu population, and they saw the Mandal strategy as a serious challenge to their ability to appeal to middle and low caste Hindu voters. The Ayodhya (or "mandir") strategy was explicitly adopted weeks after the government's 1990 decision in order to counter political mobilization around caste reservations (Parikh 1998).

The most visible manifestation of this strategy was BJP leader L.K. Advani's announcement that he would undertake a "Rath Yatra", or pilgrimage, from the temple of Somnath in Gujarat to Ayodhya in Uttar Pradesh. The Yatra was seen as a political stunt by many observers, but it drew increasingly larger crowds as it neared its final destination. When Advani was arrested in Bihar, just before he would have entered Uttar Pradesh, there were several outbreaks of violence, and the BJP's subsequent withdrawal of support led to the fall of the V.P. Singh government.

The communal conflict that accompanied the BJP's Rath Yatra in 1990, the widespread riots following the demolition of the mosque at Ayodhya in 1992, the retaliatory Mumbai bombings of 1993, and the Gujarat riots following the Godhra railway deaths in 2002, are all direct or indirect consequences of the BJP's Hindutva-based inclusion of Hindu voters at the expense of Muslim and other minority citizens. Reservation policies per se did not cause these outbursts of violence, but the politicization of reservation policies and the potential electoral consequences of this polarization have led to an environment in which political parties mobilize on the basis of either caste or religious cleavages. In both cases, ethnicity structures the terms of political discourse.

Affirmative action and immigration

Immigration is usually considered to be an issue that is most relevant for developed countries, because the policies studied involve the inward migration of people from other nations. But internal migration is a major social process in many developed countries, in particular rural-to-urban migration within regions and migration from poorer to richer regions. Immigration in India has increased substantially throughout the period in which reservations have been implemented, and the social change that immigration has created has interacted with reservation policy issues and conflicts.

First, and most obviously, immigration poses a conundrum for the implementation of reservation policies at the state and local level. Since reservation policy eligibility is based on caste and class categories that are defined by regional and local characteristics, immigrants who come from different regions are generally not eligible for employment and higher education positions even if they would be considered eligible in their home regions. While this is not a major issue for first generation immigrants, or men who immigrate without their families, as immigrants settle and raise families their children are put into a position of reservation limbo. They may be eligible for national reservations, but these are fewer in number and far more competitive. Thus, over time, immigration can create an additional layer of inequality (both in terms of resources and in terms of access) among potentially eligible citizens.

A second, less obvious consequence of internal migration is the interaction between immigrants and increased political violence. To the extent that labour immigrants are more likely to be young, male, and segregated from the rest of the society in which they are embedded, they provide a pool of participants for perpetrators of violence to draw upon, and they provide scapegoats for those who wish to attribute such violence to "outside elements". Although my own research shows no systematic quantitative relationship between immigrants and political violence, my interview data is full of anecdotal examples in which immigrants are blamed for the emergence and escalation of violent events.

The newest reservation policies: gender quotas in local government

While the focus of reservation policies in India and the focus of this study has understandably been on ethnic affirmative action, there is a need to discuss briefly a set of policies which apply to a different targeted category. India has been experimenting for more than a decade with gender reservations in local government, called *panchayats*. While the central government has repeatedly failed to pass gender reservations in electoral, employment, or educational categories at the state or national level, in the mid-1990s they passed a constitutional amendment requiring gender reservations in village government. This amendment may probably have been passed because this level of politics was thought of as relatively inconsequential and women were considered to be relatively easy to control.

However, neither of these assumptions has been borne out. The decentralization of state authority which has accompanied economic reforms has made state and local governments increasingly important in the distribution of resources, and women politicians have proved to be quite resistant to domination by their male relatives in many cases. While gender reservations are susceptible to the same types of class and "creamy layer" dominance as caste reservations, the presence of women as politicians and policy makers has been shown to increase the implementation of policies considered to be of particular relevance to women, including education, health, sanitation, and good governance (Chattopadhyay and Duflo 2004).

Conclusion

Affirmative action policies in India, both for SC and STs, and for OBCs in southern India, were initially developed to offer accelerated, guaranteed opportunities for members of ethnic groups who had endured discrimination and exclusion. When these groups formed a minority of the population the preferences embedded in the policies were justified on the grounds that abolition of discrimination was insufficient to advance the community. When the groups comprised a majority of a society's population, the preferences were justified as providing a way of establishing a new and more appropriate political and economic status quo. In both cases the programmes were designed primarily to provide access, although they were also accompanied by redistributive efforts such as scholarships and financial subsidies for members of targeted groups. In contrast to the way affirmative action policies have developed in other countries, the private sector in India has been largely exempt from reservation policy requirements.

The conclusion can be drawn that, in India, these limited goals of affirmative action have been met. There have been increased economic and political opportunities for members of the targeted groups, and in most cases social integration and minority representation have also increased. At the same time, however, many regions of India have experienced a rise in intra-ethnic inequality, increased social conflict, and the increased salience of ethnic identity in politics, even in southern states where reservations have been less controversial. But when critics "blame" affirmative action policies for these negative consequences, they often fail to recognize that these consequences are embedded in the nature of the policies themselves; they are a trade-off for the benefits of the policies, which are that they are relatively inexpensive to implement in economic terms and require a low level of intervention in existing institutions (although institutions themselves bear major costs).

While affirmative action policies have been included within the larger umbrella of redistributive policies, this categorization is not entirely accurate in the Indian context. The policies select targeted groups almost entirely on the basis of ascriptive characteristics, assuming that ascriptive identity is a reliable proxy in determining whether the beneficiaries are deserving. While this assumption was defensible in some circumstances in the early years of affirmative action, given the de facto and de jure exclusion that groups suffered, it has become increasingly untenable as affirmative action policies continue, in both minority- and majority-beneficiary contexts, but especially in the latter cases.

The limitations of affirmative action as a redistributive programme arise from two characteristics: its emphasis on access and its focus on ascriptive identity. Indian reservation policies are targeted at the highest levels of education and adult employment. Beneficiaries are expected to have been provided with the human capital that allows them to take advantage of affirmative action. If they have not, there are no provisions within the programmes to overcome this deficiency because affirmative action does not include mechanisms that build educational capital before adulthood. As a result, poorer members of targeted groups are less likely to be able to take advantage of affirmative action, and in the cases studied in India, the rise in intra-ethnic inequality reflects the targeted groups members' uneven ability to take advantage of the opportunities offered.

The limitations that accompany an emphasis on access are intensified by the programmes' stress on ascriptive identity. To the extent that an ethnic group is homogeneous, policies that select beneficiaries on that basis are more likely to provide equal opportunities to all members. But if opportunity is extended without accompanying programmes that ensure all members similar chances, then the programme shifts the competition from one between members of different ethnic groups to one between members of a single ethnic group. Ironically, a successful affirmative action programme will have fewer and fewer beneficiaries from the less advantaged segments of the designated community.

Despite these limitations it is important to recognize that affirmative action programmes have succeeded on their own terms. Previously under-represented groups have increased their representation in politics and the economy. The middle classes in these cases have been expanded through a strong focus on human capital development; this new middle class would not have emerged had its members been denied access to tertiary education. And previously excluded minority and majority populations have been integrated into a wide range of positions in mainstream society and culture. In the Indian context, the symbolic and practical importance of requiring high caste Indians to approach low and scheduled caste officials from a subordinate position should not be underestimated. It is difficult to parse the relative importance of affirmative action policies in particular (as opposed to economic growth and social change in general) but it seems reasonable to conclude that the former policies accelerated the effects of the latter.

Nevertheless, if we examine the role of affirmative action policies in present and future economic and political development, rather than its effects in the past, it is difficult to justify their continuation as currently formulated. The policies are predicated on the identification of a static form of ethnic identity even as ethnicity becomes more malleable and changeable through caste integration and social mixing through immigration, marriage, and other social processes. Proponents may have hoped that affirmative action would decrease inter-ethnic group differences, but declines in economic and social inequality have been accompanied by the increase of ethnic differentiation in politics. In turn, ethnic political divisions have increased the incentives for political parties to adopt ethnic-group-specific policy positions. In most cases these processes have led to competition and conflict between groups, and in some cases they have contributed to violence and even civil war.

A less widely recognized disadvantage of affirmative action is apparent from this study of India: policies that give the government a large role in selecting beneficiaries for access to affirmative action concessions frequently promote rent-seeking behaviour by politicians and increase the likelihood of economic development that is marked by crony capitalism. While there is nothing inherent in the policies that leads to these outcomes, the dominant role of government in the economy, and the political benefits of targeting supporters, makes implementation of affirmative action based on political rewards extremely common.

Supporters and critics of affirmative action have suggested two modifications to the policies. First, affirmative action programmes might expand the range of targeted groups and individuals to include not only ethnicity, but also class position, in determining eligibility status. This change would enhance the ability of disadvantaged members of society to have access to programmes, since they would no longer have to compete with more privileged members of their own ethnic group. However, it would probably slow the development of the minority elite population, which has been an explicit or implicit goal of reservations in India.

Second, affirmative action policies could remain focused on ethnic identity but expand to include the development of human capital at an earlier stage of development. This change would allow current programmes to continue but eventually provide access for a larger sub-set of the targeted group. However, this change would be expensive, it would be less rewarding in the short term for politicians and parties, and it is therefore less likely to decrease crony capitalism and rent-seeking by politicians.

References

Bowen, William G. and Derek Bok. 1998. *The Shape of the River*. Princeton: Princeton University Press.

Chandra, Kanchan. 2004. *Why Ethnic Parties Succeed*. New York: Cambridge University Press.

Chattopadhyay, Raghabendra and Esther Duflo. 2004. "Women and Policy Makers: Evidence From a Randomized Policy Experiment in India" in *Econometrica*, 72 (5): 1409–43.

Desai, Sonalde and Amaresh Dubey. 2011. "Caste in 21st Century India Competing Narratives" in *Economical and Political Weekly*, 46 (11): 40–9.

Galanter, Marc. 1984. *Competing Equalities*. Berkeley and Los Angeles: University of California Press.

Graham, Hugh Davis. 1990. *The Civil Rights Era*. New York: Oxford University Press.

Graham, Hugh Davis. 2001. "Affirmative Action for Immigrants? The Unintended Consequences of Reform" in John David Skrentny (ed.), *Color Lines*. Chicago: University of Chicago Press.

Jaffrelot, Christophe. 2003. *India's Silent Revolution*. New York: Columbia University Press.

Parikh, Sunita A. 1997. *The Politics of Preference*. University of Michigan Press, Ann Arbor.

Parikh, Sunita A. 1998. "Religion, Reservations and Riots: The Politics of Ethnic Violence in India" in Amrita Basu and Atul Kohli (eds.), *Community Conflicts and the State in India*. Delhi: Oxford University Press.

Parikh, Sunita A. 2001. "Affirmative Action, Caste, and Party Politics in Contemporary India" in John David Skrentny, (ed.), *Color Lines: Affirmative Action, Immigration, and Civil Rights Options for America*. Chicago: University of Chicago Press.

Parikh, Sunita A., Edward D. Mansfield, Alfred Darnell, and Martin Battle. 2006. "Riot Politics: Explaining Violent Conflict in India, 1971–2001". Presented at the annual meeting of the American Political Science Association, Philadelphia, 31 August–3 September.

Skrentny, John David. 1996. *The Ironies of Affirmative Action*. Chicago: University of Chicago Press.

Sowell, Thomas. 2004. *Affirmative Action Around the World*. New Haven: Yale University Press.

Srinivas, M.N. 1962. *Caste in Modern India*. Bombay: Asia Publishing House.

Wilkinson, Steven I. 2004. *Votes and Violence*. New York: Cambridge University Press.

2 The struggle for equality and justice

Affirmative action in the United States of America

Ralph Premdas

Debating affirmative action

Even though the practice and theory of affirmative action involving the designation of preferential rewards and benefits to the historically disadvantaged and discriminated against had been established previously elsewhere,[1] it was in the case of the United States of America (US) that the phrase "affirmative action" became fashionable. Affirmative action policies have been controversial and contentious in the US, in part because it legally permitted arbitrary preferences, especially to African-Americans and other minorities, by abridging principles of individual merit and equality suggesting reverse discrimination (Glazer 1975). The passage of the Civil Rights Act of 1964, a piece of legislation that offered equality in the face of widespread discrimination against historically disadvantaged minorities, was not enough to bring immediate benefits and relief. It was this Act, however, in its interpretation by federal civil service bureaucrats and courts, that led to preferential policies. Since the object of the Civil Rights Act was to effect change in institutions so that exclusionary practices against qualified women or minorities be put to an end, and given the lack of voluntary cooperation from employers, it was clear that stronger medicine was required. It was this fact that precipitated a series of aggressive affirmative preferential policies and programmes in the US. The courts upheld and ordered institutions to adopt "goals", "timetables", and "quotas" to take in specific numbers of minorities and women in anticipation that once these new workers were securely accommodated, the programmes would have outlived their purpose and be withdrawn. Throughout the 1970s courts and government enforcement agencies implemented this idea everywhere, requiring a wide range of employers and organizations temporarily to select minorities and women by these numerical procedures and plans. The courts engaged in practically no discussion of the justification to correct past historical wrongs or the need for compensation or remedy but focused on institutional reform to end discrimination and provide benefits and other advantages to minorities.

Controversy over affirmative action also ensued because it bestowed benefits on a group basis, contrary to embedded ideas that recognized and rewarded individual effort. Frequently this practice has tended to benefit the better off in these groups and less so the more deserving for whom the policy was originally intended. To be sure, it has in most cases substantially succeeded in creating a new middle class among the erstwhile oppressed and disadvantaged and in bestowing on them symbolic gratification, recognition, and dignity. However, in the persistent and often bitter controversy over the issue, this accomplishment is frequently forgotten.

In the US, affirmative action was voluntarily enacted by a majority through a legitimate democratic process. It was initially intended primarily for African-Americans and indigenous native peoples, but then was subsequently extended to other minorities and also to women. With the steady increase in the number of beneficiaries and the scope of entitlements, the policy drew more public ire. From the outset it was an embattled policy and would become embroiled in party politics, legislative contests, crucial court decisions and popular referendums. Focused mainly on diametrically different concepts of equality and justice over positive government intervention on behalf of the historically oppressed and poor in American society, the arguments for and against from philosophers, publicists, and opinion makers have become polarizing over the past half century and sensitive to political and sectional interests. Lawrence Bobo (2001:191), at the Du Bois Center for African-American Studies at Harvard University, describes this bipolar division thus:
The debate over affirmative action often seems to involve two warring camps.

> Defenders of affirmative action cast themselves as the champion of racial justice and the keepers of Dr. King's dream. Opponents of affirmative action cast themselves as champions of the true color-blind intent of cherished American values. In the eyes of the defenders of affirmative action, the latter are, at best, apologists for racism. Opponents see their antagonists as advancing a morally bankrupt claim to victim status and the spoils of racial privilege for African-Americans and other minorities.

American public opinion for and against affirmative action has tended to follow a hierarchical structure with the bottom (occupied by African-Americans) holding the least negative perception, followed by Latinos, then Asians, and finally whites, who hold the most negative perceptions (Bobo 2001: 200). However, there are some significant differences and nuances within these groups with blacks (especially) and Latinos more likely to favour affirmative action than whites, while Asians' views are closer to whites (Bobo 2001: 199). What is very important is that while whites, by a majority, oppose affirmative action, their views are not monolithic such that black–white differences are not diametrically opposed. About 29 per cent of whites perceive the policy as helpful to American competitiveness, a third reject the idea on the basis that it is unfair to them, and nearly 60 per cent support affirmative action of an outreach type which provides educational and training opportunities for qualified blacks to get a chance. Most whites hold negative views where they perceive affirmative action as contributing to the hiring of unqualified blacks and minorities. Clearly, those preferential programmes that improved human capital rather than equalized outcomes were most popular among whites, and public opinion surveys showed that they were most vocally opposed where affirmative action called for quotas and clear-cut numerically based racial preferences; indeed, this was also unpopular even among many blacks (Bobo 2001: 193–9). In effect, while opinions on affirmative action differed by race, with majority black and Hispanic support and a majority of whites opposing it, neither was unequivocal in outlook (Bobo 2001: 193–9). Despite these variations and nuances, public sentiments on affirmative action have been portrayed in polarized fashion, and it remains a fact that the issue has tended to be very divisive.

As a distributive policy over limited and scarce resources in American society, affirmative action policies tend to engage zero-sum contests and struggles, creating winners and losers for both individuals and groups. Noting that "the removal of affirmative action produces drastic declines in the economic and educational fortunes of Blacks and Latinos", Bobo (2001: 208) reminds us that "despite all the high, abstract, and moralizing rhetoric, affirmative action is about concrete matters of who gets what". He proceeds to point out (2001: 195) that:

> The core argument here is that racial politics unavoidably involves a nettlesome fusion of racial identities and attitudes with racial interests. It suggests that many Whites will oppose affirmative action not so much because they see race-based policy as contravening their highest values or because they have learned a new, politically relevant set of resentments of Blacks, but rather because they perceive Blacks as competitive threats for social resources, status, and privileges.

Typically, the competition is manifested in such material areas as employment (public and private) and access to educational and business opportunities; including government procurement, contracts, and licences. Also, symbolic issues are at stake related to the recognition of the dignity and identity of the marginalized and disadvantaged communities. In altering the distribution of goods and values in American society, affirmative action programmes promised more than superficial change, and called for the redesign of certain institutions in society and with it the behaviour of Americans in relation to minorities.

With the benefits being enormous, affirmative action programmes tended to attract new contestants other than those who were originally envisaged, which triggered intra-black non-white struggles. Who is a person of colour and who is exactly black? Should persons who are non-white but not of African-American lineage, such as blacks from Africa and the Caribbean and Asians from Asia, be included? With large numbers of non-white foreigners migrating from the Caribbean, Africa, and Asia, affirmative action has become enmeshed and entangled with immigration issues. The flames of the controversy would also be fanned by other emergent issues tied to political patronage and the voting interests of the Democratic and Republican parties, the two main political parties in America.

While it may be argued that affirmative action policies were necessary to integrate the disadvantaged groups into the wider society and facilitate full participant citizenship, a critical issue has emerged related to whether the policy has run its course by successfully empowering minorities and women but has now commenced on a trajectory of diminishing returns, especially by creating dependency. This argument turns on the claim that affirmative action programmes in the US, having been in existence for almost five decades, have so shielded and overly protected minority non-white groups (instead of getting them to be stronger and self-reliant) that they have become habitually dependent on unmerited preferences and thus in the long term are unprepared for equal market competition. Consequently, despite numerous tangible instances of meritorious achievements among minorities, especially African-Americans where a large vibrant middle class has emerged, communities and individuals that benefit from affirmative action preferences have become collectively stigmatized and ghettoized as genetically inferior and continue to face discrimination today. In this respect, the preferential policies embodied in affirmative action programmes, instead of integrating the society, result in exacerbating the cleavages. Some even contend that things have not changed much from the old patterns of segregation.[2]

In the US then, affirmative action became an inflammatory issue mired in ongoing heated controversy with most white Americans opposing it as well as significant numbers of minorities themselves. When it was first initiated in the mid-1960s, it moved rather innocently from what seemed a short term minor issue on behalf of African-Americans as a means of enabling equal access to jobs and opportunities, free from discrimination. But it quickly morphed, drawing ardent supporters and opponents into a heated controversy. This in turn evolved into a tidal wave of mass partisan mobilization both for and against the policy, splitting American society right down the middle. The battle that would be waged came in the form of violent street demonstrations, presidential executive orders, Acts of Congress, court decisions, popular referendums, incendiary talk shows, etc. Today, affirmative action practices are found in a variety of inter-related bodies of law which include the US Constitution, federal statutes, federal executive orders, state constitutional provisions, state statutes, state executive orders, self-imposed restrictions by state bodies, and local ordinances. This list also includes judicial decisions interpreting these laws (Malamud 2001: 314).

The American model of affirmative action, even though it has come to influence other similar international experiments in social engineering on behalf of the disadvantaged, is a very complex creature honed on the peculiar anvil of American society and politics. Affirmative action policies tended to involve a variety of programmes and strategies of implementation in different targeted areas such as employment and education, with different consequences in each sector of activity. Different affirmative action laws emerged for different domains. Over the past four decades a Supreme Court affirmative action jurisprudence saw the establishment of distinctive bodies of case law concerning affirmative action in university admissions, federal contracting and licencing, and employment (Malamud 2001: 316).

In the US, affirmative action policies, as they evolved administratively in the practices of the federal bureaucracy supported by early court decisions, were proposed and justified as a temporary preparatory measure necessary to establish peace and political stability and a level playing field for the enactment of fair competition in the long term. In practice, these temporal limits have been breached by fiat of the US Congress every ten years as programmes expanded and beneficiaries increased. Aimed in part at promoting societal unity by rectifying historical discriminatory wrongs and ameliorating inequality, these policies and programmes have left in their wake a mixed bag of setbacks and achievements. Implementation was in practice a protracted and often painful experimental process with constant revisions and redesigns, with unending legal and constitutional challenges, and threats of abandonment. Having started off as something involving mainly African-Americans, it metamorphosized into a different creature with new recipients, accumulated interests and aims, and became rooted almost permanently in the governmental administrative apparatus.

Affirmative action in history

To understand the story of affirmative action in the US, there is a need to first look at some of the peculiarities of American society and its political and constitutional institutions. One eminent commentator on the role of institutions in affirmative action, J. Edward Kellough (2206: 22), stated correctly that

> the variety of strategies that have been devised to deal with discrimination, and the evolution of those efforts, have been shaped in large part by the character of our governmental institutions, the rules by which those institutions operate, and the manner in which they have interacted

Among the most critical of these institutions and practices are those related to federalism and states' rights; the separation of powers and the system of checks and balances; judicial review; the Bill of Rights; and other features such as the 14th and 5th Amendments of the US Constitution regarding individual rights. Other embedded traditional practices relate to the paramountcy of merit and individualism; the sanctity of private property; the design of electoral and party systems; and the role of the media. There is no quick way to adequately describe the structural and behavioural architecture that characterizes the political and constitutional edifice of the American form of governance. A few facts will have to suffice. The American Constitution is the paramount document that describes the institutions that govern the country as well as setting forth a Bill of Rights that mediates the relationship between citizens and government. In a federal system that consists of 50 "sovereign" states, each with its own legislature, executive, and courts, there is a division of powers so that the federal government and the states have exclusive powers in some areas and concurrent powers in others. What is important here is that the decentralized state system has historically conferred strong state jurisdictions, "states rights", in many areas of citizen rights, that impinge on affirmative action. While the federal government has its own legislature (Congress), Executive (the presidency and the civil service bureaucracy), and Judiciary, when conflicts over jurisdiction occur, especially over the interpretation of the Constitution, they are adjudicated by the courts in a system called "judicial review". The Federal Legislature (Congress) is a two chamber parliamentary system with powerful committees that in effect control the passage of legislation. The behaviour and decisions of members of Congress are open to significant influence by a comprehensive infrastructure of lobbyists. The President, who is embedded and hemmed in by the system of separation of powers, is elected separately by the entire US population and is in constant negotiation with Congress over the passage of laws and policies. The party system, substantially dominated by a conservative Republican party and a more liberal Democratic Party, is only minimally disciplined and has enough internal variation in ideological leanings so that on occasions Democrats and Republicans unite against their own party leadership to form alliances. The Federal Supreme Court adjudicates constitutional issues and can override legislation from any level of government. The US is a vibrant democracy, with widespread participation, fed by an active and vigorous free media. The fate of legislation (such as affirmative action policies) at the federal level, requires an alignment of popular partisan forces in Congress and from within the office of the President, but even this can be overturned by the courts as part of the process of judicial review.

Although affirmative action would come to encompass African-Americans, Hispanics, Asians, Native Americans and women, it really began as a desire to rectify the discrimination that African-Americans endured for centuries of American history. African-American history commenced in the seventeenth century when in 1619 a number arrived as indentured labourers and settled in Jamestown, Virginia. The slave system did not develop until the eighteenth century. By 1775, African-Americans constituted 20 per cent of the population, the second largest after the English. In 1790, when the first US census was taken, African-Americans, including slaves and free, numbered only 760,000 or 19.3 per cent of the population. In the 1770s African-Americans helped defeat the British in the American War of Independence. Under the American Constitution of 1887, African-Americans were counted as only three-fifths of a person, politically. The slave trade ended in 1808. However, slavery within the US continued and by 1860 about 3.5 million remained enslaved.

In 1860, at the start of the Civil War, the African-American population was 4.4 million, all but 488,000 of them slaves. President Abraham Lincoln's Emancipation Proclamation of 1863 freed all slaves. However, after a post-Civil War reconstruction period, when some progress towards freedom was made, this was superseded in the 1890s by the Jim Crow laws that legally segregated and discriminated against African-Americans. The Supreme Court case, *Plessey v. Ferguson*, enunciated the doctrine of "separate but equal", which perpetuated the subordination of African-Americans. It was not until 1954, in the case *Brown* v. *The Board Of Education*, that the separate but equal doctrine was deemed unconstitutional.

Dramatic changes began to transpire with the civil rights movement in the 1950s and 1960s, led by Martin Luther King, when blacks engaged in mass demonstrations and boycotts. It culminated in the most significant civil rights legislation in US history – the passage of the Civil Rights Act of 1964. The 1966–75 Black Power Movement accelerated change, demanding jobs and opportunities without further delay. It was this threat of sustained mass protest and disruption of order that gave birth to affirmative action. The post civil rights era witnessed substantial strides that saw the election of some 8,936 black officeholders. Nevertheless, despite the emergence of a large African-American middle class, the highest incidence of poverty, 24.7 per cent, was among African-Americans. The average black income in 2007 was $33,916, compared to $54,920 for whites. The black middle class has grown so that 47 per cent own their own homes, and in the business sector they have ownership of about 1.2 million enterprises, out of a total of 23 million firms. Half of African-American households are now in the $50,000-a-year income bracket. In tertiary education, African-Americans attend college half as frequently as whites; 89 per cent completed high school, and some 556,000 were in college in 1995. About 1,314 earned doctorates in 1996. In 1910, 90 per cent of blacks lived in the South; during the Great Northern Migration between the 1890s and 1970s, a third migrated to the North to gain better opportunities. By 2005 African-Americans constituted 13.8 per cent, or about 39.9 million, of the population. Today, 58.8 per cent still live in the South. Their life expectancy is 72 years compared to 78 for whites. Among African-Americans some 70 per cent rate of the birth rate is accounted for by the children of unmarried mothers. Black men in jail in 1995 numbered about 711,600. There is a 28.9 per cent chance of blacks going to jail. The chance of whites going to jail is 2.5 per cent. A total of 54 per cent of blacks said they were victims of racial discrimination. On balance, despite the gains, the contemporary outlook for African-Americans and other minorities has been described thus (Bobo 2001: 208):

> Although differing in degrees and forms, the economic disadvantages and modern-day discrimination faced by blacks and Latinos are tangible. These groups are more likely to live below the poverty line, indeed far below it compared to whites; they are far less likely to complete a college degree, a form of certification that increasingly draws the line between middle class standard of living and a life of constant economic hardship; and they will almost certainly face racial discrimination in search of a place to live or for employment.

Affirmative action: in the beginning

While there were earlier attempts by Presidents Roosevelt, Truman, and Eisenhower to encourage employers to voluntarily engage in equal employment practices on behalf of minorities, especially African-Americans, this bore little fruit. Meaningful changes began with the election of a new government controlled by the Democratic Party in 1961, led by President John F. Kennedy. The Democratic Party owed its razor-thin victory over the Republicans to the support of African-Americans who, under Martin Luther King and the National Association for the Advancement of Colored People (NAACP), had commenced the modern civil rights movement with a series of mass marches and demonstrations in the American South. More specifically, the problem that loomed large was a history of oppression and discrimination against African-Americans that had left in its wake grave inequality, poverty, and unemployment among a community of some 10 per cent of the total population. Apart from political interests, the Democrats decided to act because they also believed ideologically in egalitarian doctrines.

On 6 March 1961, President Kennedy issued Executive Order 10925 which required federal contractors to "take affirmative action to ensure that applicants are employed and that employees are treated during employment without regard to race, creed, color or national origin". Two years later this was reaffirmed by President Lyndon Johnson's Executive Order 11246 which covered both contractors and sub-contractors and, under Executive Order 11375 of 1967, women were added to the list of beneficiaries. Both executive orders established regulatory agencies to enforce compliance, with Executive Order 0925 creating the President's Committee on Equal Employment Opportunity. This was superseded, under Executive Order 1146, by the Office of Federal Contract Compliance. Both stipulated penalties for non-compliance, including termination of contracts and debarment. However, the term "affirmative action" was imprecise and was not defined, and policy implementers did not know what it meant and what exactly to do (Kelly and Dobbin 2001). At best, it seemed to suggest positive action in the form of outreach programmes. Also, there were no spelled out criteria of what "compliance" entailed.

However, it was clear that at the time Kennedy proclaimed his executive order, he did not have in mind any sort of compulsory programme to extirpate discrimination and he did not intend to deviate from the principle of merit as the measure of allocating rewards and benefits in employment. Rather, he contemplated that the new government directive would successfully persuade employers voluntarily to assist the disadvantaged through establishing outreach programmes for training and imparting skills. This expectation of voluntary compliance was precisely what guided Kennedy's Commission on Equal Employment Opportunity (PCEEO) – which only had investigative powers in responding to complaints. When this resulted in mixed but unsatisfactory performances, Kennedy responded by imposing new obligations on employers not to engage in discriminatory behaviour in their employment practices and also for them to take some specific actions to facilitate minority employment. In practice, this meant nothing more than the deployment of outreach programmes by the federal government and by private employers with federal contracts. Outreach programmes were, however, very limited in compelling change because they only included training and skills development to enable minorities to qualify for entry-level employment. There were very limited teeth to secure compliance in that employers were required only to file periodic reports and the PCEEO was authorized to levy sanctions. The system depended upon employers, including the federal civil service and private employers with federal contracts, acting in good faith. During the Kennedy years the overall effect was that African-American employment in the federal civil service increased by only 13.1 per cent, with almost all of this in lower level jobs.

Nevertheless, the affirmative action policy that Kennedy promulgated provoked a storm of criticism that nurtured racial resentments against minorities and sustained divisive and bitter debates throughout the country. Few public issues have had such a searing effect on American society, even though the question of race seemed to have been settled by the Civil War of the 1860s. Kennedy was assassinated in the wake of the rising crescendo surrounding affirmative action. After his death the most significant civil rights legislation in the history of the country was enacted: the Civil Rights Act of 1964. Kennedy's successor, President Johnson argued, as he sought to persuade Congress to pass the Civil Rights Act, that it would represent a fitting tribute to Kennedy. Even so, with Kennedy's assassination fresh in the minds of Americans, the southern bloc in the United States Senate mounted the longest sustained filibuster in American history, a delaying tactic that was ultimately aimed at preventing the passage of the Civil Rights Bill. The tactic failed, but attested to the persistence of resistance among significant sections of American society for equality to be meaningfully extended to African-Americans.

Given the ongoing controversy, the strangest aspect of the Civil Rights Act was that it demanded nothing more extraordinary than the extension of equality to all citizens and the end of racial discrimination. The Act was colour blind and its mandate was based on merit; it did not require special preferences, quotas, set asides, timetables, numerical goals, etc., just equality and the end to deliberate and systematic discrimination. In a memorable statement by Senator H. Humphrey, as he sought to persuade Republicans to sign up to Title VII of the civil rights legislation, he said:

> Contrary to the allegations of some opponents of this title, there is nothing that will give any power to the Commission (enforcing Title VII or to any court to require, hiring, firing, or promotion of employees in order to meet 'quota' or to achieve a certain racial balance. That bugaboo has been brought up a dozen times; but it is nonexistent. In fact, the very opposite is true. Title VII prohibits discrimination. In effect, it says that race, religion, and national origin are not to be used for hiring and firing. Title VII is designed to encourage hiring on the basis of ability and qualification, not race or religion.
> (Cited in Congressional Record, 88th Congress, 2nd session, 1964, 110, Part 5: 6549)

Indeed, Title VII of the Act stated unequivocally the colour blind aspect of the egalitarian legislation, and said: "It shall be an unlawful employment practice for an employer to fail or refuse to hire or to discharge any individual because of such individual's race, color, religion, sex, or national origin." The Act established for its enforcement the Equal Employment Opportunity Commission (EEOC), which was to ensure compliance and eliminate all employment discrimination based on race, religion, sex, or national origin. One section of the Act specifically exhorted against granting special preferences:

> Nothing contained in this Title shall be interpreted to require any employer ... to grant preferential treatment to any individual or group on account of an imbalance which may exist with respect to the total number or percentage of persons of any race ... employed by any employer ... in comparison with the total number or percentage of persons of such race ... in any community ... or in the available workforce in any community.

On the surface then, the Civil Rights Act possessed no redistributive features by suggesting that any group would benefit from the corresponding loss by any other group. While the Act primarily had in mind African-Americans as the main beneficiaries of its egalitarian behests, it did extend its anti-discriminatory scope more broadly to persons of colour, to different religions, to persons of different national origin, and to women in 1967. Despite the fact that other groups were included, it would be the persons of colour who would draw much ire from various sections of the American population. Anti-black racism was clearly widespread, despite the Civil War, and it would be this factor above all that would animate much resistance against the equality motif of the Act in seeking to eliminate discrimination. It is important to note that as the proposed legislation eventually passed into law there was hint of the sort of compensatory and redemptive rectification for past wrongs that had been demanded by the more militant portions of the civil rights movement. Neither was there any compulsory redistributive programme within the Act that might deprive white Americans of their earnings or property. Bearing all this in mind, the resistance and controversy that surrounded the demands for equality in the early civil rights movement of the 1950s and 1960s, seems puzzling.

When President Johnson succeeded Kennedy, he retained the President's Committee on Equal Employment Opportunity (PCEEO). But with the passage of the Civil Rights Act of 1964, two new instruments were added in Titles VI and VII. Title VI prohibited discrimination by any organization with federal funds, while Title VII prohibited discrimination by both federal employers and all private employers, as well as labour organizations that received federal funds. Title VII also established a permanent agency, the Equal Employment Opportunity Commission (EEOC), to supervise implementation and to receive, investigate, and resolve discrimination complaints. The EEOC was the first statutory body established to combat employment discrimination. Under Title VII the

EEOC had authority over all private employers regardless of federal funding. However, the EEOC was not required to establish a positive programme of affirmative action and it was primarily an investigatory unit reacting to complaints. Despite this, Southern Congressmen attacked the PCEEO by denying it funds. Johnson responded by issuing Executive Order 11246 (in September 1965) to transfer compliance issues to the Department of Labour. Implementation became more aggressive. Executive Order 11375, established in October 1967, extended equal opportunity to women for the first time.

Yet it was abundantly clear that the Civil Rights Act was not enough. The repeated call for equality did not bring a halt to discriminatory behaviour practised by white employers and managers in both the public and private sectors. Indeed, the strict and rigorous application of equality and merit principles militated against the historically disadvantaged since they were unprepared to compete in the open market for jobs and opportunities. The established and privileged community wanted to maintain the status quo and took refuge under a strict interpretation of the equality provisions of the Civil Rights Act, refusing to yield or make the kind of concessions that might have brought an end to racial discrimination.

Lurking behind the gross sense of injustice was the recent memory among blacks that in the Second World War they had fought and died for the liberation of the oppressed in Europe and elsewhere, yet at home they returned to live in the chains of widespread and embedded discriminatory practices that made it impossible for them to live in dignity and equality. They had fought for these ideals on behalf of others abroad, but were denied them at home.

But the status quo could not continue. Peaceful marches and demonstrations gave way to the sort of open obstructionism and violence that disrupted the peace and order of American society, and the more moderate black leaders were sidelined by militants who organized demonstrations, blocked streets, burnt buildings, and crippled the normal life of cities.

It was on the anvil of violent mass protest among blacks and their supporters (who included many whites) that the system finally yielded. Riots practically brought the US to the verge of a new civil war. A militant Black Power Movement, whose members were willing to lose life and limb, emerged, and agitated for meaningful change. This was the trigger point that led to meaningful change in affirmative action.

The resort to violence forced an Establishment rethink. As Skrentny argued (1996: 67), "it was in the handling of a crisis, defined as a threat of elite control, that moral cultural boundaries limiting civil rights in employment to color blindness were expanded to allow for the building of the affirmative action model". In effect, affirmative action of a different sort, envisaging more aggressive positive action programmes, came from the centres of the American elite after the Civil Rights Act of 1964. Skrentny went on (1996: 67): "More specifically, a racial crisis, the severe rioting of the 1960s, made available a discourse of crisis management with which affirmative action or other normally risky race-targeted measures could be advocated by political and business elites."

New dispensation of affirmative action

Out of these disturbances came the Kerner Report, which described the plight of the poor and oppressed as the underlying cause of the troubles. From the violence and the legitimating Kerner Report, affirmative action was born. Something more than simple equality measures were needed to maintain the status quo. The new meaning of affirmative action required the award of preferences to the disadvantaged in apportioning jobs, and other benefits and opportunities, without reference to strict principles of merit. The disadvantaged minorities needed help by way of compensatory programmes that granted them preferential treatment for a period of time until they could engage in open competition with others for jobs, resources, and benefits. That was the crux of what affirmative action meant: not a negation of the equality principle, but a temporary suspension of it so as to enable equality to be fairly practised.

The problem was how to make the rigours of the equality provisions in the Civil Rights Act bend so that they would conform to the edicts of preferences. It would be in the application of the Civil Rights Act, specifically in the interpretation of the equality aspects of Title VII, that affirmative action was forged in the new form of special preferences. More specifically, it would be the unusual way in which the Civil Rights Act was interpreted and implemented by senior bureaucrats in the federal civil service, and eventually ratified by the courts, that would define the uniqueness of the American practice of affirmative action.

The Kerner Commission served as the legitimating instrument supporting the new meaning of affirmative action, and it justified the need to treat difference in a new way. The Kerner Report not only placed the blame for the riots squarely on the persistence of gross discrimination against blacks and other minorities, but advocated urgently that jobs and opportunities be found to help provide a remedy and thus restore law and order. Faced with the crisis of riots, and with the Kerner Report on hand, President Johnson assembled business leaders from around the country and urged them to give jobs to blacks and minorities, as well as women, immediately. They were urged in effect "to give jobs to ghetto blacks before their businesses burned down" (Skrentny 1996: 90). What the President argued was that merit and similar job qualifications be modified or even set aside and that employers, instead of being colour blind, become colour conscious in hiring blacks. Skrentny (1996: 8) went on: "Employers were now required to use group differences for hiring, that is to count minorities collectively as a group rather than as individuals in the labor force for their qualifications for a job." The President was more concerned with representation, utilization, and employment of minorities than with strict equality and merit. The President's message pleading for race-targeting in hiring and utilization was taken seriously by business leaders across the country (Skrentny 1996: 80). In the US federal public service this urgency was communicated to managers and administrators who promptly set about the business of deliberately seeking out and hiring blacks (Skrentny 1996: 7). Through these actions it was evident that affirmative action entailed something quite different from equality as stipulated in the Civil Rights Act. As

Skrentny (1996: 7) observed: "As it developed in civil rights administrative agencies and the courts, however, affirmative action as well as simple non-discrimination came to mean something quite different from any color-blind approach. It came to mean color conscious not color blind."

President Johnson's Executive Order 11246 marked a new phase towards a tougher and more stringent affirmative action programme, as witnessed by the transfer of responsibility for equal employment to the Department of Labor under Secretary Willard Wirtz. Under Wirtz and the enforcement agency, the Office of Federal Compliance Programs (OFCCP), focus shifted to the construction industry, where discrimination against minorities was rife. At the time the construction industry was enjoying a boom with federal funds of $30 billion impacting on 20 million workers through 225,000 contractors (Skrentny 1996: 38). In what became known as the Philadelphia Plan, the OFCCP required contractors to establish numerical goals, targets, and timetables. It established by 1967 pre-award reviews of equal opportunity compliance looking at the employment of minority workers. The idea of numerical goals and implicit quotas would trigger new resistance, but unexpected opposition came from the Comptroller General of the federal bureaucracy, Elmer Staats. As head of the Government Accountability Office (GAO), an arm of Congress, he rejected the Philadelphia Plan for its specification of racial preferences, goals, and timetables for the advancement of equal employment opportunity. Opposition also came from Congress, causing President Johnson to drop the Philadelphia Plan.

However, in another unexpected turn of events a couple of years later, it was a Republican, President Richard Nixon, who on coming to power in 1968, sought to divide the coalition of Southerners and the black electorate that traditionally supported the Democratic Party by reviving the Philadelphia Plan. His Attorney General, John Mitchell, ignored the Comptroller General's objections, deeming the GOA as a tool of Congress that was in violation of the principle separation of powers that confers autonomy to the executive branch. The Philadelphia Plan was applied and when it was legally challenged and taken to court, the suit was rejected in March 1970. Subsequently, Nixon, through Revised Order No. 4, extended the principles of the Philadelphia Plan to all major federal contractors. Then, in May 1971, the head of the US Civil Service Commission endorsed the timetables and goals for minority employment in federal executive offices and agencies. Kelly and Dobbin (2001: 93) note:

> The scope of affirmative action law expanded by the early 1970s through OFCC Order 4 which required employers to submit detailed reports on their employment patterns to remedy inequality. Order 4 required affirmative action programmes from government contractors based on analysis of 'underutilization' of blacks, Hispanics, Native Americans, and Orientals in major job categories. This required comparison between minorities in the job market and the numbers hired. Acceptable affirmative action plans had to include 'goals and timetables' specifying projections.

Revised Order 4 added women. The upshot thereafter was that affirmative action became tied to the concept of goals and timetables for the employment of minorities and women.

From the implementation of Titles VI and VII, the presidential executive orders, and through the actions of the civil service, the new affirmative action received much of its legitimacy. The initiatives from Johnson and Nixon culminated in the 1972 Equal Employment Opportunity Act, which amended the Civil Rights Act of 1964 by expanding restrictions on discrimination in the private sector and prohibiting discrimination by state and local governments and in federal departments and agencies (Kelly and Dobbin 2001: 83).

President Jimmy Carter transferred the equal opportunity responsibility to the EEOC under a reorganization coinciding with the 1978 Civil Service Reform Act. This Act endorsed the idea of the proportional representation of minorities for reasons of diversity and for the achievement affirmative action goals. The new EEOC placed greater emphasis on the requirement for timetables and numerical goals. However, several years later, under Ronald Reagan, the EEOC retracted this approach and new regulations introduced in 1987 no longer required agencies to have numerical goals. However, by 1976, large numbers of employers had adopted EEOC and affirmative action programmes, and had hired EEOC and affirmative action specialists and supervisors (Kelly and Dobbin 2001: 93). By 1976, 80 per cent of large firms had EEO policies. By 1980, 40 per cent of all employers had them (Kelly and Dobbin 2001: 94). By doing so employers created internal constituencies of EEO and affirmative action specialists who, by the time of the Reagan administration (which sought to dismantle affirmative action programmes), fought the President's effort to dismantle these programmes. They argued that affirmative action had successfully created a diverse and more productive workforce which improved the bottom line (Kelly and Dobbin 2001: 97).

The courts

Having passed the Civil Rights Act of 1964, and following executive orders from Presidents Kennedy and Johnson (who had instructed the federal civil service and private employers to implement various affirmative preferences on behalf of African-Americans, other minorities and women), the next step in the evolution of positive government intervention came in the form of court challenges over the legality and constitutionality of these programmes. More specifically, the problem derived from the imposition of race and gender-based numerical goals and timetables on employers that themselves seemed to transgress the non-discriminatory stipulations of the Civil Rights Act. In effect, it smacked of reverse discrimination. Sections 703 and 717 of Title VII of the Civil Rights Act of 1964 as amended by the Equal Opportunity Act of 1972 and the Civil Rights Act of 1991, defined as unlawful any employment practice that discriminates against any individual on account of race, colour, religion, sex, or national origin. Similarly, Title VI of the Civil Rights Act 1964 prohibits discrimination on the basis of race, ethnicity and sex by any organization including universities receiving federal assistance. Apart from seemingly violating the Civil Rights Act of 1964, as amended in 1971 and 1992, there were also two constitutional grounds on which race-based affirmative action seemed precariously vulnerable. First was the 14th Amendment of the US Constitution, known as the due process and equal protection clause governing actions by the federal government. Similar protections were embodied in the 5th Amendment, which applied only to states.

The task of adjudicating the legal and constitutional challenges to affirmative action programmes fell to the judiciary. It would be the final arbiter of the fate of these preferential programmes. During the course of the history of these judicial challenges, over a dozen affirmative action cases were submitted to the United States Supreme Court, and many more were contested in federal, district, and circuit courts. From all these cases, dealing with a wide range of issues including employment, university admissions, and business opportunities, from across the US, was there a clear distillation of approved principles and disapproved practices relating to what was permitted and what was not in affirmative action programmes? One commentator (Kellough 2006: 13) summed it up thus, pointing to a record of contradictions and inconsistencies:

> Ultimately, of course, the judiciary plays an important part in sorting out conflict over affirmative action. More than a dozen affirmative action cases have been heard before the US Supreme Court and scores of other cases have been addressed by federal district and circuit courts of appeal. Attempts to synthesize judicial opinions regarding the legality of affirmative action programmes are difficult, however, since it frequently appears court decisions on the issue are disjointed and inconsistent. Thernstrom and Thernstrom have argued that 'anyone who looks for doctrinal consistency in the Supreme Court's decisions on employment discrimination will be severely disappointed'. A cursory review of decisions regarding preferential affirmative action could reinforce such an opinion. In those cases, the courts have at times upheld the legality of affirmative action and at other times they have struck it down, but because affirmative action comes in a variety of specific forms and must meet a range of legal requirements, divergent rulings on its legality hardly constitute doctrinal inconsistency.

It has been argued (Kellough 2006: 13) that such inconsistencies have arisen because "different standards of review are applied when courts assess the legality of the policy and those standards vary based primarily on the nature of the legal challenge to affirmative action". Regardless, after three decades of litigation, at the end of the first decade of the twenty-first century, there now evolved a set of settled judicial interpretations that have come to define what is permitted and forbidden in affirmative action programmes in the US. In effect affirmative action continues to be legally sanctioned and practised as a programme in service of the disadvantaged in American society, but, as a result of a variety of court challenges and decisions, a number of restrictions have now been established in the administration of affirmative action.

In the area of employment, affirmative action programmes, to be legally and constitutionally valid, need to satisfy three conditions: first, they must address a manifest racial or gender imbalance in traditionally segregated job categories; second, they must not trammel the rights of majorities, or men; and third, they must be constructed as a temporary strategy. Since it was not permissible purely to appeal to race or ethnicity in the allocation of preferential benefits, nevertheless this was allowed under certain constitutional conditions that satisfied "strict scrutiny", a guideline that in turn requires demonstration of "a compelling state interest" and a requirement that the programme be "narrowly tailored". Under the equal protection clause of the 14th Amendment of the US Constitution, the courts have decided that government affirmative action programmes are to be subjected to different levels of scrutiny so that under the category of "strict scrutiny", when applied to racial and ethnic classifications, these programmes are "narrowly tailored" to meet a compelling state interest. Gender-based discrimination was subjected to "intermediate scrutiny" that required substantial reference to a government purpose (Malamud 2001: 317). The term "narrow tailoring" also became a part of the strict scrutiny regime and it also has been imposed by the courts in the award of affirmative action benefits. Its meaning was spelled out in the Corson case where the Supreme Court criticized the City of Richmond, Virginia, for extending affirmative action benefits to Aleuts who did not exist in that city. Hence "strict scrutiny" and "narrow tailoring" refer to the need to determine the beneficiary class which must be justified by demonstrating past and present discrimination as well the need to demonstrate how closely a government affirmative programme fits a compelling state purpose (Malamud 2001: 317). What is a compelling state interest? This differed from one place to another, but generally referred to the issue of proportionality since many affirmative action programmes tended to set goals and targets for minorities and women based on achieving "balanced" proportions of these groups (Malamud 2001: 317). The issue of "balance" has been particularly significant as a measure of how affirmative action expectations were met, especially among private employers. Under Title VII, private employment had been a main concern of voluntary affirmative action (Malamud 2001: 325) which had been dealt with in two major Supreme Court cases: *Steelworkers* v. *Weber* (a race/ethnicity case) and *Johnson* v. *Santa Clara* (a gender case) which established the legal standard. From these decisions employers were now permitted to correct a "manifest imbalance" in a traditionally segregated job category. In addition the programme must be temporary and it must be designed not to "trammel" the rights of non-beneficiaries.

There are two cases which offer some insight into present-day affirmative action practices. The first relates to *Griggs* v. *Duke Power Company* (1971), which led to a decision by the US Supreme Court that established a new criteria called "disparate impact". The background to this case refers to factories and businesses prior to 1964, especially in the South, applying facially discriminatory policies and rules which tended to openly relegate African-Americans to low-level jobs such as maintenance departments and channelled whites into higher echelon departments where the pay and opportunities for advancement were far better. After the passage of the Civil Rights Act the companies willingly abandoned their facial segregation policies but were still able to carry forward the effects of past segregation through other already-existing *facially neutral* rules. In the court case in question a power company that had habitually discriminated against blacks by openly using facial and physical criteria, then decided after the enactment of the Civil Rights Act of 1964 to continue the practice, less overtly, by introducing irrelevant tests for minorities. In the Griggs case the Supreme Court decided that Title VII prohibited "practices, procedures, or tests neutral on their face and even neutral in terms of intent" that seemed fair but in effect froze the status quo of prior discriminatory practices. The court in effect ruled that not only was overt discrimination illegal, so too were practices that were fair in form but discriminatory in operation. The court prohibited any employment practice that had the effect of excluding blacks which could not also be shown to be directly related to job performance. Consequently, courts began striking down facially neutral rules that carried through the effects of an employer's past discrimination, regardless of the original intent or provenance of the rules.

The Griggs decision also led to a radical break in old practices that depended on prosecutors having the impossible task of proving "intent" in discriminatory practices. Thereafter, following the Griggs decision, "intent" was nullified as proof and effectively decoupled from "discrimination". The Griggs judgement also introduced the very significant doctrine of "disparate impact", a term which applied to employment practices that appeared to be non-discriminatory and that were seemingly non-discriminatory in intent. These were now deemed to be in violation of Title VII if they had the impact of disproportionately screening out applicants or employees along the lines of race, ethnicity, or sex. Most significantly, the burden of proof simply called on employees to make a prime facie case based on statistical data that demonstrated low rates of representation of a community in that workplace. For about 18 years the doctrine of "disparate impact" greatly facilitated the advancement of affirmative action programmes. However, it was temporarily rescinded in 1989 following the case of *Wards Cove Packing Co. v. Antonio*, which once again placed on the complainant the onus of providing evidence of clearly delineated specific discriminatory employment practices. The court made a finer distinction between "disparate impact" and "disparate treatment", and the interpretation was a major setback for affirmative action programmes. In 1991, however, in the amended Civil Rights Act of 1991, "disparate impact" was restored and signed back into law by President George H.W. Bush.

A second significant contemporary case of affirmative action relates to the area of university admissions. From 1996 to 2001, five cases came up regarding university admissions in the federal courts and in the circuit and appeal divisions. In an earlier decision in the 1978 case, *Regents of California* v. *Bakke*, which involved a constitutional challenge under the 14th Amendment of the US Constitution about admissions into the medical school at the University of

California at Davis (where 16 positions were reserved for minority groups), Justice Powell permitted race to be taken into account as a compelling state interest in a programme of diversity for university admissions. However, in subsequent cases there were contradictions and inconsistencies so that in some cases the use of race as a criterion for affirmative action admissions was denied while in others it was permitted. By 2002 two circuit Courts of Appeal had decided that affirmative action in university admissions was permissible while in two others it was denied. In this two versus two split, the matter was finally resolved by the US Supreme Court decision in *Grutter* v. *Bollinger*. Applying the criteria of strict scrutiny, the court decided that race-based affirmative action as a wider part of recruiting a diverse student population did not violate the equal protection provisions of the US Constitution. It found that diversity was a compelling state interest. The Court argued that the use of race in affirmative action for college and university admissions was "narrowly tailored" only when it was combined with other factors in underscoring diversity. This procedure avoided the idea of indiscriminate group-assigned preferences as well as imposed quotas since each student application was individually evaluated on a range of diversity factors, which included, but was not restricted to, race. The Court determined that this procedure did not unduly harm white students.

Immigration and affirmative action: a continuing burning issue

With affirmative action policies and programmes in place under various legal and constitutional constraints, a number of issues continue to haunt its practice today. Among these is the issue of immigration. It is important to note that only a year after civil rights activists succeeded in getting the Civil Rights Act of 1964 enacted, the Immigration and Nationality Act was also passed. Activists for civil rights saw a connection between non-white minorities and the racial selectivity that favoured immigrants from Europe. During the passage of the Immigration and Nationality Act (1965), a new immigration recruitment regime was inaugurated that eliminated the preference for Europeans. White supporters of the Act mistakenly thought that because family reunification criteria were now to be applied as part of the immigration process, this would perpetuate the arrival of European migrants to the US. However, the immigration data paints a dramatically different picture. During the 1980s, when some 8.6 million new immigrants arrived, 78 per cent came from Asia and Latin America (Graham 2001: 64). Today about 95 per cent of all immigrants come from the Third World, which is mainly constituted of non-European non-white populations (Graham 2001: 64).

As permanent residents and citizens, under the 14th Amendment of the US Constitution and the Civil Rights Act of 1964, these new immigrants enjoyed equal access to affirmative action benefits and opportunities. This would impact adversely on relations between African-Americans and immigrants, particularly over access to business opportunities. Since African-Americans were the first beneficiaries for set asides for procurement contracts, they had obtained most of the benefits. As Graham (2001: 63) points out:

> The Small Business Enterprise (SME) administration under the SME section (8) programme, which was established to administer business opportunities to minorities in the wake of the urban riots of 1965–68, was intended mainly for African-Americans, even though it listed as eligible groups African-Americans, Hispanics, American Indians, and Asian Americans. Hence, in 1981, Black firms garnered some two thirds of $1 billion disbursed by federal agencies. Non-European immigrant groups however progressively entered the competitive scene gaining access to affirmative action benefits and much conflict would emerge. Under the Philadelphia Plan, government contractors were required to hire minority workers in rough proportion to their availability in the workforce, including all minority entrepreneurs. During the Nixon and Reagan administrations, Congress extended minority set aside requirements to the large procurement budgets of the Department of Transport and Defense so as to build minority capitalism and appeal to minority voters.

In 1980 the US Supreme Court, following *Fullilove* v. *Klutznick*, upheld minority access to business opportunities and to awards that were growing rapidly in city and state governments. Congress had set aside from competitive bidding 10 per cent of the appropriations, "earmarking businesses owned by Negroes, Spanish-speakers, Orientals, Indians, Eskimos, and Aleuts". Asians, who were dropped from the eligible groups in 1978, were restored in 1979 and this category was now expanded to include Asian Pacific Americans such as those from Cambodia, Laos, the Philippines, Samoa, Taiwan, Japan, Korea, China, and Vietnam. In the 1980s eleven additional groups petitioned to be included, among them were those from India, Tonga, Sri Lanka, Indonesia, Bhutan, and Nepal.

The Small Business Administration (SBA) rejected Hasidic Jews, women, disabled veterans, Iranians, and Afghans, using arbitrary criteria. Much controversy and acrimony ensued. These new immigrant groups were seen as lacking a long term history of oppression and prejudice in the US. Among the new eligible groups were Asians, who were ranked second highest income earners in the US (Sowell 2004: 62). In 1995 the SBA reported on the ethnic heritages of 6,006 eligible firms; they included African-Americans, Caribbeans, and Africans, 47 per cent; Hispanics, 25 per cent; Asians, 21 per cent; Native Americans, 6 per cent; and others, 1 per cent. The US census showed that in 1996, 16 million out of the 24.6 million foreign-born population were non-citizens and yet were eligible for preferences. One observer (Graham 2001: 54) concluded: "The trend was explosive with conflict possibilities."

Another area related to the impact of immigration was employment. African-Americans were reported to be facing progressive displacement by immigrants. In one case in Chicago, businesses preferred to employ immigrants to fill their affirmative action requirements rather than African-Americans. The pattern of immigrants displacing blacks was repeated elsewhere in construction, garment making, restaurant, janitorial, and agricultural activities (Graham 2001: 66). Graham offered the explanation: "The immigrant success ethos, with its emphasis on hard work, merit, and social assimilation, clashed with hard African-American's emphasis on historic victimhood, reparations, and racial entitlement." (Graham 2001: 68)

The impact of immigration on African-Americans had been gauged as destabilizing, but it has been particularly devastating for the poorest, specifically the urban poor who had benefited least from affirmative action (Graham 2001: 67). Looking at the impact of immigration on the welfare of African-Americans who were historically disadvantaged, Graham (2001: 67) concluded:

> The unique moral force of affirmative action's original public rationale, as a temporary measure to compensate for the lingering, institutionalized effects of past discrimination against descendants of slaves, was eroded when preferences were extended to newly arrived immigrants from Latin America and Asia.

Arguments for and against affirmative action

In evaluating the case for and against affirmative action, some broad observations are important to place these arguments in a wider perspective. Equality and justice are commonly shared calls evoked by both proponents and opponents of affirmative action. In part this stems from the ambiguities and contradictions that seem to accompany the meaning given to these crucial terms. In the concept, "equality", the principles which are offered to define it are neither clear nor universally shared, and frequently contested. What it may signify in theory may be quite different in practice. In practical terms, as a daily guide to action, equality is a concept that is contextually defined, anointed, and shaped by an array of cultural symbols and patterns; moulded by issues, actors, institutions, the stakes involved etc. In the same society, it may pragmatically or opportunistically shift its meaning but almost always it is a creature of struggles over power and resources, some of major and others of minor consequence.

As noted, equality is the rhetorical flourish that is unsheathed in combat between both proponents and opponents of affirmative action but the term lacks universal clarity and is in fact shrouded in ambiguity. Equality is not a neutral principle that is crystal clear. Walzer referred to it as a "procrustean bed". When unlocked, it is discovered to be infused with a conflicting and contradictory variety of principles, formulae, and procedural applications as well as results. It invariably raises controversies on the appropriate formula to be applied over what goods and resources are to be distributed, and about who the rightful and eligible recipients are. Often, in seeking to decipher the meaning through the origins of the doctrines and principles of the term, it may be shown to derive from judicial decisions serving as precedents; or from the hoary and revered cultural traditions and practices of a society; or from the sacred teachings of different religious and cultural traditions; or from ideological prescriptions such as "from each according to his ability, the prescriptions and beliefs to each according to her need" or "equal reward for equal work" etc. What is clear is that the concept is loaded with the historical meanderings of a society as it adjudicates conflicting claims applying to various justifications and historical narratives all locked in power struggles over those things that are scarce and valuable.

For some equality refers to procedural process while for others it pertains to outcomes. Even where this is a clear distinction it becomes entangled in issues of appropriate institutional procedures, or on the issue of determining correct shares of resources that are to be distributed, and to whom. To wave the flag of equality, then, is not to assume that the term is self-evident in its meaning and operationalization. It is often a red flag signalling a call to battle over vital symbols and material ends. Different ideologies adhere to radically different formulae regarding equality and its justification. For some, it is erected on the view of a shared parentage in a common progenitor, creating all as brothers and sisters. For others, Darwinian laws of descent inexorably describe a world of equality in terms of the struggle for survival of the fittest – who are the rightful inheritors of what is good and valued. For some, equality simply refers to equality of opportunity with no reference to results and outcomes. Some ideologies place private property at the very heart of claims over equality and thus beyond the scope of resources to be distributed, regarding it as a sacred natural right of individuals. Others see property as socially constructed and able to be manipulated to serve different public policy ends, including an egalitarian order. In all of this it is therefore critical to locate the meaning of equality and justice within the context of culture, historical moment, and the political rivalry over power and resources. It means different things to different people and groups.

Equality is not a clear-cut formula but a clarion call for defence of the status quo or for radical change involving struggle over scarce resources and values that may define the fate of individuals and communities. It is an invitation for unending analysis and intellectual meditation. Anyone with a particular point of view on the meaning of equality can find documentation, narratives, texts, and sources in a society's history to justify a position. It is important to listen to the arguments for equality and justice, bearing in mind that it is always partisan, ideological, religious, and charged with claims to maintain or redistribute power, resources, and statuses.

Each state where affirmative action policies are being proposed and pursued, carries its own mix of arguments for and against affirmative action with its own array of groups and interests in contention. The arguments in the first set of states practicing affirmative action tend to influence the arguments and policies and programmes of later comers. In a number of cases affirmative action claims have been stimulated into existence because of the pattern and example of earlier states. Some affirmative action programmes and policies are fundamental in scope and revolutionary in effect. Arguments for and against therefore tend to be more than legalistic artifacts and are part and parcel of a wider political struggle to restructure the society. In effect, in some states the affirmative action changes are reformist and limited in scope, while in others they are more far reaching.

In a number of cases the arguments preceded the affirmative action policies, while in others they came mainly after – democratic discourse versus domination; the effects on the legitimacy of affirmative action. Arguments are never settled once and for all but persist and evolve during implementation, with both advances and reverses.

In making the case for affirmative action there are other arguments apart from those that point to compensation, rectification, and temporary suspension of egalitarian principles, so as to effect a level playing field for all in the long term. Because affirmative action tends to occur in states that are ethnically divided into ethno-cultural groups, distribution of values and goods tend to privilege one cultural community over others. In effect, social advantages and disadvantages tend to coincide with the cultural fault lines that divide the state. Clearly, in establishing a more just and inclusive society, the need exists inter alia to recognize all groups and ethno-cultural communities within a society. Affirmative action recognizes differences, cultural and gender alike, in a multi-ethnic society instead of forcing assimilation and cultural hegemony of a particular group's values and practices. Cultural recognition bestows dignity and space for a separate identity. It is anti-hegemonic in conferring equal recognition of the cultural symbols and practices of groups other than the dominant one. In this way, affirmative action promotes equal citizenship in a divided state. It advances inter-cultural harmony and unity in a tolerant policy of multiculturalism. Affirmative action by conferring dignity, a separate space, and ending discrimination and alienation, may diminish migration of the talents and skills from a society.

It may be argued also that affirmative action tends to promote more efficient utilization of the human resources in the society. Discrimination against an ethno-cultural community tends to underutilize the potential of the discriminated group to contribute maximally to the development of the state. Discrimination based on ethno-cultural criteria leads to inefficient use of the human resources of the society. Finally, it may be argued that affirmative action via the conferring of preferences to the disadvantaged through representation in decision-making political institutions, restores justice and equality in the society. In turn this advances political participation and a commitment to a shared citizenship.

Arguments against affirmative action are numerous and incisive but as a whole they tend to pivot around the dogma of merit, which is an integral part of the edifice of egalitarian justice. Opponents of affirmative action tend to articulate an uncompromising argument that underscores the essential role of merit to maintain a society based on democratic rights and equality. They vehemently inveigh against affirmative action as detrimental to equal citizenship because it destroys the relationship between equal work for equal reward, between work and reward. It also strikes at the very heart of citizenship from another angle related to the role of the individual, since affirmative action grants rewards to groups and not individuals. This is wrong because it destroys incentives for individual effort and similarly discourages responsibility for the individual's own choices and self-determination. Merit and individual identity, responsibility, and self-determination are critical interlocking principles and values bearing doctrinal status in the edifice of the acclaimed Western democratic system of justice and governance, and define a way of life. Thus, affirmative action bears the mark of an alien strain, a deviant and subversive intervention that threatens a just equal democratic order at its very core. To invoke merit in an argument therefore, even in all of its contradictions, is to assert an article of faith that is beyond reasonable counter claims. It reverses the wrong of discrimination that cannot be remedied, by committing another wrong, it is argued.

The merit principle, however, is vulnerable to attack. The advocates of merit regard the idea as a technical exercise that can be objectively discerned (if not quantified and measurable), leading to undisputed comparisons in performance. This, however vocally and vociferously it is affirmed, is basically incorrect, as Iris Marion Young has argued, declaring that "impartial, value neutral, scientific measures of merit do not exist" (Young 1990: 193). She goes on:

> For the merit principle to apply, it must be possible to identify, measure, compare, and rank individual performance of job-related tasks using criteria that are normatively and culturally neutral. For most jobs, however, this is not possible, and most criteria of evaluation used in our society, including educational credentials and standardized testing, have normative and cultural content.

Opponents of affirmative action argue that the policy rewards the uncompetitive and unenterprising and encourages laziness and lack of motivation. Further, it tends to place into jobs the unskilled and undeserving, thereby distorting the efficient allocation of human resources. Further, and most importantly, the history of affirmative action in the many societies that have adopted it has shown that it tends to reward the wrong people within a disadvantaged group. Consequently, it creates new groups of exploiters, leaving the truly needy in a state of persistent poverty. Hence, it promotes corruption in the distribution of preferences, often enriching a small minority against the truly majority disadvantaged.

Among the repertoire of counter arguments against affirmative action are its societal and psychological repercussions. Opponents of affirmative action argue that it tends to promote divisiveness among groups in the state by bestowing preferences to those that many regard as undeserving. In many instances affirmative action programmes bestow benefits on those who are not themselves victims but are the *descendants* of victims, in the process penalizing not the real culprits but rather their innocent progenies. It thus engenders anger, bitterness, and conflict among groups. Consequently, it promotes disunity by accentuating differences, many of recent and invented vintage, and in doing so cultivates identity politics that is fraught with envy and invidiousness. In turn, this militates against cross-cultural cooperation and sustains inter-ethnic malaise and jealousy. In effect, affirmative action inadvertently culminates in counterproductive identity politics which tends to accentuate differences and ghettoize communities. It simultaneously stigmatizes entire groups with a mark of inferiority and institutionalizes prejudice indiscriminately against entire communities. It infantilizes the disadvantaged by keeping them dependent and inferior. It tends to encourage the practice of victimology and engender a culture of blaming others for lack of initiative and obtaining undeserved rewards. It implements a new form of self-inflicted discriminatory apartheid. At another level it leads to the politics of patronage, which creates political constituencies out of disadvantaged communities that become self perpetuating.

Notes

1 See Chapter 1 in this volume, by Sunita Parikh. Also see T. Sowell (2004: 1).
2 See, for example, the well-known book, *American Apartheid*, by D. Massey and N. Denton.

References

Bobo, Lawrence. 2001. "Race, Interests, and Beliefs about Affirmative Action: Unanswered questions and New Directions" in John D. Skrentny (ed.), *Color Lines: Affirmative Action, Immigration, and Civil Rights Options for America*. Chicago: University of Chicago Press.
Du Bois, W.E.B. 1903. *The Souls of Black Folks*. Boston: Bedford Books.
Glazer, Nathan. 1975. *Affirmative Discrimination: Ethnic Inequality and Public Policy*. New York: Basic Books.
Goldman, Alan. 1979. *Justice and Reverse Discrimination*. Princeton: Princeton University Press.
Graham, Hugh Davis. 1990. *The Civil Rights Era: Origins and Development of National Policy 1960–1972*. New York: Oxford University Press.
Kellough, J. Edward. 2006. *Understanding Affirmative Action: Politics, Discrimination, and the Search for Justice*. Georgetown University Press.
Kelly, Erin and Frank Dobbin. 2001. "How Affirmative Action Became Diversity management: employer Response to Anti-Discrimination Law, 1961–1996" in John D. Skrentny (ed.), *Color Lines*.
Malamud, Deborah C. 2001. "Affirmative Action and Ethnic Niches: A Legal Afterword" in John D. Skrentny (ed.), *Color Lines*.
Massey, Douglas S. and Nancy A. Denton. 1993. *American Apartheid*. Cambridge: Harvard University Press.
Skrentny, John D. 1996. *The Ironies of Affirmative Action: Politics, Culture, and Justice in America*. Chicago: University of Chicago Press.
Skrentny, John D. (ed.). 2001. Color Lines: Affirmative Action, Immigration, and Civil Rights Options for America. Chicago: University of Chicago Press.
Sowell, Thomas. 2004. *Affirmative Action Around the World*. New Haven: Yale University Press.

3 Ethnicity, economy, and affirmative action in Malaysia

Hwok-Aun Lee, Edmund Terence Gomez, and Shakila Yacob

Historical, constitutional, and political contexts

A convergence of factors have compelled and facilitated the breadth and intensity of Malaysia's affirmative action. Malaysia is one of a few countries where a majority and politically dominant ethnic group, the *Bumiputera*,[1] was socially excluded and economically disadvantaged in the aftermath of colonial rule. Bumiputera under-representation in tertiary education institutions and upper occupational positions, and in ownership and control over economic activity, was starker in Malaysia than in most nations that implement forms of affirmative action. Socio-political demands for preferential policies inevitably arose out of such conditions. At the same time, Malaysia's abundant natural endowments and relatively robust record of economic growth, development spending, and rapid industrialization have availed resources and opportunities to be redistributed. Additionally, the perpetuation of a one-party political system since independence in 1957, and exertion of Malay dominance within the ruling race-based Alliance (1957–1974) and *Barisan Nasional* (or National Front) (1974-) coalitions, coupled with the expansion of executive power from the 1980s, permitted racial preference to be instituted in more explicit and extensive forms than would be realizable in most countries. The United Malays' National Organization (UMNO) is acknowledged as the hegemonic party in the Barisan Nasional, which comprises about a dozen, mostly ethnically-based, parties.[2]

Post-independence Malaya was characterized by a social structure, fittingly termed an ethnic division of labour, in which groups were predominantly and persistently confined to certain occupations and industries (Khoo 2005). Through British colonial rule and migration processes, foreign interests came to dominate the ownership of resources and capital, while Malays, Chinese, and Indians by-and-large lived and worked in separate geographic and economic spheres (Andaya and Andaya 2001). Ethnic social stratification was reinforced by disparities in educational and job opportunities, and in access to capital.[3] Educational institutions were fragmented, again, by race and socio-political factors, and not integrated into a broader system for facilitating social interaction and coordinating school content.[4] The Malay masses were overwhelmingly excluded from these developments, except for the privileged or talented few who enjoyed access to elite schools, scholarships, and civil service appointments. Indians on plantations were excluded on the grounds that plantations were private property; hence, the educational and health needs of its workers fell outside the state's jurisdiction.

The historical timeline of affirmative action, and the basis for its continuity, are anchored in the 1957 Federal Constitution.[5] Individual equality and prohibition of discrimination is set out in Article 8, "[e]xcept as expressly authorized by this Constitution". Article 153 grants such authorization, making provision for the Yang Di-Pertuan Agong (the national king) to "exercise his functions under this Constitution and federal law in such manner as may be necessary to safeguard the special position of the Malays and natives of any of the States of Sabah and Sarawak [i.e. the Bumiputera] and the legitimate interests of other communities", through reserving places in public sector employment, scholarships, training programmes, and licences. These legal grounds for race preference have been the subject of intense debate, particularly with reference to the specific wording of the Bumiputera's "special position" – as distinct from Bumiputera "special rights" – and the delimitation of the scope of programmes to public sector jobs, scholarships, training and licencing.

The focus on semantics and scope in the discourse over special rights omits the elements of discretion and qualification in the Constitution's provisions for affirmative action. Article 153 does not confer an absolute mandate and obligation to apply reservations and quotas, but establishes those possibilities "in such manner as may be necessary". Thus, the constitutional case for affirmative action is qualified by adjudged necessity, and this is arguably a more constructive focal point for deliberating the continuity of racial preference.

Of course, given the convergence of vast disparities and available resources, and the consolidation of race-based politics over time, socio-political pressures for racially delineated redistributive policies have prevailed over the principles and limits to affirmative action as set out in the Constitution. The momentous event in the expansion and intensification of affirmative action was the racial upheaval and bloodshed of 13 May, 1969, and the subsequent overhaul of Malaysia's development regime under the New Economic Policy (NEP). Affirmative action and the NEP will be discussed in the following section. However, a few points are worth noting at this juncture. First, affirmative action is embedded in Malaysia's institutional framework. Constitutional provisions for racial preference must be situated in historical context and examined on an ongoing basis, corresponding with changing conditions. Second, affirmative action was expanded and intensified in the aftermath of racial strife, and under conditions of national emergency. Crisis provided a rallying point and galvanized resources, but also triggered the consolidation of pro-Malay political power and executive dominance, and increasingly centralized the policy regime.

Affirmative action before the NEP (1957–1971)

In the early post-independence years Malaysia's policy dispensation can be characterized as principally laissez faire, with limited state intervention in key sectors of the economy that were dominated by foreign capital. Some preferential policies and quotas were implemented in post-secondary education and public sector employment, especially in upper administrative posts. In the elite diplomatic and administrative service corps, the proportion of Malays rose from 34.6 per cent in 1957 to 86.6 per cent in 1970, on the heels of a 4:1 ratio of Malay to non-Malay quota introduced in 1953 (CPPS 2006a: 5). In federal and state government as a whole, Malays comprised 64.5 per cent of workers in 1969 (Khoo 2005: 30). However, affirmative action outcomes were less significant on a national scale. Total enrolment (in 1970) at the University of Malaya, the country's sole tertiary institution, was a minuscule 7,395 in a population of 10.5 million. Although overall enrolment in university was fairly reflective of the country's racial profile, Malays were acutely under-represented in scientific and technical fields, due in large part to deficiencies in rural schools.[6] The public sector comprised 11.9 per cent of the working population in 1970, and exerted a modest impact on the overall racial employment profile, except perhaps in bolstering the proportion of Malays among professionals and technicians.

The Malay community grew somewhat disaffected in the 1960s, in the face of uneven distribution of benefits from economic growth, continual small landholdings and indebtedness, and abuse of programmes for the poor by the wealthy (Andaya and Andaya 2001: 302–4). At the same time, pressures accumulated for state support and special programmes to develop a Malay business class. Administrative elites had cultivated close ties between government and a nascent capitalist class (Jesudason 1989: 51–2; 65–8). The mid-1960s witnessed the first budget for Malay business development in the *First Malaysia Plan (1965–1970)*, the establishment of Bank Bumiputra in 1965, MARA (the Council of Trust for Indigenous Peoples) in 1966, and other development agencies entrusted to fund or nurture Malay commerce and industry. The number of public enterprises increased from 22 in 1960 to 109 in 1970. Local business interests were free from regulatory inhibitions, although most were involved in an informal and loose nexus with the ruling coalition. Such a relationship can be characterized as a quid pro quo understanding, whereby generous issuance by the government of licences to operate, for example, was reciprocated by political donations (Gomez 1994). The presence of foreign, particularly British, businesses, continued to be tolerated and even encouraged, largely as their capital and expertise were considered important for the development of the fledgling economy. UMNO leaders also felt that British capital served as an important check on the ascendance of Chinese capital in the post-colonial period.

Inevitably, wealth and income-diverging trends persisted through the decade. Bumiputera interests owned just 2.4 per cent of total equity in 1970, while non-Bumiputera Malaysians held 28.3 per cent and foreigners 63.4 per cent. Income inequality increased on a national scale between racial groups and within racial groups, and deepening sentiments toward the failures of economic and social policies to uplift Malays made for a volatile political setting.[7]

Indeed, a political crisis shifted the policy regime onto a vastly different path. In the 1969 general elections the ruling coalition lost ground. Malays became wary of the largely non-Malay opposition's strengthened political position while non-Malays, especially Chinese, reacted against measures perceived as constricting their cultural and commercial space. In the wake of the post-election riots of May 13, Malay political dominance was reasserted and pro-Malay policies were institutionalized, somewhat legitimated by the ongoing crisis and an overwhelming sense that extensive and intensive state intervention would be necessary. The top-down approach and centralized executive control of that crisis situation also set a precedent for Malaysia's mode of governance (Ho 1992).

Affirmative action since the NEP (1971–present)

The NEP, a 20-year restructuring policy, was presented as means to achieve inter-ethnic economic parity between ethnic communities. The NEP hoped to achieve national unity by "eradicating poverty", regardless of race, and by accelerating the "restructuring" of society so as to reduce racial disproportionalities in economic participation and ownership. The policy entailed greater state intervention, characterized by the active participation of public enterprises, later called government-linked companies (GLCs), in the economy on behalf of the Bumiputera community to ensure more equitable distribution of corporate equity among ethnic groups. The NEP also stipulated that 30 per cent of the equity of all quoted firms be transferred to Bumiputeras. The initial 20-year timeline of the NEP (1971–1990) reflected a concern for the preferential programmes to be transitory and ultimately redundant. However, the NEP's primary affirmative action instruments have remained in place, with marginal alterations, and Malaysia has largely evaded a thorough discourse on transitioning away from Bumiputera preferential treatment.

Affirmative action substantially overlaps with the NEP, and the two are often equated. However, it is necessary to highlight distinctions between them, from temporal and spatial perspectives. Temporally, affirmative action measures of much smaller scope and scale were in place prior to the NEP, as outlined above. Spatially, the NEP encompasses policies involving racial preference, but also lays out a broad policy vision for economic growth, poverty alleviation, and industrialization, and pronounced that "national unity is the overriding objective of the country" (Malaysia 1971: 1). In the post-1971 era, it is more accurate to locate affirmative action as a subset of the NEP.

Tertiary education

Affirmative action interventions in education consisted of newly created post-secondary institutions and scholarships for Bumiputera students and a racial quota system for university admissions. The Ministry of Education established exclusively Bumiputera residential science colleges from the mid-1970s, in line with the goal of increasing science and engineering graduates (Lee 1994). MARA also set up junior residential colleges, principally for rural and under-privileged students, which also emphasized science subjects and designated higher standards of teaching and facilities (Leete 2007: 189).

Malaysia founded new public universities and a centralized government agency to process applications in accordance with affirmative action objectives. Supply of tertiary enrolment provision, however, did not keep up with demand. Between the early 1970s and the mid-1980s, the proportion of applicants who were offered a place in university dropped from half to one-fifth. The problem of insufficient places in domestic public tertiary institutions was compounded by the Bumiputera preference in admissions that made entry more difficult for non-Bumiputera. Some of this pressure was relieved by the growth of private tertiary education from the 1980s, mostly in the form of colleges affiliated with foreign universities or accreditation bodies, which provided pre-university diploma programmes from which students could continue towards obtaining a degree abroad. In 1985 more Malaysian Chinese tertiary level students were enrolled overseas than domestically.[8]

Major shifts occurred in the 1990s. Public tertiary education burgeoned; universities were established across the states of Malaysia. Matriculation colleges, a shorter and easier route to university entrance compared to sixth form in the national schooling system, expanded in the late 1990s (Loo 2007: 223).[9] The Private Higher Education Act of 1996, which permitted domestic private for-profit degree-granting universities, led to a proliferation of private tertiary education institutes. Private higher education thus sustained its significant role in mitigating grievance against affirmative action in public universities. In recent years scholarship programmes have become somewhat more transparent in their operation.[10] On the whole, quotas remain the preponderant mode of operation, with changes at the margins, including some allotment of non-Bumiputera admission to previously Bumiputera-only institutions.[11]

Employment

Social restructuring under the NEP pursued an overarching goal of ensuring that "employment patterns at all levels and in all sectors ... must reflect the racial composition of the population" (Malaysia 1971: 42). Emphasis was placed on managerial and professional positions, where Bumiputera under-representation was most acute. This branch of affirmative action leaned heavily on the public sector, with very limited interventions in the private sector.[12] Prior to the NEP, measures had already been taken to sustain Malay representation in government departments, especially in high level positions.

Preferential hiring and promotion continued with greater intensity under the NEP, bolstered by expansion of the public sector, especially in the 1970s and through to the mid-1980s.[13] Although the general objective was a racially representative workforce, there was no specified timeline or systematic framework for attaining proportional group representation. The mechanism and reference points for applying preference have been largely uncodified and discretionary. In some governmental bodies, especially non-administrative statutory bodies, the agenda of increasing Bumiputera proportions proceeded in the absence of formal policies. The public sector has been an extension of the university scholarship programme with Malay scholars in particular being absorbed into government employment. Mehmet and Yip's survey of graduating scholars in the early 1980s found 86.2 per cent of Malays working for government and statutory bodies, compared to 61.9 per cent of Chinese and Indians (Mehmet and Yip 1985).

Malaysia's affirmative action interventions in private sector employment have been minimal. The Industrial Coordination Act (1975) required large-scale manufacturing establishments to align their workforces more closely with the composition of Malaysia's general population. Companies were also required to use Bumiputera distributors for a minimum 30 per cent of their turnover, and could not be awarded government contracts if these quotas were not met. Meanwhile, trade unions were brought under strict control to keep labour costs down to draw direct foreign investment. It was relatively easy to fill production line positions with Peninsular Malaysian workers, particularly young Malay women from the villages who migrated to foreign-owned electronics, textile and clothing factories. However, parallel change was harder to effect in managerial positions, where Malay representation was limited and concentrated in non-technical responsibilities such as personnel management. No general legislation concerning employment practice has been instituted outside manufacturing, although some sectors strive for racial diversity in a selective manner, whether for reasons of strategy or regulation. For example, most banks employ a diverse workforce as tellers and in service jobs, although management tends to correspond ethnically with the banks' ownership. In recent years measures to raise Bumiputera representation in workplaces have continued to unfold, although in ad hoc and rather inconsequential manner.[14]

Enterprise and managerial development

This branch of affirmative action overlaps with occupational representation but focuses on commercial production of goods and services, as distinct from public administration, with a distinct agenda of cultivating a Bumiputera Commercial and Industrial Community (BCIC). Malaysia's approach to Bumiputera enterprise development has been largely state-centric. Various agencies were created to support Malay business, particularly in the 1970s and 1980s. State-owned enterprises, comprising public services departments, statutory bodies, and government-owned private or public companies, numbered 109 in 1970, 656 in 1980, and 1,149 in 1992, with the largest numbers in manufacturing, services, agriculture, finance, and construction (Gomez and Jomo 1999: 29–31). The national five-year plan expenditures on non-financial public enterprises flowed in accordance with funding needs in these entities. State Economic Development Corporations (SEDCs) were designated agencies for fostering Malay business from the early 1970s, backed by government guarantees or seed funds. However, such ventures often turned out to be unsuccessful or unsustainable – due to inexperience, inefficient management, or corruption. Relatively more effective, though less widely distributed, were the Malaysian government's efforts (from the late 1970s) through its investment arms to secure ownership of hitherto

British-owned companies, thus facilitating the entry of Malay managers and professionals into a few large firms.

The following decade witnessed major shifts in the state-sponsored Bumiputera capitalist and entrepreneurial development agenda. In the early 1980s, under the premiership of Mahathir Mohamad, a shift to a pro-business focus transpired under the NEP, along with a desire to promote heavy industrialization to secure as rapidly as possible for Malaysia the status of "newly-industrialized country". The heavy industries programme started with the incorporation of the Heavy Industries Corporation of Malaysia (HICOM), a GLC that ventured into various sectors, predominantly automobile, steel, and cement. These large firms were to be government-owned and Bumiputera-managed, with financial and operational support from Japan. The global recession of the mid-1980s curtailed the launch of Malaysia's heavy industry companies, but the emergence of excess capacity, lack of competency, and gross under-performance demonstrated the immaturity and poor monitoring of the programme. The focus shifted again, from the late 1980s, to privatization of state entities and concentration of ownership in the hands of "corporate captains", with the ultimate objective of facilitating a broad, capable, and wealthy Bumiputera business community.

The Malaysian state has also deployed licencing, contracting, and public procurement methods aimed at developing a Bumiputera capitalist and entrepreneurial class. Affirmative action programmes through licencing have operated on a sectoral basis. The Petroleum Development Act (1974) vested ownership of oil reserves in the hands of the government, and required that management of petrol stations be reserved for Bumiputeras. Taxi licences have also been restricted to Bumiputera – although this is an area of conspicuous *Ali-Baba* relationships in which a Bumiputera partner secures a licence then subcontracts the work to other persons. The vendor programme in the automobile sector set up a system for procurement from local parts suppliers. "Approved Permits" – quotas to import motor vehicles – were distributed.

The public procurement system has been utilized to stimulate and finance Bumiputera commerce, by reserving smaller contracts for Bumiputera contractors and conferring preferential conditions for larger contracts. The overall support to small and medium-scale Bumiputera enterprise, however, has been dwarfed by GLCs and large privatization projects. The fields of transportation, telecommunications, and media have seen the issuance of licences for big and politically strategic operations (Gomez and Jomo 1999: 91–100). By-and-large, political connections have affected the selection of beneficiaries of the above programmes.

Equity ownership

Equity ownership is the most highly emphasized and politically important of the NEP's objectives, and the area of starkest Malay under-representation by official measures (see Table 3.1). Although the NEP sought to reduce ethnic inequalities in wealth, income, and employment through affirmative action, the government declared that no particular group would experience loss or feel any sense of deprivation as a result of the policy. According to the government, "restructuring" was to be achieved primarily through economic growth. Asset redistribution was to be undertaken through various forms: taxation, funding public enterprises, and the banking system, which would provide Bumiputeras with preferential credit access and funding for the acquisition of corporate equity.

Progress on this front was slow in the early years of the NEP, and from the mid-1970s pressure mounted for the state to intervene more forcefully. The Industrial Coordination Act of 1975 mandated the transfer of equity into Bumiputera hands; medium- and large-scale enterprises had to obtain a manufacturing licence, which came attached with a precondition that at least 30 per cent of shares had to be allocated to Bumiputera individuals or agencies at prices approved by government authorities. Export-oriented (more than 80 per cent of output exported) firms, which were largely foreign-owned, were exempted from this regulation.

The government also moved aggressively in acquiring stakes, in the form of institutional representation of Bumiputera interest. A number of these institutions, including Khazanah Nasional, the Ministry of Finance Inc., Petroliam Nasional (Petronas), the Employees Provident Fund (EPF), Lembaga Tabung Haji, and Kumpulan Wang Amanah Pencen,[15] have become major equity shareholders. State-operated Bumiputera trust funds, notably Permodalan National Berhad (PNB, or National Trust Ltd.), were founded from the late 1970s, selling units and substantially investing in areas of national priority. One condition of Malaysia's political economy that has worked rather fortuitously to its advantage has been the large presence of foreign firms, particularly in the then lucrative fields of mining and plantations. State investment funds played a key role in taking over these hitherto foreign establishments, and substantial holdings have been maintained. Despite the high risks involved this acquisition drive was well planned and well executed and Malaysia became the exemplar of an emerging

Table 3.1 Share capital ownership (at par value) by ethnic group, 1970–2008 (%)

	1969	1970	1975	1980	1985	1990	1995	1999	2004	2006	2008
Bumiputera individuals & trust agencies	1.5	2.4	9.2	12.5	19.1	19.2	20.6	19.1	18.9	19.4	21.9
Chinese	22.8	27.2	n.a.	n.a.	33.4	45.5	40.9	37.9	39.0	42.4	34.9
Indians	0.9	1.1	n.a.	n.a.	1.2	1.0	1.5	1.5	1.2	1.1	1.6
Other	n.a.	n.a.	n.a.	n.a.	n.a	n.a.	n.a.	0.9	0.4	0.4	0.1
Nominee companies	2.1	6.0	n.a.	n.a.	1.3	8.5	8.3	7.9	8.0	6.6	3.5
Locally controlled firms	10.1	n.a.	n.a.	n.a.	7.2	0.3	1.0	n.a.	n.a.	n.a.	n.a.
Foreigners	62.1	63.4	53.3	42.9	26.0	25.4	27.7	32.7	32.5	30.1	37.9

Sources: Malaysia 1996, 2001, 2008, 2010.

Notes
Par value denotes the price at which the share was first issued; Government ownership is omitted.
n.a. = not available.

economy that did not nationalize its foreign firms, unlike neighbouring countries such as Myanmar, Indonesia, and Sri Lanka.[16]

These public agencies were quite successful in the early years. In 1975 British-owned London Tin (now Malaysian Mining Corporation), the country's leading tin mining group, was acquired by the state. The following year the Southeast Asian-based multinational Sime Darby was acquired. In 1981 British-controlled Guthrie Corporation, the largest plantation company in Malaysia, was taken over by PNB, which was soon to emerge as the country's largest institutional investor. Sime Darby has long been a well-cited example of the NEP's success, having recorded impressive growth of 15 per cent a year between 1988 and 1995. A regional magazine, the *Far Eastern Economic Review*, ranked Sime Darby as number one in "overall leadership, long-term vision" and "as a company that others try to emulate" (quoted in Khanna, Yoshino, and Melito 1996).

When public enterprises and trust agencies began actively acquiring domestic firms with increased state funding, they usually bought between 20–50 per cent of equity in companies for investment purposes. These state enterprises also incorporated wholly-owned firms across a range of business areas, and established joint ventures with Bumiputera, non-Bumiputera, and foreign firms.

Chinese capital continued to grow during the NEP period, but since affirmative action contributed to the bypassing of such enterprises during the award of contracts and projects, this served to undermine the community's entrepreneurial capacity. Inevitably there was an increasing need for Chinese businesses to accommodate the state in order to continue to expand (Gomez 1999). With the implementation of the NEP, inter-ethnic relationships became common at three levels. First, among the top Chinese-owned firms, prominent Malays were appointed to boards of directors, primarily to serve as avenues for these firms to secure access to the state or bypass government red-tape. Although these directors had equity ownership, they were not actively involved in the management and development of these companies. Second, at the level of the SMEs, unequal *Ali-Baba* partnerships were forged, with the Malays merely providing the contracts and the Chinese implementing them.[17] Third, among Malaysian elites, business partnerships were forged on a more equal basis. Notable examples include the partnership between Rashid Hussain and Chua Ma Yu who established Rashid Hussain Bhd, before the latter went on to develop his own business interests. Eric Chia worked with Mokhzani Abdul Rahim and Shamsuddin Kadir in UMW. Mokhzani and Shamsuddin moved on to develop their own enterprises (Searle 1999).

Since the Industrial Coordination Act had introduced uncertainty in business planning, this had become a disincentive for foreign and domestic investments, contributing to capital flight, even by prominent businessmen such as Robert Kuok, Malaysia's leading corporate figure. Huge protests were mounted against the Industrial Coordination Act leading to its liberalization on a number of occasions.

The Promotion of Investments Act of 1986 formally broadened the scope of exemption from equity requirements, and effectively exempted the bulk of manufacturing establishments from equity redistribution. To promote domestic private investment, in 1987 the government amended the Industrial Coordination Act's stringent Bumiputera investment and employee exemption limits for licencing of manufacturing enterprises (Yasuda 1991). These policy moves, coupled with favourable external market conditions, resulted in a resurgence of export-oriented manufacturing, largely under the auspices of foreign, especially East Asian, capital.

These liberalization endeavours of the government in the mid-1980s in response to the recession allowed for the introduction of neoliberal policies such as privatization.[18] This policy would serve to promote the rise of a Bumiputera capitalist class, implemented within the context of affirmative action. Entrepreneurial development was entrusted to a process of handing over of previously state-owned enterprises to individuals, hand-picked more through political connection than competitive selection. While the government had used public enterprises and trust agencies to acquire equity on behalf of the Bumiputeras, its aim, under Mahathir, was to shift the focus of corporate restructuring to nurturing Bumiputera individuals in control of well-capitalized companies with an international reputation, an endeavour that would constitute part of the BCIC policy. For Mahathir, parity would be achieved only if Malaysia had an equal number of Bumiputera and Chinese millionaires.

In contrast to the previous programmes that concentrated on institutional ownership, privatization concentrated capital in the hands of a small section of the Bumiputera population. Through privatization government assets were sold to private individuals when state-owned enterprises were listed on the stock exchange. There were a number of sizeable privatized public listings including the gaming firm, Sports Toto, the national airline, Malaysia Airlines (MAS), and HICOM. By the mid-1980s 24 state enterprises had been listed on the local stock exchange, and by 1995 privatized former state agencies accounted for 22 per cent of the local bourse's total market capitalization (Callen and Reynolds 1997: 15).

Over a mere decade a number of well-connected business people would emerge as owners of huge, publicly quoted, conglomerates. These business groups were controlled by Bumiputeras linked to one of the then three most powerful politicians – Prime Minister Mahathir, the then Deputy Prime Minister Anwar Ibrahim, and the then Finance Minister Daim Zainuddin. A group of well-connected non-Malays also quickly developed huge enterprises with state patronage. All had been privy to major privatized contracts.[19]

In spite of the rapid rise of the "new rich" by the mid-1990s, according to official government figures corporate equity owned by individual Bumiputeras and trust agencies amounted to only about 19 per cent. However, the 1997–1998 currency crisis resulted in many state-sponsored Malay capitalists and conglomerates foundering, after which they were renationalized. Large GLCs – both in financial and productive sectors – would re-emerge to continue to play significant roles in Bumiputera managerial employment and development, and have been reissued a mandate to drive Bumiputera enterprise.

In 2003, following a change of premiership, the government stressed that it would continue to champion Bumiputera capital, but would now place more emphasis on nurturing small and medium-sized enterprises (SMEs). The government would support potentially lucrative cottage industries dominated by poor rural Bumiputeras. A Vendor Development Programme (VDP), in which SMEs were tied to GLCs and multinational companies (MNCs), was created to help them gain greater access to both local and foreign markets. A similar vendor system had been a core component of the national car project, Proton, introduced in the 1980s. This vendor system was used to create trade links between SMEs and MNCs in the retail sector. Subsequently, an Industrial Linkage Programme (ILP) was introduced to tie domestic firms to major foreign firms such as Intel and Dell. Although the ILP was universal in orientation, it became evident that it had to be used to encourage Bumiputera involvement in this sector. A Global Supplier Programme (GSP) was created to link SMEs to hypermarkets run by MNCs, including Tesco and Carrefour, which were persuaded to allot space for locally produced goods in both their domestic and foreign outlets. There have, however, been complaints about the potentially lucrative ties between MNCs and SMEs, involving the issue of selective patronage. Critics allege that Chinese firms are seldom considered when SME–MNC ties are being contemplated, denying them access to the domestic and overseas markets the foreign companies can provide. A crucial component of this complaint is that the local firms excluded from consideration are sometimes better placed to break into foreign markets because they can produce higher quality products at lower prices.[20]

Despite inordinate attention to SMEs, including providing them access to loans, the state found it difficult to foster entrepreneurial small firms. By the late 2000s the number of local firms that could be considered dynamic, in terms of creating new technology, was small. This suggested a fundamental problem with the government's economic orientation, i.e. that it was wrong in assuming that the state could simultaneously promote Bumiputera capital and social cohesion without jeopardizing either endeavour.

In 2009 Malaysia was confronted with a profound economic downturn that revealed severe structural problems. In the first quarter of 2009 the economy shrunk shockingly, to –6.25 per cent. It was now obvious that the economy was in desperate need of foreign investment to generate growth. The government removed the 30 per cent Bumiputera equity requirement in 27 service sub-sectors – including health, tourism, computer services, and transport – and a new centralized equity agency, Ekuinas, was created to spearhead Bumiputera ownership, ostensibly with a greater emphasis on productivity and competitiveness. This was a major concession by the government as it meant that ethnic equity ownership conditions would no longer apply to these sub-sectors. In 2008 services constituted about 55 per cent of GDP and accounted for nearly 57 per cent of total employment. Bumiputera presence in services was large and members of this community were concerned that with this liberalization they would not be able to compete with Chinese and foreign firms.

Evaluation of outcomes

Table 3.2 summarizes the main affirmative action programmes, and a few notable features that have been outlined above or will be discussed in this section.

Tertiary education

Education data are scarce and dispersed, compared to employment and equity ownership statistics that are tracked across time in official publications. Nonetheless, what can be garnered from available sources indicates substantial quantitative progress in Bumiputera educational attainment. The ethnic composition of universities demonstrates the efficacy of admissions quotas and Bumiputera-only pre-university institutions. In 1970, the university student population consisted of 40.2 per cent Bumiputera, 48.9 per cent Chinese and 7.3 per cent Indian; by 1985, these figures had changed to 63 per cent Bumiputera, 29.7 per cent Chinese and 6.5 per cent Indian (Khoo 2005: 21). In 2003 the proportions were reported to be 62.6 per cent Bumiputera, 32.2 per cent Chinese and 5.2 per cent Indian (Sato 2005: 86).

Growth in tertiary education carries forth to the labour force, where data are available across time (see Table 3.3). The share of Malay and Chinese workers who have attained tertiary education in 2007 is 24.1 per cent and 22.6 per cent respectively. However, differences persist across ethnic groups. By 2007 the Indian and non-Malay Bumiputera communities continued to experience less advancement in formal education, with 18.8 per cent and 12.9 per cent of their respective workforces holding tertiary level qualifications. Overall, provision and attainment of tertiary education at degree level has increased, but the opportunities available to Indians and especially non-Malay Bumiputeras are consistently fewer.

The residential school and university scholarship programmes undoubtedly provided educational access to many Bumiputera who otherwise would not have had the opportunity. However, it is unclear whether the distribution of benefits has been conducted in a systematic way that balances merit and social position. In the mid-1970s, children of urban middle class households constituted 63 per cent of MARA junior science colleges (Selvaratnam 1988: 191). Similarly, the allocation of university scholarships has been found to follow a regressive pattern. Mehmet and Yip's (1985) survey of a graduating cohort of 1982 found the distribution of scholarships skewed towards children of high income families, more markedly among Malays. This survey was limited to domestic universities in the early 1980s, but it is probable that regressive practices have persisted, especially in the case of high-demand scholarships to study overseas. While the children of urban middle class households on average present better prospects for further academic achievement, their selection comes at the expense of other youth, particularly from rural and low-income families, for whom scholarships facilitate potentially greater upward mobility.

Table 3.2 Summary of affirmative action programmes and notable features

Area	Programmes	Notable features and outcomes
Tertiary education	- Residential colleges - Matriculation colleges - Expansion of tertiary institutions, enrolment quotas - University scholarships	- Exclusively Bumiputera (until 2000) - Exclusively Bumiputera (until 2002) - Extensive growth of Bumiputera in tertiary education; but serious concerns over decline in quality - Facilitating access to university education, but lacking systematic consideration of equitable (within Bumiputera) distribution - Restricted access to public institutions for non-Bumiputera due to racial enrolment quotas is somewhat mitigated by growing numbers of private institutions, but remains a significant factor in the 'brain drain'
Upper-level occupations	- Public sector employment - Industrial Coordination Act (ICA)	- De facto quota, largely ad hoc in practice; major role in absorption of urbanizing Malays and growth of Malay professional and middle class - Poor public delivery system - Minimal impact at professional and managerial level; no impact on SMEs
Enterprise and managerial development	- Public enterprises/government-linked companies - Takeover of foreign companies - Licencing - Public procurement	- Spanning all sectors, but largely under-performing or failed; post-1997 crisis: government-linked companies given reinvigorated mandate to spearhead BCIC - Steady development and retained ownership, but limited in scale - Confined to fields with limited technological growth; no incentive structure, particularly for SMEs - Little effect on advancing Bumiputera business; widely viewed as a patronage regime; scant incentive structure, particularly for SMEs
Equity ownership	- ICA, public listing equity requirements - Privatization - Vendor programmes (VDP, ILP, GSP)	- Modest effect, widespread profiteering, little effective control transferred - Concentrated wealth accumulation; massive renationalization in the aftermath of the 1997–1998 crisis - Capital flight; low rate of domestic investment since 2000 - Limited capacity to promote SMEs - Failure to broaden independent Bumiputera-owned conglomerates

Serious questions also loom over the quality of education, especially at the tertiary level, alongside the problem of graduate unemployment and its disproportionately greater effects on Bumiputera. Haliza *et al.* (2009) explore differentials in the academic performance of university entrants by comparing those who were admitted with the Malaysian Higher Certificate, or A-level equivalent, and those who graduated from matriculation colleges. These findings strongly indicate that the preferential programme through which the vast majority of Bumiputera enter public universities provides less rigorous and competitive preparation than the national schooling system.

A comparison of unemployment rates by educational attainment suggests differences between ethnic groups in the capacity of graduates to participate in the labour market. Table 3.4 shows that the unemployment rate of the tertiary educated labour force increased between 1995 and 2007 within the Bumiputera and Indian populations. Undeniably, these labour force data are highly aggregated and their interpretation warrants circumspection. However, inter-ethnic differentials in unemployment also prevail among young adults but not among older adults. Of those aged 20–24 in 2004, a significant proportion of whom have presumably completed tertiary education, unemployment was higher among Bumiputera (12.4 per cent), followed by Indians (8.8 per cent) and Chinese (5.3 per cent). Such disparities are not observed among workers above 30. These patterns are consistent with the view that more recent Bumiputera beneficiaries of affirmative action face greater difficulty securing employment.

Table 3.3 Percentage of labour force with a tertiary level education, by race group

	1995	1999	2007
Bumiputera	11.4	13.8	22.0
Malay	*13.1*	*15.7*	*24.1*
Non-Malay Bumiputera	*4.4*	*6.4*	*12.9*
Chinese	12.0	15.1	22.6
Indian	9.5	11.9	18.8
Malaysia	11.1	13.2	21.8

Source: *Labour Force Survey Report*, various years.

Table 3.4 Unemployment rates within ethnic group, by highest education attained, 1995 and 2007

	Malaysian		*Bumiputera*		*Chinese*		*Indian*	
	1995	*2007*	*1995*	*2007*	*1995*	*2007*	*1995*	*2007*
Primary	1.7	2.2	2.7	2.6	0.8	1.6	1.5	2.8
Secondary	4.0	3.6	6.0	4.1	1.7	2.5	3.2	4.3
Tertiary	3.1	3.9	3.8	4.8	2.3	2.2	2.6	4.0
Overall	3.1	3.4	4.6	3.9	1.5	2.2	2.6	4.0

Source: authors' calculations from *Labour Force Survey Report*.

Other survey data add further insight to the under-researched area of graduate unemployment, and indicate that domestic public university degree-holders, the majority of whom are Bumiputera, experience greater difficulty in securing employment in highly skilled positions (World Bank 2005: 94–6). In a major survey of the employers and employees of 902 firms in Peninsular Malaysia, 70 per cent of managers responded that an insufficient supply of capable university graduates was the most severe limitation in the labour market. Employees self-evaluated the most important skill that they lacked in conducting their job competently; lack of proficiency in English came first (47 per cent), followed by professional and technical skills (14 per cent). The problem of deficiency in English language was found to be more acute on the east coast, which is predominantly Malay populated. This indicates that Malay and non-Malay Bumiputera graduates are more likely to face difficulty entering the upper rungs of the occupational ladder, and reinforces the view that graduates of Malaysian public universities encounter difficulties in the transition to the labour market, especially relative to the graduates of overseas universities.

The ramifications of affirmative action in tertiary education on non-Bumiputera are considerable and complex. Curtailed access to public institutions due to racial quotas persists as a point of contention, especially for families that cannot afford overseas or local private colleges and universities. Massive expansion of Malaysian private tertiary institutes has alleviated the sense of deprivation. However, large numbers of highly educated Malaysians work abroad, signalling a significant level of dissatisfaction with the opportunities at home available to them. Official sources estimate, relatively modestly, that 350,000 Malaysians are working abroad, over half of them with tertiary-level qualifications.[21] Undoubtedly the causes of emigration are complex. The decline of Malaysia's public universities and the international mobility of this group of Malaysians – most reside in Singapore, Australia, the US, and the UK – suggests that employment prospects, quality of public services, and political sentiment, as well as university quotas, are contributing to the "brain drain".

In 2010, by the government's own admission, education in Malaysia was in need of urgent reform. Government reports, including the *Government Transformation Plan*, the *New Economic Model for Malaysia* and the *10th Malaysia Plan*, unequivocally admitted that the country's human capital was "at a critical stage", that "the education system is not producing the skills demanded by firms" and that "we are not developing talent and what we have is leaving".[22] The *10th Malaysia Plan* further revealed that only 23 per cent of the workforce was highly skilled, while the *New Economic Model* made a shocking disclosure: about 80 per cent of the workforce has only up to SPM-level – or O-level equivalent – qualifications. Graduates had limited capacity to adopt and learn about new technologies – a reflection of a poor quality education system whose institutions were not producing the necessary human capital to feed into new economic sectors.

Employment

A few patterns of change can be noted in Bumiputera representation in upper-level occupations over the official NEP timeline (1971–1990) and the subsequent period. Tables 3.5 and 3.6 present occupational data based on labour force surveys. The classification system has changed, which likely accounts for discrepancies observed before and after 2000. Bumiputera entry into professional and technical positions progressed steadily in the 1970s and 1980s, but slowed down from the 1990s through the 2000s (Table 3.6). The Bumiputera proportion in these occupational categories increased from 47.2 per cent in 1970 to 62.2 per cent in 1990, but only changed slightly in the period 1990–2000; teachers and nurses comprised a continuously high and slightly increasing share. Over 2000–2005 the Bumiputera percentage of professionals and technicians increased marginally. Table 3.7 shows more than half of Bumiputera professionals working as teachers and lecturers, considerably higher than the corresponding figures of 22 per cent for Chinese and 30 per cent for Indians. The concentration in teaching positions need not be a concern, and indeed serves vital social purposes. However, the dismal academic profile of teacher trainees reflects poorly on the academic performance of Bumiputera graduates, and does not bode well for the quality of instruction in public schools.

The public sector has been instrumental in facilitating Malay upward mobility and forming a Bumiputera middle class (Abdul Rahman 1996). Recent employment trends reflect a continuing dependence of affirmative action on government employment. Public sector employment data show how the importance of the public sector in the early 2000s was not just sustained, but in fact grew on the whole and more so in the upper echelons. In the government employment roll of June 2005, Malays comprise 83.9 per cent in top management, 81.6 per cent at management and professional level, and 75.8 per cent of support staff (CPPS 2006a). Ethnic quotas in hiring, compounded by discriminatory practices in promotion, have also led to a perceptible and systemic decline and loss of capacity in public institutions, to the detriment of service delivery.

Malaysia's achievement shortcomings are greatest in its programme of developing an independent managerial and entrepreneurial class. Bumiputera representation in management increased gradually from 22.4 per cent in 1970 to 30.3 per cent in 1990, then more rapidly to 36.8 per cent in 1995, but has remained static and hovered at around 37 per cent in the period 1995–2005 (Tables 3.5, 3.6, and 3.7). The development of Bumiputera-owned and operated SMEs remains an area of pronounced shortcoming, particularly in manufacturing activities, where reliance on foreign investment persists (Lee 2007). Licencing and procurement, beset by corruption and political influence in selection, have suffered from poor implementation, while the massive renationalization of a number of major companies in the late 1990s was a huge failure (Tan 2008).

Professional association membership offers another data source about ethnic composition. Table 3.8 shows the combined Bumiputera share of registered professionals – predominantly in the private sector – increasing from 4.9 per cent in

Table 3.5 Ethnic representation in occupation groups (percentage of Malaysian employed population), 1970–2000

1970

	Bumiputera	Chinese	Indian
Admin. and managerial	22.4	65.7	7.5
Professional and technical	47.2	37.7	12.7
Excl. teachers and nurses	n.a.	n.a.	n.a.
Teachers and nurses	n.a.	n.a.	n.a.
Clerical workers	33.4	51.0	14.3
Sales and service workers	n.a.	n.a.	n.a.
Agricultural workers	68.7	20.8	9.6
Production workers	31.3	59.9	8.6
Overall	51.4	37.0	10.7

1990

	Bumiputera	Chinese	Indian
Admin. and managerial	30.3	65.5	4.2
Professional and technical	62.2	29.9	7.9
Excl. teachers and nurses	58.0	33.2	8.8
Teachers and nurses	68.8	24.7	6.4
Clerical workers	52.6	38.8	8.6
Sales and service workers	46.4	45.0	8.6
Agricultural workers	76.5	15.3	8.1
Production workers	46.4	42.1	11.5
Overall	56.3	34.6	9.1

1995

	Bumiputera	Chinese	Indian
Admin. and managerial	36.8	52.5	4.8
Professional and technical	64.4	25.7	7.0
Excl. teachers and nurses	60.0	28.5	7.2
Teachers and nurses	72.3	20.5	6.6
Clerical workers	57.5	33.8	7.4
Sales and service workers	47.0	35.8	7.2
Agricultural workers	61.2	11.9	6.9
Production workers	44.2	33.7	9.6
Overall	51.4	29.6	7.9

2000

	Bumiputera	Chinese	Indian
Admin. and managerial	37.0	52.3	5.5
Professional and technical	63.9	25.8	7.6
Excl. teachers and nurses	59.3	29.5	7.9
Teachers and nurses	73.2	18.4	6.9
Clerical workers	56.8	32.9	8.6
Sales and service workers	47.9	35.3	7.7
Agricultural workers	61.2	10.3	6.9
Production workers	44.7	33.8	10.0
Overall	51.5	29.7	8.3

Sources: *Third Malaysia Plan* (cited in Jesudason, 1989), *Seventh Malaysia Plan*, *Eighth Malaysia Plan*.

Notes
Rows do not total 100% due to omitted category termed "Others"; n.a. = not available.

Table 3.6 Ethnic representation in occupation groups (percentage of Malaysian employed population), 2000–2005

	2000			2005		
	Bumiputera	Chinese	Indian	Bumiputera	Chinese	Indian
Admin. and managerial	36.6	55.8	6.6	37.1	55.1	7.1
Professionals	57.3	33.5	7.9	58.5	31.9	8.2
Excl. teachers and lecturers	*45.4*	*44.2*	*9.3*	*47.2*	*42.0*	*9.6*
Teachers and lecturers	*74.4*	*18.2*	*5.8*	*74.9*	*17.4*	*6.2*
Technicians and assoc. pro.	59.5	30.3	9.5	59.5	29.7	10.0
Excl. teachers and nurses	*54.6*	*34.0*	*10.8*	*55.2*	*32.9*	*11.2*
Teachers and nurses	*71.1*	*21.4*	*6.4*	*70.6*	*21.5*	*6.9*
Clerical workers	56.6	35.4	7.4	56.7	34.3	8.5
Sales and service workers	51.2	40.6	7.3	51.5	39.6	8.0
Agricultural workers	77.1	13.9	5.5	80.8	11.3	4.3
Production workers	53.2	31.5	12.3	54.4	30.9	12.0
Overall	56.4	32.5	9.1	56.5	32.4	9.3

Source: *Ninth Malaysia Plan.*

Notes
Rows do not total 100% due to omitted "Others" category.

1970 to 29.0 per cent in 1990, 33.1 per cent in 1995, 35.5 per cent in 2000 and 38.8 per cent in 2005, with some variation across occupations. These data also show the momentum of rising Bumiputera representation in professional organizations dwindling from the 1990s, although in a few sub-categories – specifically, architects, dentists, and lawyers – the proportions of Bumiputera have continued to grow steadily.

Equity ownership

Empirical evaluation of this area of affirmative action is as contentious as it is imperative. Official data sources have consistently reported equity distribution based on par value, disaggregated by ethnicity and whether the equity is held by individuals, trust agencies or nominees (Table 3.1). The Bumiputera share increased from 2.4 per cent in 1970 to 12.5 per cent in 1980, primarily through redistribution from foreign interests, in which trust agencies played a prominent

Table 3.7 Teachers and nurses as percentage of total professionals and technicians, within race, 2000 and 2005

	Lecturers and secondary school teachers		Primary school teachers and nurses	
	2000	2005	2000	2005
Bumiputera	53.2	52.5	35.6	33.6
Chinese	22.2	22.4	21.0	20.5
Indian	30.2	30.8	20.3	19.5
Overall	41.0	41.0	29.8	28.3

Source: authors' calculations from the *Ninth Malaysia Plan*.

Table 3.8 Registered professionals[a] by race, as a percentage of total

	Bumiputera	Chinese	Indian	Others
1970[b]	4.9	61.0	23.3	10.8
1975[c]	6.7	64.1	22.1	7.1
1980	14.9	63.5	17.4	4.2
1985	22.2	61.2	13.9	2.7
1990	29.0	55.9	13.2	1.9
1995	33.1	52.4	12.9	1.6
2000	35.5	51.2	12.0	1.3
2005	38.8	48.7	10.6	1.9

Sources: Jomo, 2004, *Seventh Malaysia Plan*, *Ninth Malaysia Plan*.

Notes
a Architects, accountants, dentists, doctors, engineers, lawyers, surveyors, veterinarians.
b Excludes surveyors and lawyers.
c Excludes surveyors.

role. The Chinese share also grew over this period. By 1990 the Bumiputera proportion had risen to 19.3 per cent, most of it held by individuals. The 1990s, until the 1997–1998 currency crisis, saw the share for Bumiputera and foreigners rise slightly, while the Chinese share declined. The impact of the crisis is reflected in the 1999 data, showing a proportional drop in Bumiputera and Chinese ownership and a rise in foreign ownership. Between 1999–2008 the overall Bumiputera share stabilized, with trust agencies constituting an increasing portion, while the Chinese share fell. In summary, by the official account, Bumiputera ownership barely changed in the two decades since the late 1980s.

While the official methods for estimating equity distribution have persisted, they are emphatically disputable. Particularly problematic are the usage of par value, the inadequate accounting of holdings held via nominees, and the omission of government ownership (Jomo 2004; CPPS 2006b). The usage of par value, instead of market value or net tangible assets, omits changes in asset price that contribute to wealth accumulation or contraction, and would tend to understate holdings in large corporations where Bumiputera equity ownership is known to be concentrated. The presence of holdings not assigned to an ethnic group, through nominees or others, is considerable – as high as 21.2 per cent in 1988 (Jomo 2004: 12) – and also likely understates Bumiputera ownership.

The omission of government ownership has been justified on the grounds that government does not represent one particular ethnic group. However, state policy in this area clearly specifies Bumiputera capital development as a prime objective, and executive positions in the relevant corporations are predominantly Malay. In any case, the representation of government holdings can be apportioned according to the ethnic composition of the population, e.g. 65 per cent Bumiputera. The failure to account for market value and government ownership is all the more problematic in view of the massive renationalization of privatized corporations and infrastructure projects after the 1997 currency crisis. GLCs, largely excluded from official ownership statistics, comprised 36 per cent of market capitalization in 2008.

Alternate estimates of ownership are sparse, and data are constrained. However, Jomo (2004) references published statistics of publicly listed companies which indicate that in March 1989 the market value of shares held by Bumiputera was 34.5 per cent. More recent research, incorporating the criticisms above, estimates Bumiputera ownership to be 45 per cent in 2005 (CPPS 2006b).[23] The study notes that Bumiputera presence has become substantial in some sectors, such as banking, plantations, and oil and gas.

Overall, the expansion of Bumiputera equity ownership over the 1970s and 1980s is fairly undisputed. Evidence from the late 1980s, however, is polarized, with official statistics pointing to little progress while other research indicates markedly higher proportions of equity held by Bumiputera interests. Critical comparison of both methods finds those applying market value and including government ownership to be more credible and pertinent. In other words, Bumiputera wealth accumulation – in terms of equity ownership – and empowerment in the corporate sector, reflected in substantial stakes through GLCs or private holdings in major industries, have advanced substantially. However, efforts to expand private individual equity ownership, such as Bumiputera quotas in the public listings, and to broaden participation in trust funds, have fallen short.

The promotion of Bumiputera capital has contributed to close ties between politics and business along ethnic lines, leading to the rise of a new elite signifying fresh class configurations (Gomez 2009). Since the rise of these businessmen was linked to the patronage of influential politicians, their fortunes depended on whether their patrons remained in power. After a serious political fall-out between Mahathir and his deputy, Anwar, the latter was removed from office in September 1998. Most businessmen associated with Anwar subsequently had to struggle to protect their corporate interests; many of them are no longer prominent business figures. Similarly, when Daim fell out of favour with Mahathir in 2001, the corporate assets owned by his business allies and proxies were taken over by the GLCs.[24] It is those Malay capitalists who have remained relatively independent of influential politicians that appear to have fared better in times of political crisis.

The government's leading proponent of the promotion of Bumiputera capital, Mahathir, gave a surprisingly frank appraisal of some of his less successful policies before stepping down as prime minister in 2003, arguing that long-term implementation of affirmative action had led to a "crutch mentality" among Bumiputera businesspeople (Mahathir 2002). The failure of his policies to reduce the presence of the state in the corporate sector and create a cohort of major Malay entrepreneurs is evident in firm ownership statistics. In 2010 six GLCs, but not a single Bumiputera-owned firm, were listed among the top ten quoted firms. Three were Chinese-held, and one Indian-owned. No Bumiputera owned firms in the industrial sector were among Malaysia's top 20 firms. Most Bumiputeras were involved in services: finance, construction, property development, and telecommunications. Following a serious global economic crisis in 2007 the government liberalized ethnic equity ownership regulations involving these sectors. Since Bumiputeras had a huge presence in these sectors, the liberalization of these sectors was an issue of much concern to them. The Malays in these sectors were fearful that they could not compete with non-Malays and foreign firms.

Conclusions

Affirmative action has considerably advanced the economic and social standing of the Bumiputera, indicating that the stated goals of the NEP have largely been met. Among the beneficiaries of the NEP there has been a substantial reduction in poverty. Absolute poverty among the Bumiputera reduced from 65 per cent in 1970 to 3.6 per cent in 2007. Bumiputera equity ownership increased from 2.4 per cent in 1969 to 21.9 per cent in 2008. Income disparities between the Bumiputera and non-Bumiputera narrowed significantly during the two NEP decades. Affirmative action facilitated Bumiputera access to education, especially at the tertiary level, which robustly increased their representation in managerial, professional, and technical occupations during the 1970s and 1980s.

The NEP's early capacity to contribute to the rise of a new Bumiputera middle class, one also capable of functioning independently in business, draws attention to one crucial lesson. The NEP's initial strong focus on sound early education for the poor has contributed to this positive outcome. The policy's emphasis on pulling poor children out of rural areas and sending them to residential schools equipped with good teachers proved crucial. The best of these students were sent abroad or to local public universities, a key factor contributing to the rise of a new Bumiputera middle class. A crucial lesson from the Malaysian case is the need to concentrate on nurturing human capital at an earlier stage of development, with an emphasis on quality teaching in schools, particularly in rural areas where poverty is most rampant.

But these positive outcomes of reducing poverty and creating a new Bumiputera middle class have been achieved in part rather than in full. Based on the evidence weighed above, the momentum of progress has dwindled in recent years, and the benefits have been inequitably distributed within the beneficiary group. While Bumiputera gains in access to tertiary education are evident in the share of the workforce holding formal qualifications, Indian and especially non-Malay Bumiputera attainment levels are substantially lower. Affirmative action has contributed to a decline of quality of services provided by public institutions. The government acknowledged this institutional decline when it admitted that the quality of the public delivery system was poor. Spatial differences have also been exacerbated by the limited ability of the rural poor to take advantage of access to higher education, an issue conditioned on high quality primary and secondary education.

Bumiputera representation in managerial, professional, and technical occupations has remained more or less static since the mid-1990s. Entry into these positions continues to depend on the public sector, where Bumiputeras are over-represented. Hiring quotas for Bumiputeras are practically redundant, given that applications for public sector jobs by non-Bumiputeras have steadily dwindled to small fractions. Meanwhile, unemployment rates among young adults and degree-holders have increased, disproportionately for Bumiputera, largely due to deficiencies in the sort of language and communication skills sought by private sector employers.

Serious intra-Bumiputera inequalities have emerged. Income and wealth disparities within this community have increased appreciably with the most prosperous members having made substantial economic gains. A subset of the targeted group has become politically powerful, allowing them to also become economically well off. This powerful cohort is among the most strident defenders of affirmative action, ostensibly in defence of an entire community. By the government's own admission equity redistribution, involving access to shares listed on the stock market, has benefited those who know how to obtain the loans needed to buy them; these shares have later been sold at a huge profit. Of the RM54 billion worth of quoted stock taken up since 1971, only RM2 billion remains in hands of Bumiputeras (*Bernama*, 30 June 2009).

There have also been contrasting outcomes in Malaysia's equity redistribution project. While official data suggest that ownership attributed to the

Bumiputera has stagnated over the past two decades, other sources, employing more transparent and credible methodologies, demonstrate that the share may be considerably higher. Undoubtedly, a segment of the Bumiputera population has accumulated substantial wealth. However, the shortcomings of various regulations and programmes, notably state-sponsored unit trust funds, Industrial Coordination Act equity rules, privatization of state assets, and ethnic quotas in public share offerings, pose questions on the efficacy and relevance of preferential policies in wealth distribution through these mechanisms, and suggest that priority should return to developing human capacities and skills, and raising earnings and income. Alternative measures for expanding ownership, not just of equity but various forms of assets, warrant serious consideration.

The decline in the capacity of the NEP to produce well-educated Bumiputera, and the growing intra-group wealth and income inequities among members of this community, suggests that ethnocentric type policies targeting specific groups rather than individuals tend to benefit those with the best mobilization capacity. What is also obvious is that the structure of the state and its role in the market collectively influences redistribution endeavours that can have a bearing on ethnic and spatial inequities. For example neo-liberal policies, such as privatization, introduced by the state to promote Bumiputera capital, shifted the focus of the NEP from being pro-poor to pro-business (Gomez 2009). The pro-business dimension of the NEP has contributed to close and unproductive, even corrupt, ties between politics and business. The promotion of Bumiputera capital has usually involved intra-ethnic selective patronage, ostensibly in an attempt to identify, pick, and groom "winners" (Gomez and Jomo 1999: 24–74). This non-transparent mechanism of "picking winners" has diminished the capacity of non-Bumiputera entrepreneurs to move up the technology ladder because of the latter's reluctance to invest in research and development for fear of losing ownership and control of their firms during equity redistribution exercises.

Since the NEP has contributed to the bypassing of entrepreneurial non-Bumiputera capital, this suggests that targeting has not helped develop a domestic industrial capital base in Malaysia, bringing into question the viability of policies based on race. This concerted attempt by the state to promote ethnic capital as a redistributive mechanism has led to a merger between Bumiputera business and the state elite – with such capital still highly dependent on the regime for survival. In addition to intra-group wealth inequalities, spatial inequities have worsened since the NEP's implementation because the policy has not helped develop rural Bumiputera-owned enterprises. Spatial differences have also been exacerbated by the limited ability of the rural poor to take advantage of access to higher education, an issue conditioned on primary and secondary education success.

These anomalies in the NEP can be explained in terms of the issue of the persistence of the policy across time, as well as its inability to ensure equal access for the targeted group. Determining the duration of affirmative action and abiding by this stipulation appears imperative. The short-term impact of the NEP appears positive, while its long-term consequence has been to reinforce ethnic identity in a manner that hinders social cohesion. A key point that emerges from this study is that the duration of affirmative action is fundamental. Crucially, the long-term implementation of affirmative action can have repercussions; and it is difficult to dismantle. In Malaysia the NEP was recast, though its primary objective of affirmative action along ethnic lines has remained unchanged, even in times of economic crisis.

This was evident when the economy encountered a serious recession in 2008 and the government announced numerous plans in 2010 to address it, including the *Government Transformation Plan* (GTP), the *New Economic Model* (NEM), and the *10th Malaysia Plan* (10MP). The NEM, for example, voiced three goals: to promote high income, sustainability, and inclusiveness. But it would also persist with affirmative action, though now the policy would be "market friendly" and based on class, not race. Importantly too, the NEM and 10th Malaysia Plan continued promoting neo-liberal policies such as privatization, ostensibly as part of its endeavour to support the private sector as the primary engine of growth. To ensure proper implementation of affirmative action the government would curb "rent seeking" and "patronage".

The arguments in these documents suggest the idea of a government confronting a serious conundrum. On the one hand, the GTP contends that since the proportion of shares in the corporate sector owned by Bumiputeras has "remained stagnant", there is a need to establish a private equity fund, Ekuinas, to increase Bumiputera participation in new areas of the economy. On the other hand, the GTP admits that one outcome of affirmative action has been "rising discontent", along with other problems such as a "two-speed economy", a huge brain drain, and widening inequality, including growing intra-Bumiputera wealth and income disparities. As for affirmative action, although the policy will henceforth be market friendly, this will inevitably involve state intervention. However, the government also advocates the need to free up the market, specifically to draw domestic investment that has stagnated since 2000. In spite of high savings rates the volume of domestic investment in the economy since 2000 has not increased, an issue linked to the matter of property rights involving ownership and enterprise control – specifically the need to relinquish 30 per cent equity when a firm is publicly quoted.

There is an obvious reason for the conundrum faced by the government. UMNO fears it may lose support among the Bumiputera electorate, particularly in rural areas, if any new government plan does not explicitly mention the promotion of this community's economic interests in one form or another. After all, even the GTP, NEM, and 10th Malaysia Plan draw attention to two serious problems. First, regional divides have emerged, with poverty most rampant in rural areas. Second, those areas where hardcore poverty prevails are Bumiputera majority localities, including Sabah, Kelantan, Perlis and Kedah, states where the opposition has a strong presence.

The controversial nature of affirmative action is obvious, mainly because it appears to have institutionalized discrimination even though the NEP's ultimate objective was to promote national unity. The nature of the debates about sustaining affirmative action suggests that in the long term this policy reinforces ethnic identity as a basis for continued access to privileges. Moreover, the lack of a systematic framework for limiting the duration of affirmative action perpetuates communal contentions, and compromises the ultimate objective of self-reliance and national unity. The Malaysian case suggests that, in the long term, horizontal inequality (HI) based policies are divisive, prevent social cohesion, and perpetuate the notion of the importance of ethnic identity over national identity. Policies based along HI lines have failed to create a more inclusive environment.

This assessment of affirmative action in Malaysia indicates that it can serve as a sound policy to rectify historical social injustices. However, after a short period of time the policy must expand its range of targeted groups and individuals based on class position. Non-transparent targeting and selective patronage in business have serious repercussions, including hindering domestic enterprise development and perpetuating a dependence on foreign investment to foster economic growth. The evidence suggests that, in the long term, the government must return to universal-type policies to sustain economic growth if it hopes to promote the principle of equal opportunity for all citizens.

Notes

1. Bumiputera, or "sons of the soil", refer to the Malay and other indigenous groups.
2. The other leading members of this multi-party coalition include the Malaysian Chinese Association (MCA) and the Malaysian Indian Congress (MIC).
3. European (particularly British) interests held a massive portion of Malaya's rich primary commodity production, centred on rubber plantations and tin resources. Puthucheary (1960) found that Europeans controlled over 84 per cent of large rubber estates and 60 per cent of tin output, and accounted for about 70 per cent of exports and 60 per cent of imports.
4. In 1957 literacy rates in Bumiputera-dominant states in Northern Peninsular and East Malaysia (Kelantan, Terengganu, Kedah, Perlis, Sabah, Sarawak) fell below the national average of 50 per cent, while the west coast and central Peninsula states recorded notably higher literacy rates (Leete 2007: 199).
5. As Lee (2005: 212) points out, these constitutional provisions for affirmative action were first set out in a 1948 Federation of Malaya Agreement under British colonial rule.
6. In 1970 the University of Malaya was the only university in Malaysia. In science subjects Malay graduates numbered 22 out of a total 493, one out of 67 in medicine, one out of 71 in engineering, and 15 out of 49 in agriculture (Selvaratnam 1988: 180).
7. From 1957–1970, the income share of the top 5 per cent of households increased considerably. Inter-racial disparity grew as well, with the Chinese:Malay household income ratio increasing from 1.89 in 1957 to 2.47 in 1967, and the Indian:Malay household income ratio also rising over the same period, from 1.51 to 1.95 (Anand 1981).
8. Faridah (2003: 166) reports that in 1985, out of 22,684 students studying overseas, 73.4 per cent were non-Bumiputera who failed to gain admission to local public universities or who were offered places in programmes not of their choice.
9. Enrolment in the then Bumiputera-only (a 10 per cent non-Bumiputera quota was introduced in 2002) colleges grew from 15,470 in 1995 to 46,509 in 2000, at a growth rate of 24.6 per cent per year (calculations from the *Eighth Malaysia Plan*).

10 For instance, a quota for the award of Public Service Department scholarships was formally raised from 10 per cent non-Bumiputera to 45 per cent non-Bumiputera in around 2000. However, reports found that from 2000 to 2007 the proportion of non-Bumiputera scholars at overseas institutions averaged about 15 per cent, while that for local institutions averaged 20–25 per cent.
11 A quota of 10 per cent non-Bumiputera enrolment in the 40 MARA junior science colleges was introduced in 2000. The proportion of non-Bumiputera in these colleges was 10.5 per cent in 2008 (*The Star*, 15 May 2008).
12 Zainal (1994: 612) maintains that the main instrument for increasing Bumiputera participation was through hiring quotas.
13 The public sector's share of total employment increased from 11.9 per cent in 1970 to 15.0 per cent in 1981, then dipped slightly to 14.2 per cent in 1987 (Rasiah and Ishak 2001).
14 The 2007 Federal Budget urged publicly-listed companies to pursue "corporate social responsibility" activities, such as awarding contracts to Bumiputera vendors, ensuring ethnic diversity of employment, and developing human capital. The 2008 Budget reinforced this with a requirement that firms "disclose their employment composition by race and gender, as well as programmes undertaken to develop domestic and Bumiputera vendors." However, the purpose of this monitoring, and incentives for compliance or the consequences of non-compliance, have not been specified.
15 Mehmet would refer to the rise of these institutions as "distributional coalitions", that is, cartel-like networks acting in collusion to concentrate wealth. See Mehmet (1986).
16 One key figure championing the cause was the late Ismail Ali, former governor of Bank Negara and chairman of PNB (Yacob and White 2010).
17 See Chin (2010) for a discussion on the phenomenon of *Ali-Baba* business relationships in Malaysia.
18 See Harvey (2005) for an incisive discussion of the history of neo-liberalism.
19 For an in-depth study of the rise of these well-connected Bumiputera and non-Bumiputera businessmen, see Gomez and Jomo (1999), Searle (1999), and Gomez (2002).
20 Interview with SME Association representatives, 29 June 2009.
21 NEAC (2010). The number of Malaysians residing abroad in 2010 exceeded 500,000 by other estimates (United Nations Global Migration Database, cited by Fong Chan Onn, "Tracing the brain drain trend" in *The Star*, 16 May 2010).
22 Quoted in the *New Economic Model for Malaysia, Part 1* (NEAC 2010: 6).
23 Specifically, CPPS (2006b) applied market value to publicly listed shares, and includes GLCs, to which the authors assign a 70 per cent Bumiputera stake. The study also assessed that a minute fraction of firms listed on the bourse's Main Board – 18 out of 757, or 2.4 per cent – to constitute meaningful, independently forged inter-ethnic partnerships. These findings derive from publicly-listed firms, whereas the government figures draw on a publicly inaccessible database of 600,000 companies. However, quoted firms constitute a dominant share of total share capital.
24 For details on the takeover of assets controlled by Anwar allies and Daim protégés, see Gomez (2006).

References

Abdul Rahman Embong. 1996. "Social Transformation, the State and the Middle Classes in Post-Independence Malaysia" in *Southeast Asian Studies*, 34 (3): 56–79.

Anand, Sudhir. 1981. *Inequality and Poverty in Malaysia: Measurement and Decomposition*. Oxford: Oxford University Press.

Andaya, Barbara Watson and Leonard Y. Andaya. 2001. *A History of Malaysia*. Honolulu: University of Hawaii Press.

Callen, T. and P. Reynolds. 1997. "Capital Market Development and the Monetary Market Mechanism in Malaysia and Thailand" in J. Hicklin, D. Robinson, and A. Singh (eds.), *Macroeconomic Issues Facing ASEAN Countries*. Washington DC: International Monetary Fund.

Centre for Public Policy Analysis (CPPSa). 2006a. *Towards a more representative and world class civil service*. CPPS, Kuala Lumpur.

Centre for Public Policy Analysis (CPPSb). 2006b. *Corporate equity distribution: past trends and future policy*. CPPS, Kuala Lumpur.

Chin Yee Whah. 2010. *Towards Inter-Ethnic Business Development and National Unity in Malaysia*. CRISE Working Paper No. 73. Oxford: Centre for Research on Inequality, Human Security and Ethnicity.

Faridah Jamaludin. 2003. "Malaysia's New Economic Policy: Has it Been a Success?" in William Darity and Ashwin Deshpande (eds.), *Boundaries of Clan and Color: Transnational Comparisons of Inter-Group Disparity*. London: Routledge.

Gomez, Edmund Terence. 1994. *Political Business: Corporate Involvement of Malaysian Political Parties*. Townsville: Centre for Southeast Asian Studies, James Cook University of North Queensland.

Gomez, Edmund Terence. 1999. *Chinese Business in Malaysia: Accumulation, Accommodation, Ascendance*. Honolulu: University of Hawaii Press.

Gomez, Edmund Terence. 2009. "The Rise and Fall of Capital: Corporate Malaysia in Historical Perspective" in *Journal of Contemporary Asia*, 39 (3): 345–81.

Gomez, Edmund Terence and K.S. Jomo. 1999. *Malaysia's Political Economy: Power, Profits, Patronage*. Cambridge: Cambridge University Press.

Haliza Othman, Zulkifli Mohd Nopiah, Izamarlina Asshaari, Noorhelyna Razali, Mohd Haniff Osman and Norhana. 2009. *A comparative study of engineering students on their pre-university results with their first-year performance at FKAB, UKM*. Paper presented at the 2009 Teaching and Learning Congress, National University of Malaysia, Bangi. Available at: http://pkukmweb.ukm.my/~upak/pdffile/PeKA09/P3/28.pdf (Accessed 15 October 2010).

Harvey, David. 2005. *A Brief History of Neoliberalism*. Oxford: Oxford University Press.

Jesudason, James V. 1989. *Ethnicity and the Economy*. Singapore: Oxford University Press.

Jomo, K.S. 2004. *The New Economic Policy and Interethnic Relations in Malaysia*. Identities, Conflict and Cohesion Programme Paper No. 7, UNRISD, Geneva.

Khanna, Tarun, Michael Yoshino and Danielle Melito. 1996. "Sime Darby 1995". Harvard Business School Case Study #9–797–017.

Khoo, Boo Teik. 2005. *Ethnic Structure, Inequality and Governance in the Public Sector: Malaysian Experiences*. Democracy, Governance and Human Rights Programme Paper No. 20. Geneva: UNRISD.

Lee, Hock Guan. 2005. Affirmative Action in Malaysia. *Southeast Asian Affairs 2005*, 211–228.

Lee, Hwok-Aun. 2007. "Industrial Policy and Inter-ethnic Income Distribution in Malaysia: Industrial Development and Equity Ownership, 1975–97" in K.S. Jomo (ed.), *Industrial Policy in Malaysia*. Singapore: Singapore University Press: 216–244.

Lee, Kiong Hock. 1994. "Human Resources and Skill Development" in *Malaysian Development Experience: Changes and Challenges*. Kuala Lumpur: INTAN: 819–52.

Leete, Richard. 2007. *From Kampung to Twin Towers: 50 Years of Economic and Social Development*. Petaling Jaya: Oxford Fajar.

Loo, Seng Piew. 2007. "Schooling in Malaysia" in Gerald A. Postigliane and Jason Tan (eds.), *Going to School in East Asia*. Westport, CT: Greenwood: 201–32.

Malaysia. 1971. *Second Malaysia Plan, 1971–1975*. Kuala Lumpur: Government Printer.
Malaysia. 1996. *Seventh Malaysia Plan, 1996–2000*. Kuala Lumpur: Government Printer.
Malaysia. 2001. *Eighth Malaysia Plan, 2001–2005*. Kuala Lumpur: Government Printer.
Malaysia. 2006. *Ninth Malaysia Plan, 2006–2010*. Kuala Lumpur: Government Printer.
Malaysia. 2008. *Mid-term Review of the Ninth Malaysia Plan*. Kuala Lumpur: Government Printer.
Malaysia. 2010. *Tenth Malaysia Plan, 2011–2015*. Kuala Lumpur: Government Printer.
Mehmet, Ozay. 1986. *Development in Malaysia: Poverty, Wealth and Trusteeship*. London: Croom Helm.
National Economic Advisory Council (NEAC). *New Economic Model for Malaysia (Part 1)*. Putrajaya: NEAC.
Puthucheary, James J. 1960. *Ownership and Control in the Malayan Economy*. Singapore: Eastern Universities Press.
Rasiah, Rajah and Ishak Shari. 2001. "Market, Government and Malaysia's New Economic Policy" in *Cambridge Journal of Economics*, 25: 57–78.
Sato, Machi. 2005. "Education, Ethnicity and Economics: Higher Education Reforms in Malaysia, 1957–2003" in *Nagoya University of Commerce and Business Journal of Language, Culture and Communication*, 7 (1): 73–88.
Selvaratnam, Viswanathan. 1988. "Ethnicity, Inequality and Higher Education in Malaysia" in *Comparative Education Review*, 32 (2), 173–96.
Tan, Jeff. 2008. *Privatization in Malaysia: Regulation, Rent-seeking and Policy Failure*. London and New York: Routledge.
World Bank. 2005. *Malaysia: Firm Competitiveness, Investment Climate, and Growth*. Poverty Reduction, Economic Management and Financial Sector Unit (PREM), East Asia and Pacific Region. Report No. 26841-MA.
Yacob, Shakila and Nicholas White. 2010. "The Unfinished Business of Malaysia's Decolonisation: The Origins of the Guthrie Dawn Raid" in *Modern Asian Studies*, 44 (5): 919–60.
Yasuda, Nobuyuki. 1991. "Malaysia's New Economic Policy and the Industrial coordination Act" in *The Developing Economies*, 29 (4): 330–49.
Zainal Aznam Yusof. 1994. "Growth and Equity in Malaysia" in *Malaysian Development Experience: Changes and Challenges*. Kuala Lumpur: INTAN, pp. 591–616.

4 Coerced preferences
Affirmative action and horizontal inequality in Fiji

Steven Ratuva

Affirmative action, the state and society

Fiji celebrated its 40th year of independence from Britain in 2010. In all this time Fiji had only 13 years of continuous democratic rule by the Alliance Party (except for a brief lull in 1977). The other 27 tumultuous years saw the execution of six coups. These coups were violent manifestations of political and sociocultural tensions associated with horizontal inequalities, real and perceived, between indigenous Fijians and Indo-Fijians who were brought to Fiji in the late nineteenth century by the British under an indentured labour scheme to work on the sugar plantations (Ali 1982; Lal 1992). The potentially explosive impact of inter-ethnic differences were recognized by colonial and post-colonial elites who consciously devised pro-indigenous Fijian affirmative action programmes that preceded and followed the coups in a desperate attempt to asphyxiate further aggravation of iridescent ethnic tensions (Ratuva 2002, 2005).

Affirmative action is often justified by the need to correct historical wrongs, resolve conflict, address inequality and provide social justice for disadvantaged groups, especially if the designated categories are minorities or marginalized (Sowell 1990; Ratuva 2000). However, in cases where a group is politically, culturally and demographically hegemonic as in Fiji, political elites from this group take the initiative to construct and implement affirmative action as they see fit for their own group. This study loosely distinguishes between the two broad categories of affirmative action: namely Minority-Based Affirmative Action (MIBA) and Majority-Based Affirmative Action (MABA). Some countries which come under MIBA include the United States, India and Brazil, while MABA countries include Fiji, Malaysia and South Africa. Since the designated categories in these three cases are the majority indigene, the political and ideological slant of affirmative action has a close association with indigenous rights and politics.

While it is true that Fiji's affirmative action has addressed economic disparity by benefiting various sections of the designated categories, some unintended consequences, such as escalated ethnic differentiation and tension, continue to linger on. One paradox of ethnic-based affirmative action in Fiji is the consolidation of ethnic discourses which further strengthen ethnic differentiation, the very condition that the policy was introduced to address.

Of pertinence here is the symbiotic relationship between affirmative action and ethnicity, in particular how ethno-politics shapes preferential discourses and how, in turn, special preferences reinforce political claims to special rights and special political positioning of the designated group within the state. In the case of MABA, the state assumes an "ethnocratic" identity while attempting to maintain an image of impartiality. In such cases affirmative action could become a means for ethno-political "inbreeding", as policies are designed primarily to serve the self-perpetuating interests of the dominant community. However, as the experiences of Fiji show, the elites and privileged individuals from the designated groups are often the biggest beneficiaries.

This study examines the dynamics and dilemmas of preferential policies in Fiji that are designed to address the socio-economic disadvantaged position of indigenous Fijians in the context of an ethnically contested political situation. Affirmative action in Fiji had a number of significant interrelated characteristics. First, it was driven by real and perceived horizontal inequalities, or inequality based on cultural markers and grouping such as ethnicity (Stewart 2009). Second, as a result of this, the policy had close association with ethno-nationalism and the notion of paramountcy of Fijian interest which were articulated through coups. This was especially so in the 1987 and 2000 ethno-nationalist coups when capture of power by indigenous Fijian elites provided the state the political fulcrum for appropriation of state resources in favour of indigenous Fijians (Cotrell and Ghai 2007). After the anti-ethno-nationalist coup in 2006, there was a reversal of the process as the notion of pro-indigenous affirmative action was curtailed by the military in favour of a multi-ethnic poverty alleviation approach (Ratuva 2010).

Third, affirmative action was more than simply a policy prescription. It entailed major social engineering to create an indigenous Fijian business and bureaucratic class to balance the bourgeoning Indo-Fijian entrepreneurial class (Ratuva 2010). Fourth, because of this and the constant preoccupation with horizontal inequality, there were minimal attempts to address intra-communal inequality and poverty (Chand 2007).

The affirmative action debate

The affirmative action debate in Fiji has largely revolved around a few key issues, including the need for equity, nation building, conflict resolution, natural right as indigene and the definition and composition of the "disadvantaged" as the designated category. One of the dominant arguments, based on the ILO Convention of Indigenous Rights 169, was that indigenous Fijians, because of their relative lack of entrepreneurial participation, educational and professional achievement, and socio-economic development, and by virtue of their being indigene, should be the main designated category (Fiji Constitution 1990; FIG 1992; Qarase 1995). Herein was a veiled warning that failure to address the Fijian question would continue to create conditions for ethno-political volatility and conflict (Fisk 1995; Fiji Government 2001).

So affirmative action was seen as serving multi-dimensional interests: as a means of redressing inequality, as an unquestioned natural right of indigenous Fijians and as a conflict resolution mechanism. Contrary to this position was the argument that the disadvantaged category should be de-ethnicized and inclusive so as to include anyone from any ethnic group considered to be socio-economically disadvantaged, a principle that was seen to reflect the spirit of multiculturalism, inclusivity and social justice enshrined in the 1997 Constitution (Fiji Constitution-Section 44, 1997: 32–3).

The third argument was that affirmative action should be specifically targeted at addressing poverty because this is trans-ethnic and worsening as a result of a number of factors including the contraction of the local economy, lack of opportunities and the global economic crises (ECREA 2005; Chand 2007).

The fourth argument, now advocated by the current ruling military regime, is that affirmative action is a tool for rent-seeking and corruption by indigenous Fijian as well as non-indigenous Fijian elites (Ratuva 2010). The military regime abolished virtually all affirmative action programmes associated with the previous governments and established the Fiji Islands Commission Against Corruption (FICAC) to investigate cases of corruption associated with the policy. The focus has now turned to poverty reduction and rural development carried out within the ambit of the People's Charter, a social engineering framework for socio-economic and socio-political transformation (Fiji Government, 2008).

The question of inequality is shrouded in complexity and controversy because of the contending discourses as to what it means in what context. Competing groups would use different variables to define their social location within the political, economic or socio-cultural hierarchy to justify their subordinate and exploited position. Indo-Fijians tend to focus on their political subordination and lack of access to land to indicate how they are being disadvantaged (Lal 2010), while indigenous Fijians point to control of the business sector by Indo-Fijians as a manifestation of their economic subordination (Qarase 1995). There have also been attempts to focus on vertical inequality, to shift debates away from horizontal inequalities, through a study of poverty across ethnic boundaries (Chand 2007).

Genesis of pro-indigenous programmes

Horizontal inequality between indigenous Fijians and other ethnic groups had its origin in the colonial development process. The indigenous were ruled through a highly controlled and paternalistic system of development which kept them locked in communal and semi-subsistence existence for decades. Europeans controlled the civil service and commerce, while life for Indo-Fijians revolved around the rigours of cane plantation life. Only Europeans had the right to vote, and voting rights were only extended to indigenous Fijians as late as the mid-1960s. Lawson (1991) argues that the constant urge by indigenous Fijian elites for extra-legal regime change through coups was a consequence of this relative inexperience in the culture of democracy.

There were two contesting discourses on the question of indigenous Fijian development. The first was the "protectionist" and social Darwinian evolutionary approach advocated by Sir Arthur Gordon, who became the first Governor of Fiji in 1876 (two years after Fiji became a British colony in 1874) and later by Ratu Sir Lala Sukuna, an indigenous statesman who preferred a communal system which would facilitate the gradual change of the indigenous Fijians from direct paternalistic control to greater autonomy. Implicit in this argument was the ideological frame of "paramountcy of Fijian interest". In its original connotation, this referred to the protection and advancement of indigenous interests as a major priority of the state, premised on the belief that indigenous Fijians, like other colonized "natives", were towards the lower end of the human hierarchy and needed special attention lest they perish in the face of modernity. In the aftermath of the 1987 coup, and associated ethno-nationalistic posturing, the connotation of "paramountcy" changed from protection to hegemony of indigenous interests.

The second development approach, advocated by Governor im Thurn in the early 1900s, and enthusiastically supported by white farmers eager to lay their hands on native land, was liberalization and reform of the land tenure and indigenous Fijian social systems to ensure greater commercialization and individualization of land ownership (France 1969). Im Thurn observed that the communal system restricted indigenous Fijian vertical social mobility within the colonial economy. These restrictions contributed to indigenous Fijians' lack of participation in the market economy and progress in education (Lawson 1991). This proved to be decisive in creating the socio-economic gap between indigenous Fijians and other ethnic groups, and helped fuel ethno-nationalist grievances in later years.

To break away from the communal system, im Thurn, at the turn of the century, sought to institute dramatic changes aimed at liberalizing the rigid communal system instituted in 1876 by Gordon, in what may be termed the very first preferential system for indigenous Fijians. In a speech to the Great Council of Chiefs[1] in 1905, im Thurn accused chiefs of unfairly becoming prosperous through impositions of exaction that prevented ordinary Fijians "from gaining anything for themselves – any property to make life interesting to them". He advocated "individuality" as "the habit of thought which we (government) and you (chiefs) should encourage in the Fijians" (Fiji 1905: 2–3).

The social reforms suggested by Im Thurn included teaching English in village schools and the freeing up of communal land for individual ownership and settlement by indigenous Fijians under the Native Land Ordinance No. 14 of 1905. The latter was resisted by chiefs who preferred to continue ruling over a subservient community (Grattan 1963). Meanwhile, European settlers had begun indulging in land speculation rather than just settlement as originally envisaged. Between 1905–1908, about 105,000 acres were sold as freehold land and an additional 170,000 acres were put on long term lease before its cessation in 1911 (Scarr 1984: 112). Land liberalization was later stopped after a fierce campaign in London by Gordon (who later became Lord Stanmore), who saw im Thurn's reforms as a threat to his native policy. Lord Stanmore vigorously defended his policies in Britain's House of Lords, and won (Routledge 1985). It was the end for reform, and the protectionist school declared itself triumphant.

Among the earliest attempts to boost indigenous Fijian participation in the market economy were the establishment of the co-operative movement under the Co-operative Ordinance of 1947; setting up the Fijian Banana Venture in 1950; incorporating the Fijian Development Fund in 1951; the creation of Economic Development Officers' positions in 1954 (following the incorporation of the economic development agenda into the Fijian Administration); and more rigid control of the *galala* (independent farming) system which had been encouraged by im Thurn. These changes were part of attempts to gradually introduce indigenous Fijians into the market economy but within the context of communalism under the supervision of the Fijian administration. These were deliberate pro-indigenous policies which served two seemingly contradictory purposes: first to strengthen communalism and second to introduce indigenous Fijians to capitalism, at least in its peripheral form.

The Co-operative Society was seen as a viable alternative to fully-fledged individualism. The co-operative system was based on the assumption that because of their "communal" orientation, "Fijians were naturally inclined to co-operative effort" (Fiji Co-operative Dept. 1948: 49). A decade after the Cooperative Society was formed, of the total number of co-operatives, 51 were for indigenous Fijians, five for Indo-Fijians, and 22 for other ethnic groups and mixed membership (Fiji Co-operative Dept. 1958). The co-operative movement had mixed success and in a major review in 1959 Spate concluded that "the movement's history of difficulties illustrates perhaps better than anything else the inherent obstacles to economic advance imposed by the traditional system" (Spate 1959: 55).

Other development projects were designed specifically for indigenous Fijians. The Fijian Banana Venture (FBV) was to enhance banana cultivation and marketing amongst indigenous Fijians. The Fijian Development Fund (FDF) was to encourage copra production. The Economic Development Officers (EDOs), who were mostly chiefs, were tasked with bridging the divide between the development policies of the government's Agricultural Department (which encouraged individual farming) and the Fijian Administration (which encouraged communal farming) (Burns 1963; Belshaw 2004). The role of the EDO was part of a bigger design to help indigenous Fijians engage in the cash economy but within the ambit of state, provinial and chiefly control.

These reforms merely crystallized communal hegemony by reinforcing chiefly control, and did little to advance the economic situation of indigenous Fijians at a time when the colonial economy had progressively shown a clear link between ethnicity and socio-economic position. The class structure in the 1940s and 1950s had a distinctive ethnic dimension. The economy was dominated by expatriate and local European capital; below was a growing class of Indo-Fijian and Chinese petit bourgeoisie, and at the bottom was a large mass of impoverished Indo-Fijian cane farmers and indigenous Fijians in the semi-subsistence sector (Narayan 1984; Plange 1996). However, among indigenous Fijians was a class of comprador chiefs who were co-opted into the civil service or who through native regulations wielded substantial power over the indigenous community.

A heavy dependence on expatriate capital to develop the commercial sector characterized the post-war export-oriented economy (Knapman 1987). Europeans dominated agricultural production despite the increase in Indo-Fijian and indigenous Fijian farmers. In the late 1950s, for instance, 557 Europeans were able to produce and export to the value of £2,159 each; 22,000 Indo-Fijians about £337 each; and indigenous Fijians £72 and 10 shillings each. Europeans had much larger and more productive commercial estates, while at the other extreme, indigenous Fijians were mostly subsistence village farmers with occasional semi-commercial farming (Narayan 1984).

By the 1950s little had changed in relation to indigenous Fijian participation in commerce. The Fijian administration still played a hegemonic role and largely controlled the political and economic direction of indigenous Fijian "development", in a way that promoted communalism and undermined independent enterprise. In this, communal ownership of land proved to be a challenge. By 1956, a mere 0.2 per cent of available freehold land, which constituted the most productive commercially useable land, was owned by indigenous Fijians. Within the commercial farming sector ethnic distribution of per capita acreage holdings (land under commercial farming) in 1958 showed that there were 131 acres for each European, seven acres for each Indo-Fijian, 6.4 acres for each Chinese and other Islanders, and only 4.8 acres for each indigenous Fijian. If 36,000 acres of improved pasture land and 600 acres of fodder crops under European ownership were included, the average per capita area in use by the average European was more than 192 acres, or 27.7 per cent of the total farm land in Fiji (Narayan 1984: 67). In sugar production (the largest industry in the colony), in terms of tons harvested, indigenous Fijians made up only 3.25 per cent in 1957 (Colonial Sugar Refinery 1959).

One drawback for indigenous Fijian farmers was the difficulty in getting commercial loans. In the 1950s and 1960s European borrowers who accounted for only 15 per cent of the total number of loans received 53 per cent of the total loan value; Indo-Fijian borrowers accounted for 53 per cent of the total number of loans and received 34 per cent of the total loan value; and indigenous Fijians received 25 per cent of the total number of loans but only 7 per cent of the total value (Sutherland 1998). The figures for the financial year 1960–1961 showed that the average size of an indigenous Fijian loan was half that of Indo-Fijians' loans and a tenth that of Europeans (Fiji Development Bank 1960, 1961). The bank was generally blamed for "favouring" Indo-Fijians. But a major problem was that indigenous Fijian land was communally-owned and could not be used as collateral for loans. Legally, the bank could not make a claim on communally-owned land. Even houses could not be used as collateral since they were built on communal land.

Many indigenous Fijians joined credit unions because of their distrust of banks. The credit union movement was introduced by Father Garney in 1954. At the end of 1957 there were 231 unions with a membership of 24,148, mostly indigenous Fijians. Many of the loans went to communal obligations (Schulze 1982).

The communal cocooning of indigenous Fijians under the native policy contributed to the relatively low achievement of this group in various areas of the economy and professional services. In 1953 the per capita cash income of Europeans and Part-Europeans (F$468) was the highest, followed by Chinese (F$279), who were mostly shopkeepers, and then the Indo-Fijians (F$113), while the indigenous Fijians had the lowest per capita of only F$60. However, differences in per capita income for cash and subsistence between indigenous Fijians (F$121) and Indo-Fijians (F$128) was not very significant due to the substantial involvement of indigenous Fijians in the subsistence economy (Fiji 1956). The figures show a low level of indigenous Fijian participation in the capitalist sector of the economy compared to other ethnic groups.

Despite their shortcomings in the area of commerce, indigenous Fijians seemed, by virtue of their preponderance in small-scale, semi-subsistence agriculture, to perform well in crop cultivation for local consumption. For instance, they cultivated about 45 per cent of the 80,000 acres of crops for local consumption. But they only produced about 32 per cent of export crop acreage (Wright and Twyford 1959). Indigenous Fijians dominated banana cultivation, but a relatively low number were involved in rice and sugar farming.

In 1967, three years before independence, the proportion of indigenous Fijians receiving a cash income above F$5,000 a year was only 4 per cent, compared to 16 per cent Indo-Fijians, 38 per cent Europeans and 24 per cent of Chinese. In other words, indigenous Fijians were the least represented in the higher socio-economic strata. Indigenous Fijians predominated in the low income bracket (F$0–1,000), and were represented in almost equal proportion with Indo-Fijians within the F$1,001–2,000 range.

Around the same period (1966), the ratio of lawyer, doctor and dentist occupational categories between indigenous Fijians and Indo-Fijians were: 0:38, 1:12 and 1:8, respectively (Fiji 1966).

By the late 1950s and 1960s the promotion of the forestry and tourism industries provided some hope for the future development of indigenous Fijians. These industries became important to indigenous Fijians because of the use of native forests, labour for logging, as well as the employment of native land in the area of tourism development. However, the investors were foreign companies, sometimes with local shareholders. The Forestry Department was largely Fijian staffed. This created some difficulties with local chiefs, who saw it as their right to direct department officials as to which forests to log. The 1956 Census showed that about 600 out of the 1,000 workers in lumbering and saw-milling were indigenous Fijians. Indigenous Fijians accounted for two-thirds of the supervisory and clerical workers, and all 192 skilled workers. But over half the managerial positions were held by Indo-Fijians and Europeans (1956 Census Report).

Tourism went through a period of unprecedented boom after the 1962 legislation to allow duty free trading, while the 1964 Hotel Aids Ordinance was designed to encourage tourism investment. The growth of the service industries associated with tourism (travel services, taxis, duty free outlets, etc.) largely benefited European entrepreneurs, the Indo-Fijian petit bourgeoisie and indigenous Fijian chiefs whose land was leased to hotel companies. The lowest paid jobs were reserved for ordinary indigenous Fijians recruited from villages around hotel resorts. They were (and still are) largely used as marketing exhibits for the "smiling" and "friendly" Fijian image on which Fiji's tourism has thrived (Ratuva 2010).

The continuing disparities and lack of indigenous Fijian progress was the subject of two major investigations. In his report *The Fijian People: Economic Problems and Prospects*, Spate argued that the lack of progress of indigenous Fijians in commerce could be attributed to the rigid communal system under the native policy (Spate 1959). A year later the Burns Report concurred with Spate's findings and emphasized that communal ownership of land undermined indigenous Fijian economic progress (Burns 1963).

Post-independence preferential development

From independence in 1970, economic policy was geared toward growth through import substitution. Among the indigenous Fijian community, the rhetoric of *veivakatorocaketaki ni i Taukei* (Fijian development) was gaining currency within rural communities, Fijian institutions and indigenous elites. This was encapsulated in the Sixth Development Plan (DP6) for 1970–1975, which aimed to "improve distribution of incomes, including bridging of rural/urban and inter-ethnic disparities" (quoted in DP8: 4). The DP6 emphasized "rural development", specifically the promotion of industries where indigenous Fijians were mostly concentrated. The idea of rural and indigenous development was based on the assumption that progress entailed transformation from a subsistence to a market economy. This did not strictly apply to Indo-Fijians because although most were rural-based as sugar cane farmers producing for the sugar industry, they were already mainstreamed into the market economy. Rural development projects included pine planting, the Seaqaqa sugar cane project for indigenous Fijians and cattle projects in Uluisauvou and Yalalevu, both on the main island of Viti Levu. These rural development projects were continued in the Seventh Development Plan (1976–1980) which emphasized expansion and redistribution. The affirmative action intent of DP7 is summed up in one of its objectives, thus:

> The main beneficiaries of policies aimed at achieving more equitable distribution of income and wealth will be the rural population generally and the *Fijian population in particular* (my emphasis). Powerful economic forces have tended to concentrate economic activity and hence prosperity in the urban centers – especially Suva and Lautoka. This concentration has tended to perpetuate existing business and commercial specialization along ethnic lines. A major objective in the Seventh Plan period and beyond will be to

decentralize economic activity by location and broaden involvement by race and to enhance opportunities, material living standards and the social and cultural amenities of the rural areas.

(DP7: 5)

The strategy to reconfigure the structural association between ethnicity and socio-economic status or class was directly borrowed from Malaysia's affirmative action-based New Economic Policy (NEP). But unlike the Malaysian NEP, which was a massive social engineering undertaking involving politically imposed structural reconfiguration (Gomez 2009), the Fiji experiment was a much smaller and softer version which operated more at the policy level. The Eighth Development Plan, 1981–1985 (DP8), toned down the Fijian development strategy and focused more on diversification, generalized equity, self-help and promotion of national unity. This was an interesting shift because while the principles of equity and national unity were promoted, the ethnic factor was not made explicit, although it was implicitly assumed in the objectives.

Diversification was to take the risk burden away from the Indo-Fijian dominated sugar monoculture which, during the five years from 1975–1980, increased production by over 55 per cent. Between 1970–1980 the contribution of sugar and its by-products to domestic exports rose from 66 per cent to 81 per cent, the share of contribution to Gross Domestic Product (GDP) from 12 per cent to 16 per cent, and the share of employment from less than 18 per cent to over 22 per cent (DP8 1980).[2] The productive capacity by ethnicity in the sugar industry varied considerably. For instance, in 1989, Indo-Fijians produced F$161.91 million (95 per cent) worth of sugar while indigenous Fijians produced only F$25 million (0.5 per cent). In 1993 the production figures were F$156.99 million (86 per cent) for Indo-Fijians and F$22 million (0.5 per cent) for indigenous Fijians (Fiji Sugar Corporation 1994).

The emphasis on primary industries was due to the perception that indigenous Fijians were more at home on the land. There was also the view that given the preponderance of Indo-Fijians in the sugar cane farming sector, indigenous Fijians could learn agricultural skills and do equally well either in cane or other areas of farming. However, the Ninth Development Plan, 1986–1990 (DP9), totally de-ethnicized the development framework with the main focus on "real economic growth" (DP9: 8). This was during a global recession and when structural adjustment policies (SAP) were being introduced in Fiji. On the World Bank's recommendation, public service salaries were frozen and the market liberalized. This provoked the wrath of trade unions that had formed the Fiji Labour Party in 1984 as a vehicle to fight for their rights after the Tripartite Forum – a consultative body consisting of unions, employers and the state – was unilaterally disbanded by government.

In the mid 1980s the disparity between indigenous Fijians and other ethnic groups increasingly became contentious as political parties focused on ethnic aspects of economic development. The Fiji Bureau of Statistics' 1986 Census on "economic activity" showed the relatively disadvantaged position of indigenous

Fijians in the "white collar" employment category (Fiji Bureau of Statistics 1986). In the administrative and managerial category, 23 per cent were indigenous Fijians compared to 77 per cent Indo-Fijians. For clerical and related workers, 38 per cent were indigenous Fijians and 62 per cent Indo-Fijians, while in the sales workers category, 26 per cent were indigenous Fijians and 74 per cent Indo-Fijians (calculated from Fiji Bureau of Statistics 1989: 52).

At the other end of the socio-economic continuum, about half (55 per cent) of those engaged in rural agriculture (both subsistence and cash), such as animal husbandry, forestry and fishing, were indigenous Fijians compared to 35 per cent Indo-Fijians. The figures indicated a preponderance of Indo-Fijians in the middle class socio-economic categories, and indigenous Fijians in rural primary production. Most rural indigenous Fijian producers were village-based semi-subsistence farmers, living within the communal setting. Only 10 per cent of the independent rural settlements, for fully-fledged commercial farming outside the rural village, belonged to indigenous Fijians. To compound the problem, indigenous Fijians had a higher urban unemployment rate of 15.6 per cent (compared to 9.7 per cent for Indo-Fijians) and over 70 per cent of the prison population were indigenous Fijians even though they made up only 46 per cent of the population (Adinkrah 1995).

The 1987 coups and coerced affirmative action

Fiji experienced its first coup in May 1987, led by Lt. Col. Sitiveni Rabuka. The Indo-Fijian dominated Labour Party–National Federation Party coalition was overthrown a month after it come to power in this nationalist coup by the indigenous Fijian-dominated military. The second coup occurred on 25 September 1987 after the military refused to accept a multi-party arrangement as a solution to the political crisis under the Deuba Accord. This Accord threatened to undermine the nationalist agenda of the coup leaders for indigenous political paramountcy. The coups were coercive expressions of ethno-nationalist grievances wrought by the dynamic interplay between horizontal socio-economic inequalities and political-cultural demarcation which characterized the colonial and post-colonial milieu.

With the capture of state power and with national resources within their grip, indigenous Fijian elites were eager to fast-track the community's commercial ownership, to catch up with other ethnic groups. The thrust of affirmative action included: control of the state by indigenous Fijians and use of the bureaucracy and political machinery to drive affirmative action programmes; the harnessing and channelling of state resources towards indigenous Fijians; increasing the number of indigenous Fijians in business and civil service; and creating and expanding an indigenous Fijian middle class to balance the established Indo-Fijian middle class (FIG 1992; Qarase 1995).

Unlike the earlier period, affirmative action was now no longer just a policy prescription but a framework for major restructuring and social engineering on an unprecedented scale to ensure at least 50 per cent control of commercial activities by indigenous Fijians. To facilitate this the new 1990 Constitution guaranteed indigenous Fijian hegemony. To ensure a "pure" indigenous Fijian identity, and to control claims to land as well as membership of the affirmative action designated category, the Constitution crafted a definition of a "Fijian". The two contentious variables used were: a direct grand-patrilineal blood link and acceptance by one's *mataqali* (traditional socio-cultural group) for registration in the *Vola ni Kawabula*, the indigenous Fijian genealogical registry (Fiji Constitution 1990: 120). Criticism of this provision was most pronounced within the indigenous community itself as it was seen to be sexist and racist since it discriminated against those with indigenous Fijian mothers but with non-indigenous fathers.

This legal ethnic definition was closely tied to the Constitution's affirmative action thrust (Fiji Constitution 1990, Section 21), which provided that

> [P]arliament shall, with the object of promoting and safeguarding the economic, social, educational, cultural, traditional and other interests of the Fijian and Rotuman people, enact laws for those objects and shall direct the Government to adopt any programme or activity for the attainment of the said objects and the government shall duly comply with such directions.

The indigenous "Fijian" had an elevated privileged position that opened the door for political special status and priority access to economic benefits.

Fijianization of the civil service

The 1990 Constitution provided the framework for the formulation of a number of affirmative action legislations such as the controversial Public Service Commission Regulation that reserved a minimum of 50 per cent of civil service positions for indigenous Fijians.[3] Affirmative action in the civil service had dramatic results. Just a year before the coup in 1986, 52 per cent of civil service staff were Indo-Fijians, 43 per cent indigenous Fijians and 5 per cent from other minorities. As Table 4.1 shows, a year later there was a significant turnover rate

Table 4.1 Civil service staff turnover, 1987–1994

Year	Fijian/Rotuman	% (of total)	Indian/others	% (of total)	Total
1987	258	20.5	1003	79.5	1,261
1988	486	31.8	1041	68.2	1,527
1989	676	40.0	959	60.0	1,635
1990	532	48.8	560	51.2	1,092
1991	393	40.9	567	59.1	960
1992	740	52.6	666	47.4	1,406
1993	697	54.9	573	45.1	1,270
1994	701	58.6	497	41.4	1,198

Source: Fiji PSC, 1995:16.

amongst Indo-Fijians: 79.5 per cent of those who left the service were Indo-Fijians and other minorities, compared to 20.5 per cent indigenous Fijians; in 1988 it was 68.2 per cent and 31.8 per cent respectively (Fiji Public Service Commission 1995). However, between 1992–1994 the situation started to stabilize as there were attempts to slow down the loss of Indo-Fijians in the civil service. In the 1992 election, in an ironic political twist of events, the Soqosoqo ni Vakavulewa ni Taukei (SVT), led by the coup leader Rabuka, came to power with the support of Mahendra Chaudhry, one of the Indo-Fijians deposed during the 1987 coup.

By 1991, 55.8 per cent of the civil service staff were indigenous Fijians (compared to 43 per cent before the coup) and 44.2 per cent were Indo-Fijians and other minorities (compared to 52 per cent before the coup). This pattern continued from 1991–1994. In 1995, the proportion for indigenous Fijians had increased to 57.32 per cent, Indo-Fijians had decreased to 38.57 per cent and minorities and expatriates decreased to 4.11 per cent (Reeves *et al.* 1996). The 50 per cent minimum target for indigenous Fijians in the civil service was achieved (Fiji Public Service Commission 1995).

By 1997 only one of the ten heads of government departments was Indo-Fijian, compared to the relatively equal numbers prior to the coup. Most of those who left the civil service (about 80 per cent) migrated overseas. The net departure in 1987 was 18,563, a threefold increase compared to the 6,490 who left in 1986 and the 6,193 who left in 1985 (Chetty and Prasad 1993: 10). Of these, 78.1 per cent were Indo-Fijians (compared to 41.2 per cent in 1980), 6 per cent indigenous Fijians and 12.5 per cent other minorities. However, by 1989 the total number of Indo-Fijians migrating had declined to almost half the 1987 figure (about 7,412). But the proportion still stood at 79 per cent of total Fijian migration. Some 50,104 people migrated between 1987–1991, compared to 26,529 between 1982–1986. About 80 per cent of these were Indo-Fijians (Chetty and Prasad 1993).

The control of the police force was important for political reasons, so major changes were initiated immediately after the 1987 coup. The Indo-Fijian Commissioner of Police was removed. A more junior indigenous Fijian was appointed Commissioner and later a senior military officer was appointed. A year before the coup, in 1986, the ethnic distribution of the police force was 50 per cent indigenous Fijian, 47 per cent Indo-Fijian and 3 per cent other minorities. Almost a decade later, in 1995, the figures for indigenous Fijians had shot up to 58 per cent and Indo-Fijians had reduced to 40 per cent, with 2 per cent from other minorities (Fiji Police Force 1996). The police, like other areas of the civil service, became militarized as colonels took over senior positions and strengthened their links with the military command structure. The military did not need any affirmative action because it was always an indigenous Fijian-dominated institution with a proportion of more than 90 per cent. The changes in the civil service involved the twin processes of indigenization and militarization and this had a long term impact on the structure and capacity of the public service system.

Creating an indigenous business class

Some of the first proposals for increased indigenous Fijian participation in commerce were contained in the *Nine Points Plan*, conceived in 1992 by the Fijian Initiative Group (FIG), comprising indigenous Fijian professionals, civil servants and entrepreneurs under the chairmanship of former Prime Minister, Ratu Sir Kamisese Mara. The major proposals included: F$20 million equity to be injected from the Fijian Affairs Board (FAB) to the Fijian Holdings Company (FHC), an indigenous trust company based on the Malaysian bumiputera trust company concept; a unit trust for indigenous Fijian financial investment was to be established; a Compulsory Savings Scheme (CSS) for Fijians to be set up; government concession for indigenous Fijian business to be enhanced; a Management Advisory Services Department (MASD) to be established in the Fijian Affairs Board (FAB); and indigenous Fijians to have 50 per cent minimum ownership of resource-based industries. Certain sectors of the economy were to be reserved exclusively for indigenous Fijian investment; there should be ownership of a daily newspaper by indigenous Fijians; and the Fijian Affairs Board should be restructured and strengthened to consolidate indigenous Fijian identity and unity (Fijian Initiative Group 1992).

Three years later another document, *Ten Year Plan for Fijian Participation in Business (Ten Year Plan)*, authored by Laisenia Qarase[4] with Savenaca Siwatibau, the head of the United Nations Economic and Social Commission for Asia and the Pacific (ESCAP). The report recommended that the focus of affirmative action "should be the achievement of overall parity between Fijians and other communities in all spheres of activities within the shortest period of time possible" and should "ensure that indigenous Fijians achieve 50 per cent ownership of the corporate sector and other business sectors by the year 2005" (Qarase 1995: 4).

To achieve this, a number of strategies were proposed and these included appropriate legislation to promote and safeguard indigenous Fijian interests, the reorganization and strengthening of the Fijian administration, establishing a savings scheme and promoting indigenous Fijian interest in investment, entrepreneurship, business education and training. These were meant to complement the *Nine Points Plan* with the aim of achieving the target of 50 per cent indigenous Fijian business ownership by 2005. This aim was not realized because of the dramatic changes in the political arena which undermined the stability and consistency of future planning.

The *Ten Year Plan* recommended the privatization of a number of government entities to indigenous individuals. Some of these were monopolies such as Fiji Post and Telecom, Fiji International Telecommunications Limited, Fiji Forest Industries Limited, Fiji Pine Limited, Tropic Woods Limited, the Pacific Fisheries Company and the National Bank of Fiji.

The post-coup government quickly implemented a number of the *Ten Year Plan* recommendations. These included the reorganization of the Fijian administration to separate the Fijian Affairs Board from the Ministry of Fijian Affairs, expansion of Fijian Holdings Limited, continuation of the Commercial Loans to Fijians Scheme by the Fiji Development Bank, the setting up of the unit trust investment, establishment of a Small Equity Fund within the Ministry of Fijian Affairs and a management training scheme for indigenous Fijians in the private sector. The separation between the Fijian Affairs Board and the Ministry of Fijian Affairs was meant to make indigenous communities more autonomous.

These reforms were driven by the small size of the indigenous Fijian entrepreneurial class and the preponderance of Indo-Fijians in the area of commerce. In 1987, indigenous Fijian companies registered by the Registrar of Companies Office only constituted 15 per cent of the total of 700 companies, while 50 per cent were owned by Indo-Fijians, 20 per cent by Europeans and Chinese, and 15 per cent joint ventures by other ethnic groups (Registrar of Companies 1987).

The relationship between ethnicity and economic activity showed an interesting pattern with indigenous Fijians being concentrated in primary agricultural activities and Indo-Fijians in the white collar professions. As shown in Table 4.2, in 1986 about 60 per cent of those working in agriculture, animal husbandry, forestry and fishing were indigenous Fijians, and 40 per cent were Indo-Fijians and other minorities. In contrast, Indo-Fijians and other ethnic groups dominated various white collar occupation categories including: professional, technical and related workers (55 per cent); administrative and managerial (74 per cent); clerical and related workers (62 per cent); and sales (74 per cent) categories (Fiji Bureau of Statistics 1986).

To address these inequalities the government aggressively put in place a range of preferential programmes in a piecemeal manner using state political and financial institutions as guarantors and facilitators. These included a F$20 million soft loan to the Fijian Affairs Board in 1992 for the purchase of B-Class shares from Fijian Holdings Limited (FHL) which would hold the equity in trust

Table 4.2 Occupational categories of the economically active population by ethnicity (Indians and Fijians only), 1986

Occupational category	Fijians (percentage)	Indians (percentage)	Total
Professional, technical and related workers	45	54	15,574
Administrative and managerial	23	76	2,090
Clerical and related workers	38	62	13,726
Sales workers	26	74	13,832
Service workers	60	40	14,479
Agriculture, animal husbandry, forestry workers and fishermen	60	40	102,614
Production, related workers, transport equipment operators and labourers	56	44	28,268
Workers not classified by occupation and unemployed	70	30	13,407
Total	56	44	203,991

Source: calculated from Fiji Bureau of Statistics, 1989: 52.

for indigenous Fijians. The FHL, which was set up by the Great Council of Chiefs in 1982, was modelled on the National Equity Corporation of Malaysia, a company which held equity on behalf of the Bumiputera.

In addition, a number of concessions were provided for indigenous Fijian loans in 1989 under the Commercial Loans to Fijians Scheme (CLFS), which was set up in 1975 to assist indigenous Fijians in small to medium sized businesses by the Fiji Development Bank. CLFS loans increased sharply after the 1987 coup. Between 1975–1988 there were only 4,720 loans totalling about F$25 million. But from 1989–1994, the number of loans shot up to 6,189, totalling F$99 million (Fiji Development Bank 1996). Due to poor governance of the scheme it had to close down as arrears of between 19 per cent and 23 per cent began to accumulate.

Another target for affirmative action was the taxi business, which had been virtually monopolized by Indo-Fijians who had 87 per cent control of the business compared to only 11 per cent for indigenous Fijians. A ministerial directive on 22 October 1993 ensured that no new permits were to be issued to Indo-Fijians and as a result, by 31 December 1994, the Indo-Fijian licences had decreased to 61 per cent and the indigenous Fijian share had increased to 34 per cent (LTA 1995). Some indigenous Fijian taxi licence holders used the opportunity to sell or lease their licence to Indo-Fijians who could not get them. Some went on to run very successful taxi co-operatives.

One of the main indigenous Fijian commercial acquisitions was Fiji Television Limited (FTL). The government granted a 12-year exclusive television broadcast licence to FTL on the understanding that indigenous Fijian control of the firm would increase. In 1995 the main shareholders in FTL were the Fiji Development Bank, 51 per cent; Television New Zealand (TVNZ), 15 per cent; Fiji Post and Telecom (FPTL), 14 per cent; and the general public 20 per cent. The 51 per cent FDB shares were held in trust on behalf of indigenous Fijians, represented by the 14 Provincial Councils (Qarase 1995). The Provincial Councils owned Yasana Holdings Limited (YHL), a company established by the Fijian Affairs Board to look after provincial investment. This was one of the many affirmative action projects which were based on communal ownership.

The Fiji National Provident Fund (FNPF) was also involved in a project called the Village Housing Scheme (VHS) set up in 1987 to provide homes for rural villages. A total of 27,373 applications amounting to F$53.91 million were approved and paid out. This also had to stop due to unsustainable loans. In addition, the FNPF set up the Small Business Equity Scheme in 1990 to provide finance for small businesses, especially those run by indigenous Fijians. Since it started a total of 4,621 members were assisted, representing F$17.22 million in payments. In 1996 a total of 1,379 applications, amounting to F$3.5 million, were approved. Of these, indigenous Fijians constituted about 90 per cent: 1,200 applications totalling F$2.76 million in payments (FNPF 2006).

As a way of mobilizing resources and maintaining ethno-cultural solidarity, indigenous Fijians were encouraged to engage in communal investment through their extended kinship or administrative social groups such as *tokatoka* (group of nuclear families), *mataqali* (group of *tokatoka*), *tikina* (district), *yasana* (province) or other forms of collective groupings. These groups then bought shares in Fijian Holdings, the Unit Trust and other investment groups (Ratuva 2000). Even political parties and politicians formed investment groups on behalf of indigenous Fijian entrepreneurs. An example was the Gaunavou Investments Company Limited (GICL).[5] The GICL, which was incorporated as a public company on 11 November 1994, was set up by the Suva City Fijian Urban Constituency branch of the ruling Soqoqsoqo ni Vakvulewa ni Taukei Party (SVT) "with the positive intention to start and promote indigenous Fijian enterprise and business activities" (*Daily Post*, 13 March 1999: 3). Amongst the shareholders were Sitiveni Rabuka (the 1987 coup leader and later Prime Minister) and a number of government cabinet ministers.

Affirmative action in education

Education was probably the most successful area of affirmative action. In 1969, a year before independence, the Royal Commission on Education recommended "positive discrimination provisions" for indigenous Fijians. The government provided subsidized fees for indigenous students at the secondary level, and later in 1997 proposed a controversial scholarship quota of 50 per cent for indigenous Fijians and 50 per cent for other ethnic groups for entry into the University of the South Pacific, the Pacific's regional university based in Fiji.

Over the years a number of initiatives for indigenous Fijian education were put in place. This included the setting up of the Fijian education unit within the Ministry of Fijian Affairs, and provision for indigenous scholarships under the Fijian Affairs Board. There was a concerted effort to upgrade facilities for indigenous Fijian schools and training of teachers. These were aimed at the "development of basic education, particularly improvement of access to secondary education for rural students" (Fiji Ministry of Education 1993: 130).

Preferential provision of tertiary scholarships for indigenous Fijian students was pursued in earnest. The proportion of government scholarships awarded by the Public Service Commission (PSC) for university education to indigenous Fijians from 1970–1992 increased over the years thus: 1970–1974 (34 per cent); 1975–1979 (39 per cent); 1980–1984 (44 per cent); 1985–1989 (49 per cent); and 1990–1992 (52 per cent). However, only about a third of the indigenous Fijians were qualified to enter university. When affirmative action accelerated after the 1987 coup, an average of 62 per cent of all in-service training scholarships were allocated to indigenous Fijians (PSC 1995), although they made up just a little over 51 per cent of the population. Between 1984–1988 the FAB awarded 1,181 local scholarships and 150 overseas scholarships. This was increased to 1,719 and 108 respectively from 1989–1992. Within the 16 years up to 2001, the FAB provided more than 7,000 scholarships and about half of these graduated within the prescribed time (People's Coalition Government 2001). More than 90 per cent of these graduates entered the labour market and contributed to the expanding indigenous middle class.

Affirmative action dilemmas

While some affirmative action programmes, such as education, were successful, the rush to create an indigenous business class by forcing through an entrepreneurial culture within a short time had its tragic shortcomings. In 1992, when Fijian Holdings was reclassified as a limited liability company, a group of indigenous Fijian professionals and bureaucrats who worked in state banks and senior government positions were able to form companies using insider information to buy shares, even before the rest of the country knew what was happening (Korovulavula 1993). This led to a huge scandal which was covered widely in the local press and even debated in Parliament. The group had direct links to the military and state leadership, and had significant influence on important boards dealing with state finance and investment. They had direct access to influencing state policies and the operation of state institutions, and had a virtual monopoly of information and control of equity acquisition in Fijian Holdings. Some of the illegal and unethical business practices were condoned because they were seen to be politically acceptable in the general sentiment of speeding up indigenous Fijian entry into the business world. A number of these cases continue to be the subject of investigation by the Fiji Independent Commission Against Corruption, which was set up by the Fiji military after the 2006 coup.

There was an even worse scenario when the state-owned National Bank of Fiji (NBF) collapsed as a result of extravagant loans to indigenous Fijians to fund their entrepreneurial projects, middle class lifestyle (housing, cars, credit cards, etc.) and other things. After the 1987 coup, its leader, Rabuka, personally went to the bank and told the Australian bank general manager that he was to be replaced by a local. To the military regime, the NBF held the key to financing affirmative action projects and had to be secured by all means. Millions of dollars were given out without security in a "cargo cult" type loan programme which spanned the entire structure of the indigenous community, from the President and his family (who loaned more than F$5 million) to unemployed youths. Gold credit cards, car loans, business loans, housing loans and even personal loans were liberally given out in the name of indigenous advancement. Within a few years the bank became insolvent, debts were written off and more than F$200 million was lost. A subsequent investigation unearthed a complex web of deals between politicians and businessmen involving money transfers and political patronage (Grynberg *et al.* 2002).

One of the ironies was that although the NBF collapsed, the loans provided the means for a large number of indigenous Fijians to break into the middle class, at least in terms of lifestyle and self-perception, and expanded the indigenous middle class in a significant way. Another effect of the affirmative action policy was that it created an illegal trade in the leasing and selling of licences. Many indigenous Fijians who were issued taxi licences sold them to Indo-Fijians, and many of those who were issued with fishing licences sold them to Chinese businessmen. This practice was later discouraged after it was identified.

The "trickle down" strategy of the state was to get rural communities to invest in Fijian Holdings Limited (FHL) through communal investment. The initial fund for this was provided by the government through the Fijian Affairs Board and this was distributed to provinces, districts and villages. The problem was that the interest generated from this investment system was minimal and this had to be shared among members of these communities. After a year of investment, the average return was about F$1 per person (Ratuva 2000). The communal investment programme was more a political strategy for indigenous mobilization than indigenous economic advancement. Although the FHL concept was borrowed from Malaysia, where the investment in Bumiputera investment trust institutions was individually based, in Fiji it was communally based.

Apart from the FHL and education, almost all post-1987 coup affirmative action policies initiated by the government, failed. This included the Fiji Development Bank projects on special housing and business loans for indigenous Fijians, as well as the Equity Investment Management Company Limited's (EIMCOL) supermarket management trainee project and the Fiji National Provident Fund indigenous loans. The FHL now stands as the flagship of indigenous business and from humble beginnings it expanded to become a major player in the Fijian corporate sector. By 2008 FHL had nine subsidiaries including Basic Industries Limited, Fiji Industries Limited, Blue Lagoon Cruises Limited, Clariti (South Pacific) Limited, FHL Securities Limited, Fijian Property Trust Company Limited, Fijian Holdings Trust Management Limited, Merchant Finance and Investment Company Limited and FHL Retailing Limited. It also had 12 associated companies and a total of 842 shareholders. FHL has a total investment portfolio of F$142 million with annual group revenues of F$213 million and group net assets worth F$166.8 million (Fijian Holdings 2008).

Part of the affirmative action initiative was an attempt to incorporate Malaysian firms that had emerged through the implementation of this policy, in the Fijian economy. This started well in the 1980s and 1990s, with Malaysian acquisitions including South Pacific Textile (Fiji) Ltd, employing 250 people; the SIA Cash and Carry, a joint venture with local employees operating a retail outlet for imported garment and fashion accessories and the Malayan Banking/National Bank of Fiji partnership; and massive equity in the Carpenters Corporation, one of the largest wholesale and retail outlet in Fiji. In tourism, Malaysia's Berjaya Corporation owned the Berjaya Inn in Suva; Sateras Resources Limited owned the Tokatoka Resort near Nadi International Airport and the Suva Motor Inn in Suva; and the Malaysian Shangri-La owned the Mocambo Hotel and the Fijian Hotel, Fiji's largest five-star tourist resort (Ratuva 2010). In encouraging Malaysian investment in Fiji, Ahmed Ali, Fiji's High Commissioner to Malaysia in the early 1990s, said:

> businessmen in both Malaysia and Fiji can tap the huge opportunities available in each other's countries.... We want to welcome Malaysians to Fiji to do business and even share their knowledge and experience with us both in the public and private sectors. We also want to give something in return, not merely take.
> (*Business Times* 1994: 10)

Part of the training programme through the bilateral agreement was the sponsoring of the Chief Executive of the Fijian Holdings Company to study affirmative action in Malaysia, in particular how the Bumiputera trust agency, NEC, worked, and how these lessons could be learned by Fijian Holdings. The Malaysian "helping hand" came to an abrupt end after the 1997 Asian financial crisis which crippled Malaysia's economy and threw its own affirmative action programme into uncertainty. As a result most of the Malaysian companies folded and left Fiji.

The failure of many post-1987 affirmative action projects was due to a number of reasons. First, there was a mismatch between political will and entrepreneurial conceptualization. The political drive to implement affirmative action policies was not guided by a systematic understanding of the socio-cultural context of the business environment. No prior study of the situation was carried out. Second, the indigenous Fijian loan recipients were not provided with the right training in commercial and investment techniques and had to rely solely on their own initiative. Third, the Indo-Fijian business community strengthened their networks to keep indigenous business out; they saw such businesses as potential competitors and kept a tight control over the market though pricing. As a result some of the indigenous initiatives, such as the supermarket experiment, failed.

The failure of these projects was a big blow to the ambition and self-esteem of the indigenous elites behind the affirmative action projects. They had high expectations, driven by state rhetoric, that the economic renaissance of indigenous Fijians was at hand. The failure of many affirmative action policies contributed to a demise in support for the Rabuka's Soqosoqo ni Vakatulewa ni Taukei (SVT) party and a fragmentation in the political allegiances of indigenous Fijians.

The dramatic political changes led to the review of the 1990 Constitution, and eventually led to a new and more inclusive Constitution coming into being in 1997, ten years after the first coup. The new Constitution redefined the affirmative framework under the rubric of "social justice" and expanded the designated category to include not only indigenous Fijians and Rotumans, but also other disadvantaged groups. A new Ministry of Multi-ethnic Affairs was established, which provided scholarships for Indo-Fijian and other minorities, based on their socio-economic situation.

Did middle class social engineering work?

The question of whether affirmative action has helped build and consolidate a middle class is not an easy one to answer, given the complexity of the situation. But some comparative assessment can be made in terms of the 1986 (pre-1987 coup) and 1996 (post-1987 coup) national census figures. There was an identifiable increase in the number of indigenous Fijians in the managerial category, from 487 in 1986 to 1,292 in 1996. The real significance of this was much less than it appeared (Fiji Bureau of Statistics 1986; 1996). This threefold increase in number was due to two main reasons: first, the definition of a managerial category incorporated various other sub-categories which were not included in the 1986 Census; second, since there was an increase in the number of loans to indigenous Fijians by the CLFS from 1992–1996, there was a proliferation of companies formed to formalize business ventures, although a lot of these failed. This would have inflated the number of indigenous Fijian companies.

Nevertheless, the pattern of ethnic disparity in 1996 was almost the same as that of ten years earlier. Indo-Fijians still dominated managerial positions with 76 per cent in 1986, slightly increasing to 78 per cent in 1996 (Fiji Bureau of Statistics 1989; 1998). Despite affirmative action, the gap in the managerial category had increased slightly. The 1996 Census further disaggregated the managerial category into four sub-categories: director/chief executive; small business manager; specialist managers; and other department managers. In all sub-categories Indo-Fijians and other ethnic groups dominated with between 60 and 82 per cent of the total. The largest difference was for chief executive positions; 82 per cent were held by Indo-Fijians and other ethnic groups, and 18 per cent by indigenous Fijians.

The only area where there was a marked increase for indigenous Fijians was in the professional and technical category. There was an increase from 45 per cent in 1986 to 53 per cent in 1996 (Fiji Bureau of Statistics 1998). This relative increase was due mainly to two reasons: first, the large-scale migration of Indo-Fijian professionals after the 1987 coup; and second, the post-coup affirmative action in employment and education which led to the marginalization of Indo-Fijians in the public service. Most indigenous professionals and technical experts were in the public sector.

Very little progress had been made in terms of significant indigenous Fijian penetration into the corporate sector, despite the concerted affirmative action drive. Other available figures tend to confirm this. Prior to the 1987 coup, only 15 per cent of the companies registered by the Registrar of Companies belonged to indigenous Fijians, compared to 50 per cent for Indo-Fijians, 20 per cent by others and 15 per cent joint ventures including all other ethnic groups. In 1997, of the 101 local companies registered under the Tax Free Zones (TFZ) up to 1997, fewer than 10 per cent were indigenous Fijian-owned. Of the 71 local companies in operation within the same period, in the TFZ, only seven were indigenous Fijian-owned (FTIB 1997).

However, the post-coup economy, after 1990, went through a period of contraction, and was not favourable for investment. Although the growth rate between 1989–1990 was a high 8 per cent, a period of low growth followed. From 1991–1995, real per capita output growth averaged only 1 per cent per year. Despite this, the unfavourable investment climate affected everyone, including Indo-Fijian and indigenous Fijians. Thus it cannot be taken as the explanation for the continuing ethnic disparity in socio-economic performance. While there was an expansion of the indigenous Fijian middle class in public service and in the professions, the corporate sector was still virgin territory.

The 2000 coup and affirmative action

The ethno-nationalist coup in 2000 was seen as evidence by some indigenous elites of a need for a more concerted effort to speed up indigenous Fijian development. The interim government, led by Qarase, put together a comprehensive affirmative action framework to respond to the broad ethno-nationalist sentiments. This was captured in the *Blueprint and Government Policy for the Enhancement of Indigenous Fijians and Rotumans' Participation in Commerce and Business* (Blueprint) which called for the mobilization and integration of state political and administrative mechanisms and resources into an overall macro-economic framework that would guide government policies (Fiji Government 2000).

The operational details were outlined in an even more comprehensive document, *50/50 by year 2020*. This Plan aimed at the "enhancement of participation of indigenous Fijians and Rotumans in the socio-economic development of Fiji" (Fiji Government 2001). As part of the exercise the entire civil service machinery was mobilized to identify and operationalize potential approaches that might advance indigenous Fijians in education, human resource development, commerce and finance, public enterprise reform, health, resource-based industries, tourism, culture, and heritage and rural development. The Plan identified two major pressing issues confronting Fiji: "narrowing the socio-economic disparities between ethnic groups through more equitable sharing of resources and socio-economic restructuring; and maximizing indigenous Fijian economic productivity in relation to resources such as land" (Fiji Government 2001: 1).

Learning from previous affirmative action attempts, this document, using an Equity Index (EI) formula, attempted to analyse the state of inequity using official national census data and calculating how much the indigenous Fijian level of achievement should be accelerated before reaching the desired 1:1 (50/50) Target Equity Ratio (TER), calculated on the basis of the approximate 50/50 population proportion for indigenous Fijians and other ethnic groups. The EI is calculated using the Distribution Ratio (DR) value, that is, the extent of inequality at a given point in time, which should be used to calculate how many times it would take to achieve the TER ratio. For the corporate manager category, there is one indigenous Fijian to six Indo-Fijians and other ethnic groups (1:6 DR); therefore the EI is 6, meaning that affirmative action should ensure that the number of indigenous Fijians in the corporate manager category should be increased by six. The EI for the various occupational categories varied widely (see Table 4.3).

The 50/50 Plan contained a number of integrated assumptions including equality creation, national wealth redistribution, indigenous Fijian economic advancement and conflict resolution. But political circumstances changed the situation dramatically. During the 2001 election the new Fijian political party – Soqosoqo Duavata ni Lewenivanua (SDL) – under Qarase's leadership, used the 50/50 Plan as the major political campaign tool to mobilize indigenous Fijian votes through unauthorized delivery of goods ranging from lawnmowers to

Table 4.3 Equity index for selected different professions

Occupational category	Distribution ratio	Equity index
Corporate manager	1:6	6
Physics, mathematics, engineering, science	1:3	3
Business and legal	1:3	3
Finance, sales, business	1:3	3
Extraction, building trade	1:3	3
Plant and machinery	1:3	3

Source: calculated from *50–50 Plan*: 40–5.

fishing boats; to an aggregated value of more than F$20 million to voters. The politicization of the Plan drew widespread criticism, even among indigenous Fijians, after it was revealed that after it had won the election the SDL government had "planted" individuals within the system as "distributors" of affirmative action goods to favoured customers. A number of people, including the CEO for Agriculture and Fisheries, were convicted and imprisoned in relation to what came to be known as the "Agriculture Scam".

The continuing drive to indigenize the political process led the SDL government to push for two significant bills. The first was the Reconciliation, Tolerance and Unity Bill, which included, among its other provisions, the release from prison of indigenous Fijian activists involved in the 2000 coup. The second, the Qoliqoli Bill,[6] attempted to transfer ownership of the coastal fishing grounds and seashore from the state to indigenous landowners. Both these bills were very unpopular among the business community and other ethnic groups, and created considerable tension within the country. The most significant reaction was from the military, which saw Qarase's pro-indigenous policies not only as racist but also as a security threat (Ratuva 2007). The tension between the SDL government and the military escalated, with the military telling the Prime Minister to rescind the "racist" policies and "corrupt practices" of his government. Qarase tried to remove the military commander, Commodore Frank Bainimarama, several times, but to no avail, and the continuing tension culminated in Qarase's displacement by the military on 5 December 2006.

Re-invention of affirmative action

The military regime literally undid what the Qarase government had put in place in a programme they called the "clean up campaign". The political and institutional mechanisms for affirmative action and indigenization were forcefully dismantled, including the removal of a large number of indigenous Fijian CEOs in the statal and para-statal institutions that had been beneficiaries of the affirmative action programme in the public service since 1987. The military saw the pro-indigenous affirmative action as racist, corruption-riddled and against the noble values of multiculturalism. In place of the Plan, the military established a National Council for Building a Better Fiji (NCBBF) whose task was to put together a "People's Charter", a document which provided for integrated national socio-economic development, security reform, governance reconfiguration and socio-cultural cohesion. Instead of targeting indigenous Fijians only, the designated category for the People's Charter was broadened to include all marginalized groups.

The military also put in place an anti-corruption body called the Fiji Independent Commission Against Corruption (FICAC) to investigate activities by the previous government and others the regime deemed to be "corrupt". A number of high profile players including the sacked CEO of Fijian Holdings, Qarase, and other proponents and beneficiaries of the affirmative action programmes, were hauled into court and put on trial for corruption. In 2012, Quarase was sentenced to twelve months imprisonment. The military used coercive tactics to institutionalize its economic and political reforms and remove opposition, and the anti-affirmative action witch-hunt has transformed the connotation of this policy from something positive to something socially regressive and morally evil.

The People's Charter was more than just a blueprint for development. It was a framework for social engineering and socio-political reconfiguration as part of the revolutionary process of erasing the old order and creating a new one with new institutions and norms. In addition to the dismantling and reconfiguration of state structures, powerful institutions such as the Great Council of Chiefs and Methodist Church were paralysed and lost significant power and control over indigenous Fijians. The unilateral abrogation of the Constitution in 2009 was no doubt the most extreme manifestation of the post-coup transformation (Ratuva 2011).

Part of the new hegemonic process was the use of rural development programmes by the regime to mobilize support. This was important for the military because at the time of the coup in 2006, indigenous Fijians saw the military as pro-Indian and anti-Fijian, especially after the weakening of indigenous Fijian institutions such as the Great Council of Chiefs. To appease the indigenous Fijians, coup leader Commodore Bainimarama used a complex but clever tactical manoeuvre that consisted of direct visitation: the doorstep service delivery of goods in the form of roads, bridges, coconut biofuel factories, etc. This worked wonders as chiefs and villagers presented their *matanigasau* (traditional apology) for opposing him earlier and promised to support his reforms.

During his visits to the villages Bainimarama emphasized that there would be no more Qarase-type "handouts", through affirmative action, and that the military government would not fund any more community halls and churches but would focus only on economically productive projects, infrastructure and education. In all the development projects, there was no mention of the word "affirmative action" or "indigenous Fijian" as target groups. The language of development was de-ethnicized as part of the social engineering. Terms such as "rural and outer island development" were used instead of "rural indigenous Fijians", even though most of the rural development efforts were geared towards indigenous Fijians. The allocation for the promotion of rural and outer island development programmes are shown in Table 4.4. The only category which did not directly benefit rural indigenous Fijians was "multi-ethnic affairs".

To bolster indigenous Fijian development, land reform was now being envisaged as a major socio-economic fulcrum for development. Land reform included setting up a "land bank" where land owners could "deposit" their land to be administered by the government, rather than the Native Land Trust Board. The reforms were part of the broader development framework encapsulated in the Ten Point Economic Plan (TPEP), which set out specific targets to be achieved by 2020. These are: (1) GDP to be increased twofold; (2) balance of payments current account deficit to be eliminated; (3) poverty to be reduced from current levels to less than 5 per cent of the population; (4) visitor arrivals to increase to six million; (5) financial sector to be liberalized with a view to eliminating exchange controls; (6) Fiji to grow its communication services sector business by 100 per cent; (7) Fiji to achieve self sufficiency in rice, meat and liquid milk; (8) Fiji to convert up to 90 per cent of all electricity generation from fossil fuel to renewable sources; (9) Fiji to convert up to 80 per cent of all arable land area into productive use; and (10) Fiji to reduce the unemployment rate to less than 3 per cent (Ministry of Information, 16 April 2010).

Paradoxically, the new shift in the affirmative action paradigm is basically a resurrection of the late 1970s and 1980s development plans which garbed the policy in the language of rural development. Unlike the post-1987 and post-2000 affirmative action policies, the pro-indigenous policies after the 2006 coup were fundamentally integrated into the national development plan rather than a separate and distinguishable policy framework. The de-ethnicization of the language did not mean that ethnic preferential intent had disappeared. It simply made it less conspicuous. One of the distinguishable features between past affirmative action policies and current ones is the class dimension. Whereas the previous ones were targeted at consolidating the indigenous Fijian middle class, the post-2006 coup strategy was first to weaken the indigenous middle class created after the earlier affirmative action policies, and at the same time to target the rural poor as a designated group.

Table 4.4 Allocations towards rural and outer island development programmes: 2009 budget

Sector	Amount (F$ million)
Fijian affairs	0.9
Agriculture	21.4
Fisheries and forestry	1.15
Provincial development	5.5
Multi-ethnic affairs	1.6
Lands and mineral development	0.4
Youth development	0.2
Heath	2.5
Infrastructure and works	38.3
Total	71.95

Source: Government Budget, 2009.

The de-ethnicization of affirmative action was an attempt to de-politicize it. However, this goal was not attained as it merely led to a repoliticization of affirmative action, but in a different context.

The weakening of the indigenous middle class was a politically deliberate policy to undermine the power base of Qarase and indigenous Fijian ethno-nationalism. A large number of indigenous middle class professionals were removed from their positions in government and state corporations, and investigated for corruption. Since 1987 the affirmative action policies had created a class of wealthy and powerful indigenous Fijians who continued to feed on state patronage and resources. The military regime tried to curtail the privileges of the middle class and shifted the focus on infrastructural development for the benefit of rural villagers. This tactic had dual consequences in that it made the middle class isolated and vulnerable, while at the same time consolidating support among village-level indigenous Fijians. Isolating the liberal and vocal middle class was a tactic aimed at curtailing their power and influence. Isolating and weakening the indigenous middle class, paralysing the Methodist Church, neutralizing the Great Council of Chiefs and winning the hearts of the indigenous Fijian villagers, was a way of controlling the power of ethno-nationalism at the grassroots level and harnessing it to the advantage of the government.

Disintegrating the indigenous Fijian middle class was a grave mistake because it would undermine the skills base and the national intelligentsia, as well as weakening the middle class' buying capacity – which is crucial for the market. Contrary to its own avowed anti-ethno-nationalist and anti-affirmative action sentiments, the military has re-invented a new form of local level ethno-nationalism amongst indigenous Fijians using rural-targeted projects which some may say is tantamount to another, alternative, form of affirmative action.

Access and duration

Access to affirmative action itself was ultimately influenced by an array of factors. The first was obviously ethnicity – one had to be officially categorized as a "Fijian" through registration in the *Vola ni kawabula*, the public register for indigenous Fijian tribal members. In reality, only some indigenous Fijians had access to affirmative action. For instance, those who had access to preferential loans were political elites, urban middle class individuals, or those in the state bureaucracy or banking community. Because of the limited resources available and the geographical spread of the islands, these groups were able to use their linkages and power to access funds. Those in the rural areas did not have any access at all, except when farming implements were distributed to them as part of the SDL's political campaign strategy.

Many business ventures failed due to the inability of the individual beneficiaries to take advantage of the opportunities to maximize the outputs. One could argue that even if the concessions were given out in a transparent manner, the result of business affirmative action would not have been very different since the potential for success was predicated upon individual entrepreneurial skills and not ethnic aspirations. Those who succeeded took advantage of the opportunities and circumstances better.

One of the paradoxes was that some non-indigenous Fijians benefited from business affirmative action. The FHL, although based on the notion of indigenous equity trust, survived through purchase of shares in non-indigenous owned companies. These companies directly benefited from capital raised through state finance and indigenous Fijian equity. What FHL, like many indigenous investors, quickly learned was that while capital could be distributed politically along ethnic lines, its productive capacity was determined by the skills of investors themselves, and the complex dynamics of the market, and not ethnic identity.

In education, most beneficiaries were children who already had access to privileged primary and secondary schools. Most of the privileged schools were located in urban areas. The provinces with better developed schools were more likely to receive more scholarships and as a result there was a disparity in the distribution process. Children of the established middle class, by virtue of their access to better schools and better levels of educational achievement, had better chances of receiving scholarships.

The issue of access is closely linked to that of duration because, given the limited resources, the question of how long the designated category would continue to receive concession had to be addressed. The 1987 affirmative action projects did not have a time frame because they had been spontaneous in their implementation after the military coup. However, after the 2000 coup, affirmative action was more systematically designed and built into it was a 20-year timeframe with mid-term reviews to be held after every ten years and internal quarterly reviews every five years. The aim was to achieve the 50/50 share of the economy between the indigenous Fijians and other ethnic groups within 20 years (by 2020). The hope was that after equity in various sectors was achieved, concessions would slowly be phased out. The first quarterly internal review by the government was carried out in 2006, the same year the latest military coup took place. The military government terminated affirmative action and in its place instituted a rural development scheme as part of the People's Charter aimed at taking the country towards the proposed election in 2014.

Conclusion

Although one major justification for affirmative action in Fiji was conflict resolution, the extent to which this has been achieved is questionable. What we do know is that ethnic-based affirmative action, propagated by the 1987 coup makers as the panacea for Fiji's ethnic problems, later contributed to the 2006 military coup. Affirmative action created long-lasting challenges, in terms of worsening not improving ethnic relations, despite attempts to address the issue of horizontal inequality. By emphasizing horizontal inequality and the urgent desire to create a bourgeoning entrepreneurial class, indigenous elites' preferential policies did not pay proper attention to intra-communal inequality. While the indigenous middle class expanded, poverty also increased in a significant way.

While many indigenous Fijians benefited from affirmative action, there were disastrous projects as well, which had both short and long-term consequences. One of the emerging challenges was the appropriateness of targeting programmes purely on the basis of horizontal inequality without recognition of intra-communal diversity. The dream of building a large entrepreneurial class quickly, that would control 50 per cent of the national business share and compete with Indo-Fijian dominance, heightened expectations. When this dream did not eventuate there was disappointment and recrimination. Many programmes failed, including the demise of the state-owned National Bank of Fiji, because of their political nature; corruption was rampant. This led to tensions within the indigenous Fijian community.

While access to concessions was based fundamentally on ethnicity, in reality there were factors that favoured some groups within the indigenous Fijian category. Members of the middle class, by virtue of their knowledge of the system and links to the state and corporate sector, had greater access to loans, scholarships and permits. Since some of the beneficiaries were non-indigenous Fijian companies, this ethnic convergence was characteristic of the "embourgeoisment" process. Entrepreneurs from both sides of the divide developed similar interests as they became part of the same entrepreneurial class where political and ideological differentiation took secondary importance. Qarase, a banker and one of the fathers of contemporary Fijian affirmative action, was a living manifestation of this elite convergence. On one hand he had close affinity with Indo-Fijian businessmen who shared similar economic interests; on the other hand he was actively involved in ethno-nationalist mobilization against Indo-Fijian political elites. Related to this was the belief that access to state concessions was not going to be indefinite and a timeframe was needed to determine its longevity. The 2001 affirmative action plan had a specific duration – 20 years. However, the 2006 coup ensured that the plan would only be in place for about five years.

Individually-owned companies were not very successful because they were left to their own devices to compete in the market. In contrast, state-supervised and subsidized companies, such as FHL, were very successful and gave affirmative action a visible face.

Perhaps the most pertinent ideological driver for pro-indigenous policies was the notion of the paramountcy of Fijian interests. The assumption that indigenous Fijians had an inalienable right to special treatment did little to advance the self-realization and innovation of many indigenous Fijians who had to rely on state handouts to facilitate their development. One of the reasons for dismantling the post-2006 coup affirmative action programme was precisely to terminate the dependency syndrome. This inspired internal debate and soul-searching within the indigenous community as they tried to fathom the transformation from state dependency to self-sufficiency.

In the civil service, where affirmative action was most marked, the loss of skilled Indo-Fijian personnel and a deterioration in service levels had long-term consequences. The Fijianization of the civil service meant that the moral inducement for other ethnic groups to join the civil service was taken away. Many left the country in dismay and with them was lost valuable expertise and skills which Fiji has still not recovered today.

The association between affirmative action and violent regime change did a lot to change the image of affirmative action as a cousin of ethno-nationalist violence. The failure of the colonial and post-colonial states to provide equitable development and integrated ethnic politics created conditions for tension and made coups a historical possibility. However, in hindsight, large-scale affirmative action would not have been possible without the coups because reforms would most likely have been rejected by the Indo-Fijian opposition in a parliamentary system. The coups themselves have embedded permanent dents on Fiji's political and economic institutions, political culture and socio-cultural relations.

One issue persistently at the centre of affirmative action debates is the contestation of the definition of inequality between indigenous Fijians and Indo-Fijians, especially their use of different variables to define the other as being more "advantaged" and themselves as being "disadvantaged". Indigenous Fijians would point at the dominance of Indo-Fijians in commerce as evidence of their superiority and dominance, while Indo-Fijians would point at indigenous Fijian ownership of more than 80 per cent of the land and their control of the military, civil service and political power as evidence of their dominance as "oppressors". To indigenous Fijians, political power and land ownership are meaningless without an increased share of national wealth, but for Indo-Fijians control over entrepreneurial activities is easily overshadowed by lack of political power and land; they see real wealth being in the land, which remains to be unlocked. The coups in 1987 and 2000 were attempts to wrestle political power away from Indo-Fijians because of the view that their political dominance would signal their total control of both the economic and political processes. Meanwhile, the rate of poverty for both ethnic groups continues to rise.

The People's Charter claims to provide a trans-ethnic equity-based development approach. However, the problem is that the Charter is associated with violent regime change and this association will continue to haunt Fiji's future unless the Charter proves economically and politically workable enough to win nationwide acclaim and acceptance.

Notes

1 The Great Council of Chiefs (GCC) was set up by Governor Gordon in 1876 as a consultative body to discuss issues and advise the governor on indigenous Fijian matters.
2 DP8 emphasized the need for more exports, as well as the expansion of domestic production, as a part of the import-substitution policy. Large-scale agricultural enterprises were encouraged with the direct involvement of a number of actors; private corporations, the Native Land Development Corporation, the government in co-operation with the landowners; groups of smallholders; and groups of smallholders organized into larger units. A key aspect of this was the involvement of the indigenous Fijians to ensure that they were able to free up their land for development purposes. The involvement of the indigenous Fijians was to ensure that some of their land was to be opened up for cultivation and also to have them directly involved in the cultivation and management process themselves.
3 See the *Fiji Republic Gazette*, 4 (83), 1990: 910.

4 Qarase, a committed nationalist, was then the Managing Director of the Fiji Development Bank and he was later appointed by the military after the 2000 coup to be interim Prime Minister. Later, after two elections (2001 and 2006), he became Prime Minister until he was overthrown in a coup in December 2006 on the grounds that his policies were too nationalistic.
5 "Gaunavou" literally translates as "modern times".
6 "Qoloqoli" literally refers to traditional fishing grounds and rights.

References

Adinkrah, M. 1995. *Crime, Deviance and Delinquency in Fiji*. Fiji Council of Social Services, Suva.
Ali, A. 1982. "The Politics of Plural Society" in R. Crocombe and A. Ali (eds.), *Politics in Melanesia*. Institute of Pacific Studies, Suva.
Belshaw, C. 2004. *Under the Ivi Tree: Society and Economic Growth in Rural Fiji*. London: Routledge and Keegan Paul.
Burns, A. 1963. *Fiji*. HMSO, London.
Chand, S. 2007. "50–50 by 2020: Poverty and Redistributive Politics in Post-Independence Fiji" in *Pacific Economic Bulletin*, 22 (2): 22–35.
Chetty, K. and Prasad, S. 1993. *Fiji's Immigration: An Examination of Contemporary Trends and Issues*. UNDF, Suva.
Colonial Sugar Refinery. 1959. *Annual Report*. Colonial Sugar Refinery, Suva.
Cottrell, J and Y. Ghai. 2007. "Constitutionalising Affirmative Action in the Fiji Islands" in the *International Journal of Human Rights*, 11 (1 and 2): 227–57.
Daily Post, March 13, 1999.
ECREA, 2005. *Affirmative Action and Poverty in Fiji*. Policy paper.
Fiji Bureau of Statistics, 1986. *National Census*. Fiji Bureau of Statistics, Suva.
Fiji Bureau of Statistics, 1989. *Household Income and Expenditure Survey*. FBS, Suva.
Fiji Bureau of Statistics, 1996. *National Census*. Fiji Bureau of Statistics, Suva.
Fiji Bureau of Statistics, 1998. *Household Income and Expenditure Survey*. FBS, Suva.
Fiji Co-operative Dept. 1948. *Annual Report*. Fiji Co-operative Dept., Suva.
Fiji Co-operative Dept. 1958. *Annual Report*. Suva, Fiji Co-operative Dept., Suva.
Fiji Development Bank. 1960. *Annual Report*. Fiji Development Bank, Suva.
Fiji Development Bank. 1961. *Annual Report*. Fiji Development Bank, Suva.
Fiji Development Bank. 1996. *Commercial Loans to Fijians Scheme-Review*.
Fiji Government. 1905. *Great Council of Chiefs Proceedings*. Fiji Government, Suva.
Fiji Government. 1956. *Census Report*. Fiji Government, Suva.
Fiji Government. 1960. *Fiji Legislative Council Paper No. 1 of 1960*.
Fiji Government. 1966. *Employment Figures*. Fiji Government, Suva.
Fiji Government. 1967. *Inland Revenue Department, National Accounts Report*. Fiji Government, Suva.
Fiji Government.1970. *Fiji Development Plan 5*. Fiji Government, Suva.
Fiji Government. 1975. *Development Plan 6*. Fiji Government, Suva.
Fiji Government. 1980. *Development Plan 7*. Fiji Government, Suva.
Fiji Government. 1985. *Development Plan 8*. Fiji Government, Suva.
Fiji Government. 1990. *Constitution of the Republic of Fiji*. Fiji Government, Suva.
Fiji Government. 1990. *Development Plan 9*. Fiji Government, Suva.
Fiji Government. 1997. *Constitution of the Republic of the Fiji Islands*. Fiji Government, Suva.

Fiji Government. 2000. *Blueprint and Government Policy for the Enhancement of indigenous Fijians and Rotumans Participation in Commerce and Business*. Government of Fiji, Suva.
Fiji Government. 2001. *20 Year Plan for Fijian Participation in Business*. Fiji Government, Suva.
Fiji Government. 2008. *People's Charter*. Fiji Government, Suva.
Fiji Government. 2009. *Fiji Budget 2009*. Fiji Government, Suva.
Fiji Government. 1990. *Fiji Republic Gazette*, 4 (83).
Fiji Government. 2009. *Government Budget*. Suva, Fiji Government.
Fiji Ministry of Education. 1993. *Annual Report*. Fiji Ministry of Education, Suva.
Fiji Ministry of Information, 16 April, 2010.
Fiji Ministry of Information Press Release, 16 April, 2010.
Fiji National Provident Fund. 1996. *Annual Report*. Fiji National Provident Fund, Suva.
Fiji National Provident Fund. 2006. *Annual Report*. Fiji National Provident Fund, Suva.
Fiji National Provident Fund. 2006. *Annual Report*. Fiji National Provident Fund, Suva.
Fiji Police Force. 1996. *Annual Report*. Fiji National Provident Fund FPF, Suva.
Fiji Public Service Commission. 1986. *Annual Report*. Fiji Public Service Commission, Suva.
Fiji Public Service Commission. 1995. *Annual Report*. PSC, Suva.
Fiji Sugar Corporation. 1994. *Annual Report*. Fiji Sugar Corporation, Suva.
Fiji Trade and Investment Board. 1997. *Annual Report*. FTIB, Suva.
Fiji. 1956. "The Pattern of the Fiji Economy, The National Income. 1950–1953" in *Council Papers*, 44.
Fijian Business Initiative. 1992. *Nine Points Plan*. Fijian Business Initiative, Suva.
Fijian Holdings Ltd. 2008. *Annual Report*. Fijian Holdings Ltd., Suva.
Fisk, E.K. 1970. *The Political Economy of Independent Fiji*. ANU Press, Canberra.
France, P. 1969. *The Charter of the Land*. Melbourne: Oxford University Press.
Gomez, Edmund T. 2009. "The Rise and Fall of Capital: Corporate Malaysia in Historical Perspective" in *Journal of Contemporary Asia*, 39 (3): 345–81.
Grynberg, R., D. Munro and M. White. 2002. *The Collapse of the National Bank of Fiji*. University of the South Pacific Library, Suva.
Knapman, B. 1987. *Fiji's Economic History, 1874–1939: Studies of Capitalist Economic Development*. Pacific Research Monograph, No. 15.
Korovulavula, M. 1993. Senate speech.
Lal, B. 2010. *In the Eye of the Storm: A Biography of Jai Ram Reddy*. Canberra: ANU E Press.
Lal, B. 1992. *Broken Waves: A History of the Fiji Islands in the 20th Century*, Honolulu: University of Hawaii Press.
Lawson, S. 1991. *The Failure of Democratic Politics in Fiji*. New York: Oxford University Press.
Narayan, J. 1984. *The Political Economy of Fiji*. South Pacific Review Press, Suva.
Office of the Registrar of Companies. 1987. *Company Records*. Office of the Registrar of Companies, Suva.
Plange, N. 1985. "Colonial Capitalism and Class Formation in Fiji: A Retrospective Overview" in *Journal of Pacific Studies*, 11: 91–116.
Fiji Public Service Commission. 1986. *Annual Report*. Fiji Public Service Commission, Suva.
Qarase, L. 1995. *The Ten Year Plan for Fijian Participation in Business*. ESCAP, Suva.

Ratuva, S. 2000. "Addressing Inequality? Economic Affirmative Action and Communal Capitalism in Post-Coup Fiji" in A. Akram-Lodhi, *Confronting Fiji Futures*. Canberra: Asia Pacific Press.
Ratuva, S. 2002. "Economic Nationalism and Communal Consolidation: Affirmative Action in Fiji, 1987 to 2002" in *Pacific Economic Bulletin*, 17 (1): 130–7.
Ratuva, S. 2005. "Politics of Ethno-National Identity in a Post-Colonial Communal Democracy" in A. Allahar, *Ethnicity, Class, and Nationalism: Caribbean and Extra-Caribbean Dimensions*. Oxford: Lexington Books.
Ratuva, S. 2007. "Pre-election Cold War: The Role of the Fiji Military during the 2006 Election" in S. Firth and J. Fraenkel (eds.), *From Election to Coup in Fiji*, Canberra: Asia Pacific Press.
Ratuva, S. 2009. *Affirmative Action and the Labour Market: The Case of Fiji*. Paper presented to international research group on affirmative action, British Academy, London.
Ratuva, S. 2010. "Vakatorocaketaki ni taukei: The politics of affirmative action in post-colonial Fiji" in *Pacific Economic Bulletin*, 25 (3): 168–92.
Ratuva, S. 2011. "Fiji military coups: Reactive and Transformative Tendencies" in *Asian Journal of Political Science*, 19 (1).
Reeves, P., T. Vakatora and B. Lal. 1996. *The Fiji Islands: Towards a United Future. A Report of the Fiji Constitution Review Commission*. Fiji Government, Suva.
Routledge, D. 1985. *Matanitu*. Institute of Pacific Studies, Suva.
Scarr, D. 1984. *Fiji: A Short History*. Sydney: George Allen & Unwin.
Schulze, D. 1982. "Credit Unions in Fiji" in *South Pacific Forum*, 2 (1): 10–17.
Sutherland, W. 1998. *Globalization, Nationalism and the National Agenda: The Problematics of Reform in Fiji and the Fijian Question*. Occasional Paper.
Sowell, T. 1990. *Preferential Policies*. New York: Morrow.
Spate, O.H.K. 1959. *The Fijian People: Economic Problems and Prospects*. Council Paper 13 of 1959. Government Press, Suva.
Stewart, F. 2009. *A global view of horizontal inequality: Inequalities experienced by Muslims world-wide*. MICROCON Research Working Papers, Paper 13. Institute of Development Studies, Brighton.
Wright, A. and I. Twyford. 1959. *The Soil Resources of Fiji*. Department of Agriculture, Suva.

5 Affirmative action in South Africa
Disadvantaging the many for the benefit of the few

Anthea Jeffery

Introduction

Racial discrimination in the apartheid era was profoundly unjust and damaging to black South Africans. It not only pervaded every aspect of their lives but also made upward social mobility inordinately difficult by obstructing access to adequate housing and living conditions, good schooling, skilled employment, home ownership, business operation, and the accumulation of capital over time. Black South Africans were thus dealt cruel and crippling economic blows, while also suffering the daily humiliations engendered by these restrictions, the denial of the franchise, and the pervasive sense of being 'second-class' citizens.

However, from the early 1970s onwards, redistribution from whites to blacks via the budget increased significantly, while the apartheid system began to crumble under the weight of its own contradictions. More and more racial laws became unenforceable and were quietly abandoned. In the 1970s and 1980s, African incomes, education, and housing substantially improved. In 1979 Africans were given the same trade union rights as others, while in 1986 the pass laws were abolished. In 1991 all key remaining apartheid laws were repealed, including the Population Registration Act of 1950, which had earlier divided the population into four racial groups and provided the foundation for racial discrimination. In 1992 whites voted for the continuation of a reform process certain to result in majority rule and the loss of their political power. In 1994 that political transition took place in a country in which incremental reforms had already had great impact.

Enormous backlogs in the living standards of Africans nevertheless remained, generating widespread agreement on the need for effective measures to help overcome poverty and inequality. When President Nelson Mandela came to power in May 1994 to worldwide acclaim and with the support of most South Africans, it seemed the time had finally come when the country could marry its extensive resources to sound policies, thereby stimulating growth and jobs, improving education and living conditions, and giving the African majority the realistic prospect of a better life for all. There remains widespread support for such goals which, sadly, have yet to be achieved. Growth rates have remained moderate, at around 3 per cent a year on average (2009/2010 *Survey*: 81).

Unemployment among Africans has become very much worse, the number of jobless Africans having risen from 1.64 million in 1994 to 3.7 million in 2010, an increase of 126 per cent (2009/2010 *Survey*: 215). Mainly because of the introduction by the African National Congress (ANC) of a flawed system of outcomes-based education (OBE), the quality of public education has declined since 1994 to the point where more than half of the country's matriculants are functionally illiterate and innumerate (*The Times* 7 July 2010). Public health care has also deteriorated since the political transition, while the country's rate of HIV/AIDS infection has become the highest in the world (National Planning Commission 2011: 20–1).

These failures have had predictable consequences in hobbling the fight for greater opportunity and an end to racial inequality. They are also largely the result, not of apartheid deficits, but of misguided policies adopted by the ANC since 1994. Many of these policy failures have ideological roots, reflecting the ANC's preference for redistribution over growth along with its determination to put more and more emphasis on 'transformation' laws.

These laws have trumped an earlier consensus in the mid-1990s on the need for 'soft' forms of affirmative action aimed primarily at increasing inputs such as skills development. Instead, transformation laws have increasingly focused on outputs: on requiring the fulfilment of hard numerical quotas imposed by the state with little regard for skills shortages and other binding constraints. Predictably, such measures have deterred direct investment and restricted growth and the generation of new jobs. They have also had very little positive impact on the majority of unskilled and impoverished black South Africans, who will never be eligible for management jobs, empowerment equity deals, or state procurement contracts. Transformation laws have thus benefited only a small black elite while leaving the majority of Africans worse off than they might otherwise have been.

Triggering event for affirmative action

Affirmative action and black economic empowerment (BEE) policies have their origins in the political transition from minority to majority rule in April 1994. This brought the ANC to power as part of a Government of National Unity committed to improving the lives of all South Africans and providing redress for more than four decades of statutory racial discrimination under the National Party government.

Since the consequences of pervasive racial laws could not simply be waved away, there was wide acceptance of the need, in the post-apartheid era, for a 'soft' form of affirmative action based mainly on training and mentoring. This form of affirmative action seemed also to be what was envisaged by the equality clause (Section 9) of the 1996 Constitution, which generally requires strict adherence to equality before the law, but authorises appropriate remedial measures to advance the victims of past disadvantage. However, most affirmative measures adopted since 1996 have focused on outputs rather than inputs, putting their emphasis on numerical targets intended to achieve an elusive equality of outcomes.

Employment Equity Act of 1998

The first affirmative action law to be introduced was the Employment Equity Act of 1998. According to the government, the statute is intended to:

- provide redress for the pervasive racial discrimination of the apartheid era;
- put an end to persistent white racism;
- bring about demographic representivity at all levels of employment;
- stimulate economic growth by encouraging the creation of a black middle class;
- reduce black:white inequality; and
- help stabilise a deeply divided society and prevent a revolt by the poor and marginalised (*Business Day* 5 May 1998; *The Star* 5 August 1998).

When the Employment Equity Bill was before Parliament, the measure was generally endorsed by journalists and other commentators. A *Business Day* editorial described the bill as an 'unobtrusive measure requiring no more than the sensible affirmative action programmes good managers should be implementing in any event' (*Business Day* 12 February 1998). An article in the *Financial Mail* added that the measure would play a vital role in requiring 'employers to abandon irrational prejudices and, equally important, to undertake the planned training and development' of black people (*Financial Mail* 13 February 1998).

In fact, there were many disturbing features to the measure which most commentators seemed to overlook. The statute's emphasis on demographic representivity was particularly worrying, for (contrary to ANC assertions) it is not in fact the norm in any multi-ethnic society for each ethnic group to fan out into the workforce in accordance with its share of the population. On the contrary, as Thomas Sowell and other scholars have shown, though different groups have the same innate potential, in practice they differ in median age, education and human capital, and these differences affect their eligibility for management posts (Sowell 1989: 22, 23; Horowitz 1985: 677). Moreover, when these variables are taken into account, the alleged 'under-representation' of particular groups often becomes far less marked or even disappears (Sowell 2004: 6).

In South Africa, salient differences in age and education are consistently overlooked by proponents of demographic proportionality. In 1999, the year the Employment Equity Act came into operation, Africans accounted for 70 per cent of the economically active population: those people between the ages of 15 and 64 who were working or seeking jobs. According to the Act, Africans ought thus to constitute 70 per cent of managers. However, in the same year, only 15.3 per cent of the total African population fell within the 40–64 age bracket normally considered eligible for high-level occupations. In addition, though degrees are often required or advisable for management posts, only 270,000 Africans, or 1.5 per cent of the African population, held a tertiary qualification at that time. This meant that the pool of African people from which managers could realistically be drawn was far smaller than the Act assumed. This situation has improved in the past decade, but only by a small margin.[1]

The Act also seemed to overlook a number of other considerations. In particular, it ignored:

- the general skills shortage which had long bedevilled the country and the resulting need to harness all skills available, both black and white, in order to boost productivity, build infrastructure, and ratchet up the rate of economic growth;
- a major shift in white attitudes towards black people, which had become evident even under apartheid, and;
- the extent to which black:white inequality had been decreasing since the 1970s under the impact of these and other changes (Pienaar 2000: 2–3; Kane-Berman 1991: 8–10).

In addition, the Act betrayed the colour-blind ideal by requiring that South Africans should again be classified (this time on a supposedly voluntary basis) into the apartheid-era categories of African, Indian, Coloured and White (Department of Labour 1998: 1). However, the Population Registration Act of 1950 which had previously defined these racial categories had been repealed by the National Party government in 1991. In the post-apartheid era, there were thus no rules laying down how the envisaged racial categorisation was to be carried out, while the renewed need for classification seemed to breathe new life into racial categories which had earlier been rendered obsolete.

Core provisions of the Act

The Employment Equity Act prohibits unfair discrimination on racial and other grounds. It also requires all 'designated' employers – generally those with 50 employees or more – to apply affirmative action measures aimed at ensuring that black people (along with women and the disabled) are 'equitably represented' at all levels of the workforce. African representation is thus expected to increase to 74 per cent (the current African share of the economically active population) at every level. In addition, Africans, Indians, and so-called 'coloured' people cumulatively make up 87 per cent of the economically active population, making this the ultimate goal in terms of demographic proportionality (2008/2009 *Survey*: 208; Jeffery 1998: 5–6; Commission for Employment Equity 2009/2010: 6).

Only those black people who are 'suitably qualified' are entitled to preferential treatment, but this criterion is broadly defined. It may depend on formal qualifications or relevant experience, but it also suffices if a black person has 'the capacity to acquire, within a reasonable time, the ability to do the job'. Failure to make 'reasonable progress' towards demographic representivity is punishable by significant fines (Jeffery 1998: 5–6).

Designated employers must report to the Department of Labour on their progress towards demographic proportionality. Their reports are analysed by the

Commission for Employment Equity (CEE), a statutory body responsible for tracking the implementation of employment equity. CEE annual reports are thus potentially an important source of information on affirmative action in employment, but the methodology used by the CEE often fails to compare like with like, while its data is sometimes at odds with that from other sources (Jeffery 1998: 5–6; Solidarity 2010 (b): 3–6; P-E Corporate Services, 2009: 10–12).

Affirmative action in the public sector

The initial goal was 50 per cent black representation among senior managers in the public sector, but in 2003 this target was increased to 75 per cent, to be attained by March 2005. By then, 30 per cent of senior managers were also to be black women. By 2005 these targets had almost been met, for black people held 70 per cent of senior management posts and women 29 per cent. Targets for black women were thereafter increased to 50 per cent, prompting Mpho Letlape, head of human resources at Eskom (a parastatal with a monopoly over the generation of electricity) to say: 'Over the next five years, as it embarks on its R84 billion infrastructure programme, Eskom has to appoint two new staff every working day – and it is adamant that one of them will be a black woman' (*The Citizen* 15 February 2008). However, this approach ignored the skills shortage among Africans – and especially among black women – and contributed to crippling electricity outages in 2008 which cost the country an estimated R50 billion, equivalent to US$6.67 billion at the then prevailing exchange rate.

According to the CEE's report for 2009/2010, Africans hold 59 per cent of top and senior management posts in government, while whites hold 24.5 per cent of such positions. However, other organisations give different figures, making accurate assessment difficult. In April 2010, a report by the trade union Solidarity found that Africans hold between 80 per cent and 82 per cent of the top posts in various government departments (Commission for Employment Equity, 2009–2010; *Business Report* 9 April 2010). Overall, Africans have advanced rapidly into senior positions in the public sector, even though only 17 per cent of the total African population fell within the 40–64 age cohort in 2010, while only 1.8 per cent of Africans held a tertiary qualification at that time (2009/2010 *South Africa Survey*: 15, 375).

Rapid implementation of the Employment Equity Act in the public sector has resulted in the loss of many experienced people and their replacement by others with less experience. In practice, white men have been virtually excluded from appointment for senior positions, even in instances where no suitable 'equity' candidate can be found. The upshot is that 306,000 posts (21 per cent of the total) remained vacant in 2009, adding to a crippling skills deficit within the public service (*The Star* 27 May 2010).

By 2007 criticisms of affirmative action in the public sector had grown sharp. Many commentators warned that the policy had done little more than lead to a damaging loss of institutional memory, while driving out the people who were needed to train and mentor new appointees. Former state president F.W. de

Klerk said that the country's problems with crime and many other issues had their origins 'in the very fast rate of affirmative action' since 1994. During the negotiating process from 1993 to 1996, he added, there had been wide agreement on the need for affirmative action, but 'there had never been any talk about imposing demographic representivity'. Nor had it been intended that 'people without the appropriate qualifications would be appointed to posts merely on racial grounds'. Instead, it had generally been accepted that 'the most important and effective form of affirmative action was through the provision of excellent education and training and the creation of employment' (*Business Report* 16 July 2007).

By 2008 the problems were generally worse. Sue Brown of the Institute of Justice and Reconciliation (IJR) warned against the high vacancy rate and limited capacity for delivery in the public service, adding that the problem was not a lack of money but a lack of capacity to implement programmes. Said Brown (*Finweek* 28 February 2008):

> Budget allocations [are made without considering] who will carry out [the work]. For quite a while there's been a feeling that skilled people will somehow turn up. Yet what we're witnessing is a high churn and juniorisation of posts, which results in poor delivery.

In May 2010 the Public Service Commission (a body established by the Constitution to promote public service efficiency) published a report on the 'Effectiveness of Public Service Leadership'. The report warned that 'incompetent human resource managers, unskilled employees, nepotism, and hiring people without verifying their qualifications are putting the government at risk of not delivering services to the public' (*The Star* 27 May 2010).

The impact of affirmative action on public sector efficiency has been especially marked at Eskom. Here, a rapid loss of skills – coupled with a decision to procure coal from black economic empowerment (BEE) firms with limited experience – contributed to four months of widespread blackouts. The blackouts not only cost the country an estimated R50 billion but also resulted in a number of large investment projects being put on hold because of doubts as to the reliability of electricity supply.[2]

Affirmative action in the public sector has also contributed to:

- a rapid decline in the quality of the country's roads. In 1988 some 71 per cent of South Africa's national and provincial roads were in good or very good condition, but by 2008 only 16 per cent of roads still fell within this category (2008/2009 *Survey*: 610–11); congestion and delays at the country's ports, run by the Transnet parastatal, to the extent that a number of companies have begun shifting the movement of their goods from Durban, South Africa's largest container terminal, to a revamped Maputo in Mozambique (*Financial Mail* 11 July 2008); a rapid deterioration in South Africa's rail network and rail services (also operated by the Transnet parastatal), together with a worrying rise in accidents and derailments (*Business Day* 26 October 2010); a general inability to maintain infrastructure or expand this fast enough to meet the needs of the economy (*Sunday Times* 22 March 2009); and

- a crippling shortage of engineering and other skills within municipalities, which has resulted in the collapse of local government services in many small towns. In some of these areas, as the president of a business association commented in December 2008: 'Sewerage runs down the street, street lights don't work, roads are disintegrating, refuse is not collected, water supply is erratic, and water from taps is unsafe' (*Sunday Times* 10 December 2008).

Affirmative action in the private sector

As for affirmative action in the private sector, the government assumes that the key problem is a racist lack of demand for black people at senior levels in business. However, the real difficulty lies in a chronic shortage of black people with the requisite skills and experience for management posts. Despite this, many firms have significantly increased the proportions of black people in management positions, as shown by P-E Corporate Services, a human resources consultancy.

In September 2010, based on its survey of some 850 employers cumulatively employing more than one million people, P-E Corporate Services reported that 26 per cent of senior management posts were held by black executives. This was a significant increase from 1994, when fewer than 5 per cent of such posts were held by black people. As for middle management, the report showed that 33 per cent of such positions were held by blacks in 2010, well up from 7 per cent in 1994. At junior management level, the proportion of black people had risen from 26 per cent in 1994 to 57 per cent in 2010 (P-E Corporate Services 2010: 12–14).

However, current penetration levels have improved little since 2004, mainly because of 'the continuing severe skills shortage'. The skills shortage also explained why half of the employers surveyed in 2010 paid significant premiums (between 10 per cent and 20 per cent above established pay scales) to attract and retain black managers. The 'poaching' of black professionals was also increasing, 64 per cent of respondents saying this phenomenon undermined their ability to meet employment equity targets (P-E Corporate Services 2010: 15–17).

Statistics compiled by the Commission for Employment Equity (CEE) are broadly in line with the findings of P-E Corporate Services. However, the CEE rejects the importance of the skills shortage. In 2007, for instance, the then chairman of the Commission, Jimmy Manyi, dismissed the skills shortage among black people as nothing but 'an urban legend'. Manyi also questioned whether existing penalties were strong enough to end white racism, saying a fine of up to 10 per cent of annual turnover might be more appropriate (Jeffery 2010 (a): 157). The government is now busy tightening up the Act's provisions, in keeping with Manyi's views. The Employment Equity Amendment Bill of 2010 raises fines for non-compliance to 10 per cent of turnover in certain circumstances. The bill also removes many of the key defences on which business has thus far been able to rely. The new penalties, as the government's own regulatory impact analysis has warned, could push many firms into bankruptcy, curbing growth, and adding to unemployment levels already standing at 24 per cent in general and at 50 per cent among young people (Jeffery 2011: 6).

Preferential procurement

Under the Preferential Procurement Policy Framework Act adopted in 2000, organs of state must generally award contracts to the tenderer with the highest points, but may allocate either ten or 20 points (depending on the contract's value) to 'historically disadvantaged' people tendering for state contracts. The remaining 90 or 80 points must be assessed on the basis of price and functionality.

What the Act means, in practice, is that the government is paying 10 to 20 per cent more for goods and services procured on a preferential basis, while the intended beneficiaries (often the poor and marginalised) are getting that much less. In addition, the emergent black businesses awarded government contracts on a preferential basis often have little experience or financial acumen and have sometimes failed to meet their delivery deadlines or maintain standards.

In August 2009 Thami Mazwai, director of the Centre for Small Business Development at the Soweto campus of the University of Johannesburg, warned that some blacks were 'using "the black ticket" to charge exorbitant prices'. Said Mazwai (*Business Day* 28 August 2009):

> At times the price by the black tenderer is close to double the lowest tender, but he still wins the business. In some instances, black organisations must be bailed out as ... their workmanship is below par. The contract often ends up costing more than was budgeted for.

Poor workmanship and a failure to complete projects have been particularly rife as regards the government's subsidised low-cost housing programme for the building of millions of 'Reconstruction and Development', or RDP, homes. These construction contracts have often been awarded to black contractors, but with poor results. In 2011 the Minister of Human Settlements, Tokyo Sexwale, acknowledged that R58 billion has been wasted on RDP homes that are of such poor quality that they will often have to be rebuilt (*Business Day* 9 May 2011).

Similar problems have arisen in many other spheres. Wrote journalist Jovial Rantao (*The Star* 26 January 2007):

> Government at national, provincial and local levels is spending billions of rands on a two-pronged mission: to deliver much needed services and, in the process, empower black business. However, it is clear that government is

not getting value for money.... One would have thought that our black business people, knowing first-hand what the suffering and needs of their people are, should, in the name of correcting the wrongs of apartheid, deliver the best service available. Instead, what these providers of inferior services do once they pocket the millions from the tenders is to buy the biggest and flashiest 4×4 by far, move into a bigger and better house, and then spend what is left on the delivery of the service they are contracted to provide.

Preferential procurement has thus contributed to the wasting of government revenues. In September 2009 Finance Minister Pravin Gordhan warned that the government was paying more for everything than a private business would: 'R40m for a school that should have cost R15m, R26 for a loaf of bread that should have cost R7.' On an annual state procurement bill worth hundreds of billions of rands, vast sums were being frittered away (*Business Day* 18 September 2009; *Sunday Times* 20 September 2009).

Little comprehensive information is available on the sums being spent on preferential procurement, either by the state or the private sector. Government departments and parastatals have led the way, while the private sector has become more heavily involved over time. The business role in preferential procurement has been spurred on, in particular, by the Broad-Based Black Economic Empowerment Act of 2003.

Black economic empowerment (BEE)

The government's policy of black economic empowerment builds on affirmative action in employment and preferential procurement, incorporating both into an expanded initiative. This includes five other elements as well, and is intended to accord the black majority the economic power needed to complement its political power.

Early years of BEE

The first BEE company to be formed was New Africa Investments Ltd (Nail). This was formed in 1992, before the ANC took power, when one of South Africa's major conglomerates, Sanlam, transferred control of a subsidiary to various black people, many of whom were prominent figures in the ANC. This was followed by further BEE deals which brought the market value of listed companies in which control had been transferred to black people to R70 billion by November 1998. This amounted to almost 7 per cent of the total market capitalisation of the Johannesburg Stock Exchange (JSE), as it was then called (Cargill 2010: 10–11).

Then, however, came the Asian crisis of 1998. Prime interest rates rose to 23 per cent, while share prices on the JSE dropped sharply, making debt repayments earlier financed by dividend payments and rising share prices unaffordable. Many BEE deals were now under water and a number of them collapsed, leaving the banks which had financed the transactions holding shares worth less than the amount owing to them. Financial losses and acrimony followed, bringing an end to the first wave of BEE deals (Cargill 2010: 11).

The Asian contagion highlighted the key problem with BEE: that of funding. As Jenny Cargill (a BEE consultant who was earlier a strong proponent of empowerment) writes in her book *Trick or Treat*, the policy at first seemed to offer black South Africans 'the opportunity to accumulate what they had long been denied – the capital necessary to leave the economic ghettos created by apartheid and influence the destiny of the First World economy' (Cargill 2010: 10). However, once bad times struck, the truth of a warning earlier sounded by Laurie Dippenaar, chief executive of FirstRand Bank, came strongly to the fore: 'Trying to sell equity to those with no capital is like building a house from the fifth floor up' (quoted in Cargill 2010: 46–7).

A shift to statute and codes

Despite the major funding obstacle, the black elite continued to seek ways to give fresh impetus to BEE. In 1998 it formed the Black Economic Empowerment Commission (BEECom) which spent three years drafting a comprehensive BEE framework. The Commission's report, published in 2001, drew heavily on Malaysia's New Economic Policy and sought a comprehensive blueprint for BEE aimed at giving black South Africans a major stake in the economy.

However, it was not until 2003 that the Broad-Based Black Economic Empowerment Act was adopted. The 2003 Act did little more than set out a basic framework for BEE. However, it also made clear that its provisions were to be supplemented by ministerial codes of good practice, which were to have the same force in law as the statute itself. An initial draft of the codes was published in 2004, but it was not until February 2007 that the codes were gazetted, and not until August 2008 that they came into force (*The Citizen* 1 September 2008).

The codes set out seven different elements of BEE. Large companies, defined as those with annual turnover exceeding R35 million, are expected to comply with all seven. Smaller companies – defined as those with an annual turnover of between R5 million and R35 million – may choose four out of the seven to pursue. Micro businesses, with turnover of less than R5 million, are officially exempt. However, many companies with turnover of R35 million a year are effectively small businesses which cannot easily shoulder empowerment obligations (Cargill 2010: 200–1).

The codes assume that the BEE can be reduced to a series of simple numerical targets, and that performance against these targets can be measured by accredited verification agencies applying uniform methodologies for accurate and comparable outcomes. In fact, however:

- The rules are so complex and vague that they have (in the words of BEE analyst Reg Rumney) 'created a whole new industry of interpreters and soothsayers' with diverse views as to their meaning (*Mail & Guardian* 24 August 2007).

- No common standards of measurement apply within the mushrooming verification agencies mandated to score BEE performance against the requirements of the codes; while measuring BEE performance is more complex and more demanding than anything the National Party government attempted, for the current rules require the racial identification not only of people but also of money and shares while providing no rules as to how this should be done (South African Institute of Race Relations, *2007/08 Annual Report*: 24).

Element 1: Ownership

The BEE scorecard allows companies to score 20 points out of a possible 100 for the transfer within ten years of 25 per cent of their equity or assets to BEE investors. In practice, the transfer of ownership has predominated over all other empowerment endeavours until recently.

The emphasis on ownership arose partly from procurement rules but also from the expectation that 25 per cent black ownership would give black shareholders substantial control over corporate decision-making, resulting in a greater emphasis on transformation. In practice, however, in the modern corporate world, most minority shareholders have little influence on operational decisions and BEE shareholders are no exception – especially as the 25 per cent shareholding is often spread among a number of individuals and entities who have diverse interests and rarely act in concert (Cargill 2010: 62–3).

BEE ownership deals have also been greatly complicated by the challenge of how to finance them. Having burned their fingers in the first wave of BEE deals before the Asian crisis of 1998, banks now generally insist on the vendor company providing guarantees. Since BEE investors lack the capital to buy at market value, most vendor companies also provide discounts of between 20 and 30 per cent on the full market price (Cargill 2010: 41). Deals are commonly structured over ten years, during which dividends are expected to cover both the interest on the loans and, over time, a substantial portion of the capital as well. Hence, BEE investors are generally 'locked in' to their transactions for this ten-year period and prohibited or constrained from selling their shares within this time (Cargill 2010: 47).

The idea is to prevent BEE investors cashing in their shares, as this would leave the vendor company without BEE ownership and needing to conclude fresh empowerment deals to regain ownership points. However, many BEE investors complain about lock-in clauses, saying these are discriminatory (white investors are not subject to them), reduce the value of their shares by restricting their marketability, and prevent them avoiding losses when share prices drop precipitously, as happened in the 2008/2009 global financial crisis (Cargill 2010: 47).

In addition, even if a company performs well over the ten-year period and is able to pay the BEE investor substantial dividends, these payments are unlikely to cover the repayment of both interest and capital. In practice, as a financial model drawn up by Cargill shows, the BEE investor is likely, at the end of a ten-year lock-in period, to have to sell off 60 per cent of his shareholding to pay off his remaining debt. This would leave him with a 10 per cent equity interest at the end of the day (Cargill 2010: 43).

However, if BEE investors are ultimately left with a mere 10 per cent of equity after ten years, this is sure to raise criticisms that BEE is proving meaningless and will never give black South Africans the economic power they deserve. This could lead to political pressure for the ownership target to be raised from 25 per cent to something significantly higher (Cargill 2010: 43).

Further conundrums arise from the fact that listed companies on the JSE are mostly owned by pension funds (in which black South Africans already hold substantial stakes) and foreign shareholders. The codes attempt to deal with this by providing that 15 per cent of a 25 per cent BEE shareholding must be owned directly by black people, while 10 per cent may be indirectly owned by institutions such as pension funds, via 'mandated investments'. The codes also allow state-owned shares, along with the 'foreign operations' of South African businesses (*Financial Mail* 10 September 2010), to be excluded in calculating the proportion of equity needing to be transferred to BEE investors. However, the application of these rules remains contested, with the result that different studies have yielded very different measures of the extent of black equity ownership (Cargill 2010; Solidarity 2010 (b)). Cargill, for example, includes 'low' and 'high' assessments of the total black share of JSE corporate wealth (excluding foreign shareholdings), which ranges from 37.5 per cent to 63.75 per cent in 2008/2009 (Cargill 2010: 204).

The JSE thus commissioned a study of black ownership of listed firms, which focused on South Africa's top 100 companies (which together account for 85 per cent of the JSE's overall market capitalisation of R5.7 trillion). The study, released in September 2010, put direct black ownership of these companies at 8 per cent, valued at R460 billion. However, when mandated investments (pension funds), state-held shares, and foreign operations were excluded, as the codes allow, the black ownership figure amounted to 18 per cent of the available share capital. In addition, if shares in foreign ownership were excluded, then the black shareholding amounted to 36 per cent of the share capital available (*Business Day* 2 September 2010; *Financial Mail* 10 September 2010). On this basis, the BEE ownership target of 25 per cent had already been more than met.

However, this interpretation was rejected by BEE proponents such as Empowerdex, a BEE rating agency. According to Empowerdex, the JSE research overstated the extent of black ownership by excluding the debt underpinning most JSE deals. Once this was taken into account, only 1.8 per cent of the JSE was black-owned, it said (*Financial Mail* 10 September 2010).

BEE ownership deals have made a small number of beneficiaries – mostly individuals with close ties to the ruling party – extremely wealthy, but have brought few benefits to most black South Africans. In addition, the amount of capital allocated to BEE deals since 1994 has been enormous.

The full value of BEE deals cannot be quantified, as many transactions involving unlisted companies have not been disclosed. Figures which are available put the value of the BEE deals concluded in the past decade at somewhere between R550–R600 billion. To put this in perspective, the government has spent a much lower sum of R87 billion on housing and land reform over the same period (Cargill 2010: 205).

How much capital still needs to be allocated to BEE deals to bring black ownership up to the 25 per cent mark also remains uncertain. On the Empowerdex view that black ownership of the top 100 public companies remains at less than 2 per cent, the value of the BEE deals still needing to be done could be as high as R700 billion (Cargill 2010: 59). On this basis the price tag for BEE ownership transactions could rise to R1,300 billion by 2017.

Elements 2 and 3: Management control and employment equity

The codes regard management control and employment equity as two separate elements and set out different targets and points for both. Ten points can be gained for management control if black people make up 50 per cent of the board and 50 per cent of executive directors, while also holding 40 per cent of top and senior management posts. Full marks can be scored only if companies also have a significant proportion of black women among their executive directors (Cargill 2010: 235, 239; 2008/2009 *South Africa Survey*: 340).

A further 15 points can be gained for meeting employment equity targets requiring black representation to rise to:

- 43 per cent at top management level by 2012 and 60 per cent by 2017;
- 63 per cent at middle management level by 2012 and 75 per cent by 2017, and;
- 68 per cent at junior management level by 2012 and 80 per cent by 2017 (Jeffery 2010 (a): 275).

In practice, both of these two elements of BEE are governed by the Employment Equity Act. As noted, this requires demographic representivity at every tier, including management and the board of directors, but is difficult to implement because of the skills shortage.

Element 4: Skills development

Firms can also score 15 points for skills development. Most employers already pay a levy amounting to 1 per cent of payroll for a bureaucratic and ineffective system of on-the-job training introduced in 1998. Under the codes, companies must now contribute an additional 3 per cent of payroll for skills development for black staff in order to qualify for these additional BEE points (2008/2009 *South Africa Survey*: 340).

Since on-the-job training offers more value to business than equity transfers, the gazetting of the codes in 2007 prompted many companies to shift attention away from the ownership element towards skills development (*Business Day* 25

April 2007). However, despite the additional monies being put into the training of black employees, overcoming the skills shortage is no easy task.

Before 1994 South Africa's education system was not only racially segregated but also discriminated against black people in general and Africans in particular. Since the political transition, legal segregation has been terminated and the earlier gap in per capita expenditure on white and black pupils has been eliminated, if not reversed. However, despite these important gains, the schooling system has been undermined by poor teaching and the introduction in 1996 of a badly conceived system of outcomes-based education (OBE). As a result, some 80 per cent of public schools are currently dysfunctional (Jeffery 2010 (a): 331; 2009/2010 *South Africa Survey*: 418).

The schooling system has become so bad that more than half of those matriculating from public schools in recent years have been functionally illiterate and innumerate (*Business Day* 7 January 2011). Moreover, though the BEE assumes that employers can overcome the skills deficit through on-the-job training, there are important limits as to what such instruction can achieve when basic schooling is so poor.

Element 5: Preferential procurement

Twenty points out of 100 can be scored for preferential procurement: for buying goods and services from suppliers which themselves have good BEE scores (Cargill 2010: 59). The codes make it clear that, the better the BEE score of the supplier, the more BEE points a company can earn for every rand it spends with that supplier. If the company, for instance, procures goods from a 'level one' BEE supplier (one which has a score of 100 per cent under the codes), then every rand which that company spends with that supplier counts as R1.35 in calculating its BEE procurement spend (*Business Report* 5 February 2007).

Procurement obligations are intended to have a 'cascade' effect throughout the economy. Big firms seeking to do business with the state will insist on good BEE scores from their suppliers, who in turn will insist on such scores from the smaller companies from which they buy goods and services, and so on down the procurement pipeline. The compliance targets set by the codes for preferential procurement are ambitious, requiring that BEE procurement should rise to 50 per cent of total procurement within five years and to 70 per cent of such procurement within ten years (2008/2009 *South Africa Survey*: 341). According to Rumney, 'preferential procurement is thus the sharpest tool in government's transformation armoury' (*Mail & Guardian* 24 August 2007).

Controversy has, however, arisen over the contradiction between the 2000 Act and the much broader ambit of the codes. The key difference is that the 2000 Act entitles the state to give procurement preferences on the basis of black ownership alone, whereas the BEE codes provide six other criteria for measuring empowerment. The 2000 legislation thus reflects a 'narrow' approach to empowerment, while the BEE codes are broader in their focus (*Finweek* 11 December 2008).

Regulations amending the 2000 Act and requiring a more broad-based approach to state procurement have now been gazetted. In the interim, the government has taken further steps to help small black business win state contracts. Under these rules, approved in November 2007, national and provincial government departments are obliged to spend 85 per cent of their budgets, in ten listed spheres, with small and micro enterprises. The ten spheres in issue include advertising, maintenance, and cleaning services, along with clothing, computer equipment, furniture, and office space (*Business Day* 9 November 2007).

Element 6: Enterprise development

Fifteen points out of 100 can be obtained for spending 3 per cent of net after-tax profit on developing businesses which are 25 per cent black-owned or more. This contribution can be either in cash or via mentoring and secondments. However, as Cargill notes, staff secondments and other forms of training also entail costs (Cargill 2010: 59–60).

Available figures suggest that firms may have to contribute R9 billion every year to enterprise development, which is an enormous sum. Comments Cargill (2010: 60):

> To see the scale of the task, consider the fact that it took the [state-funded] National Empowerment Fund five years to disburse R1 billion of lending [to small black businesses] up to 2009. Anglo American's small business initiative, Anglo Zimele, invested some R300m over a 15-year period to 2008.... So it's not easy to spend large amounts of money on effective enterprise development. As Anglo Zimele's Nick van Rensburg emphasises: 'You can't just create a business without a market. If the market is not there to service all that enterprise development money, then what?'

The codes also overlook many other obstacles to the success of small businesses in South Africa, among them:

- crippling shortages of skills;
- high levels of armed robbery and other crimes;
- poor transport and infrastructure, and;
- the overall regulatory burden on small business, to which BEE now adds (Jeffery 2010 (a): 305–15).

Unless all these major challenges can be overcome, the R9 billion or so required for enterprise development every year is likely to be wasted.

Element 7: Socio-economic development

The seventh element, for which five points can be claimed, is socio-economic development. This requires business to devote 1 per cent of net after-tax profits to socio-economic projects approved by the state. This aspect of the codes is pressurising companies to move away from traditional forms of corporate social investment (CSI) to brick-and-mortar projects within the scope of what government officials are likely to approve.

Such initiatives are no longer CSI, for they are neither voluntary nor philanthropic in intent. Instead, the aim for most firms is simply to score additional BEE points, irrespective of the dangers of corporate giving (as one commentator has put it) 'becoming part of a patronage system tied to politicians' (Jeffery 2010 (a): 401).

Verification industry

One of the immediate consequences of BEE has been the growth of the 'verification industry' of BEE ratings agencies mandated to score the performance of companies against the requirements of the codes. In the early 2000s, there were only three or four ratings agencies, of which Empowerdex was one of the first (*Business Report* 24 August 2008). After the first draft of the codes was released in 2004, the number of ratings agencies rapidly increased. A key difficulty was that there were no common standards for assessing BEE status and that different ratings agencies applied different criteria.

To overcome this problem, the Department of Trade and Industry (DTI) established the South African National Accreditation System (Sanas) to develop a set of accreditation criteria by which would-be ratings agencies would be assessed. In July 2008 the DTI also gazetted a verification manual, which then became legally binding on verification agencies and was supposed to introduce uniformity in ratings procedures (*Business Report* 24 August 2008). But in January 2010 it was evident that verification agencies were still applying different interpretations of the BEE rules. Said Keith Levenstein, chief executive of EconoBEE Consulting: 'Every verification agency has a different interpretation of the codes, every consultant has a different viewpoint'; he urged Rob Davies, Minister of Trade and Industry, to 'appoint a BEE adjudicator to give rulings on interpretations that would be binding on all verification agencies' (EconoBEE, *Newsletter*, 13 January 2010). Different agencies were producing BEE certificates that differed by up to 15 points and companies were now shopping around for the verification agency likely to give them the highest score.

In August 2009 firms were barred from conducting self-assessments of their BEE status, with the DTI announcing that 'only certificates from accredited BEE verification agencies would be accepted as valid' (*Business Day* 20 April 2009). However, very few ratings agencies had yet been accredited by Sanas. Some six months later, in February 2010, only 26 agencies had been accredited to carry out the annual BEE assessments required by an estimated 500,000 firms. In addition, verification agencies were battling to find the skills required and often had to rely on whites to do the job. Verification was also expensive, costing about R150,000–R300,000 for a large company and sometimes taking as long as three months (*Business Report* 6 Aug 2009). Verification costs are also likely to increase, given the magnitude and complexity of the process and the imbalance between the demand for verification and the supply of agencies accredited to undertake this task.

Compliance with the codes

After the codes were gazetted in 2007, the Presidential Black Business Group commissioned a survey of more than 2000 companies to establish a baseline of BEE compliance. This survey was conducted by the University of Pretoria Business Enterprise Unit and examined the performance of 1,700 companies on the seven BEE elements. The research showed that compliance levels were low.

According to this report, four in ten companies had no BEE plan and had made no progress towards drawing one up, while only two in ten companies had an approved plan. The study reported that there was 78.2 per cent non-compliance across the seven elements of the codes, and that levels of compliance were as follows:

- on ownership, only 17.9 per cent of firms were compliant and 74.8 per cent were not;
- on management control, figures were 8.5 per cent and 80.5 per cent;
- on employment equity, the figures were 11.6 per cent and 60.3 per cent;
- on skills development, they were 11.8 per cent and 82.8 per cent;
- on preferential procurement, they were 6.7 per cent and 85.4 per cent;
- on enterprise development, they were 5.6 per cent and 83.9 per cent;
- on socio economic development, they were 6.2 per cent and 80 per cent (*Business Report* 6 August 2007; *FinWeek* 30 August 2007).

However, this report was at odds with other BEE assessments, including one conducted in the same year by KPMG, an auditing firm. KPMG has continued to track BEE compliance every year and its most recent survey, released in September 2010, shows:

- average scores for both ownership and preferential procurement were 11.8, against a target of 20;
- the average score for management control was four points, against a target of ten;
- most firms scored poorly on employment equity (fewer than seven points against a target of 15);
- the average score for skills development was seven points (against a target of 15);
- most firms scored around 11 points for enterprise development (against a target of 15), and;
- the average score for socio-economic development was 3.7, against a target of five (KPMG 2010).

BEE in the mining sector

The South African mining sector is the fifth largest in the world and is vital to the country's economy. It contributes 9.6 per cent to GDP,[3] while its exports of primary and beneficiated products account for more than 50 per cent of South Africa's merchandise exports. In addition, the industry provides about one million jobs on which some ten million people rely (*Sunday Times* 26 July 2009). The sector's economic predominance – coupled with limited black ownership or control of it – has made it a prime target of empowerment policies.

In the apartheid era, two-thirds of mineral rights were privately owned. These private rights were of unlimited duration and could freely be sold or used as collateral. By contrast, the Mineral and Petroleum Resources Development Act (MPRDA) of 2002 (which became operative on 1 May 2004) makes the state 'the custodian' of all mineral rights. It also requires mining companies to apply for the conversion of their 'old order' mining rights into 'new order' rights (Jeffery 2010 (a): 284).

Conversion is contingent on compliance with extensive BEE requirements and the lodging with the Department of Mineral Resources (DMR) of suitable 'social and labour plans'. Mining companies were required to transfer 15 per cent of their assets or equity to BEE partners within five years in order to convert their old order rights, and must have 26 per cent BEE ownership by 2014 if they are to retain those converted rights. An estimate of the cost of transferring the initial 15 per cent was put at around R100 billion, of which empowerment partners are unlikely to have contributed more than a small portion, leaving the balance to be financed through debt. Despite the shortage of skills, mining companies are also expected to ensure that 40 per cent of management posts are held by black people by 2014 (Jeffery 2008: 2; Cargill 2010: 96).

Many of the criteria for conversion are vaguely phrased, allowing great scope for ministerial discretion in deciding whether the requirements have been met. According to Peter Leon, an expert on the country's mining laws, the discretionary element makes for a 'very unpredictable regulatory environment'. In 2007 the government pledged to reform the MPRDA by reducing discretionary powers and making the relevant rules more certain, but nothing came of this undertaking (*Financial Mail* 26 January 2007).

Instead, the government in 2009 gazetted a code of good practice requiring that mining assets transferred to BEE partners should no longer be encumbered by debt within two years. This suggests that mining firms will virtually have to give away equity or face the risk of losing their mining rights. In Cargill's words, 'this catapults investment risk in South African mining into the stratosphere' (Cargill 2010: 45). Following the mining sector's objections, the code is currently on hold, as is an amendment Act adopted in 2008 (but not yet implemented) which gives the Minister of Mineral Resources still greater discretionary power to impose new conditions on mining companies for the benefit of local communities (Jeffery 2010 (c): 13).

Meanwhile, unhappiness has grown with the application of the existing rules. Particularly damaging has been the DMR's system for publicising applications made for rights, for this has consisted of physically pinning notices on public boards, from which they can easily be removed. Notes Cargill: 'This has enormous significance since applications are supposed to be processed on a first-come, first-served basis. If a notice goes "missing", where is the proof of who applied first?' (Cargill 2010: 93, 97–8).

Negotiations between mining houses and DMR officials are often protracted and difficult, causing further frustration. As Cargill writes: 'DMR officials ... regularly reject proposals submitted by mining companies, which get worn down by the repeated revisions required of them', especially in compiling their social and labour plans (Cargill 2010: 100). The DMR also lacks the capacity to deal with the volume of applications being received (some 20,000 in the 2008/2009 financial year, for example). Hence, delays commonly run to 18 months, while some applications have taken up to five years to process (Leon 2010: 7).

In practice, the licencing system has encouraged rent-seeking behaviour, partly because rights are allocated to individuals with no demonstrable capacity for productive mining. In addition, the rights allocated are often not commercially viable in themselves, having value only as part of a larger base of reserves. In one instance DMR officials approved part of a mining company's applications for the conversion of its rights, but gave the other rights in issue to a number of unknown BEE groups. These groups, in Cargill's words, thus acquired 'patches of reserves', which fell within the midst of the mining company's much bigger holding and were too small to be commercially viable on their own (Cargill 2010: 98–9). These small reserves had no value for the BEE partners except to trade with the mining company which needed them.

Recent attempts to snatch mining rights from two major companies – the South Africa iron ore mining company Kumba Resources and the international conglomerate, Lonmin – have added to local and international concerns. In both cases, valuable prospecting rights were allocated to BEE 'shelf' companies with tainted applications and no mining experience, but with good political connections (Leon 2010: 7–13).

Though reforms have again been promised (*Business Report* 16 November 2010), the overall result has been a sharp decline in South Africa's ranking on the Fraser Institute's international policy potential index, which measures the attractiveness to investors of different mining countries. In the 2002/2003 Fraser survey, before the MPRDA came into effect, South Africa ranked at 27 out of 47 countries. By the time of the 2009/2010 Fraser survey, South Africa had fallen to a ranking of 61 out of 72 countries. Its ranking was the third worst on the African continent, placing it only above the Democratic Republic of Congo and Zimbabwe, both of which are widely regarded as failed states (Leon 2010: 3).

Investment in the mining industry in South Africa has also fallen significantly since the MPRDA was adopted – and this in the face of an extraordinary global commodities boom (Johnson 2009: 413). While the boom generated 5 per cent annual growth in the global mining industry between 2001 and 2008, in South

Africa the mining sector, in real 2005 rand terms, shrank from R103 billion in 1993 to R92 billion in 2009. By contrast, if the mining sector had managed to match growth in the South African economy as a whole (of some 3.3 per cent between 1993–2009) its value in 2009 would have been R173 billion, 87 per cent more than the R92 billion it was in fact worth (*Sunday Times* 12 September 2010).

BEE and the regulatory environment are not solely to blame for the lack of growth in the mining sector. Other relevant factors include the skills shortage, concerns about the supply and cost of electricity, and the country's inadequate rail networks and ports (*Sunday Times* 12 September 2010). But in the face of all these obstacles – sufficient in themselves to deter investment – the regulatory environment needs to be as enticing as possible, rather than the opposite.

BEE deals in the mining sector have been very costly, yet have failed to bring about the desired shift in equity ownership. Although an estimated R280 billion has been allocated to BEE mining deals over the past decade, a government review put the proportion of equity in black ownership at a mere 9 per cent in August 2010 (*Business Day* 14 and 15 September 2010). Mining Minister Susan Shabangu criticised this poor performance, saying it stood in sharp contrast to the mining charter's target of 15 per cent black ownership by March 2009 (*Sunday Times* 12 September 2010). The Minister's review of the mining charter also showed that the mining industry had generally failed to fulfil interim targets for employment equity, procurement, and skills development, along with other social and labour obligations. In September 2010 Shabangu gazetted a revised charter which explicitly gives her the right to cancel mining and prospecting rights for failure to fill targets in any of these spheres (*Business Day* 14 September 2010).

Costs of affirmative action and BEE

The BEE is so ambitious a programme of affirmative action that its costs and consequences are difficult to measure or foresee in full. For present purposes the analysis is confined to four key issues:

- growth of the black middle class;
- direct and indirect economic costs of BEE;
- role of BEE in fuelling corruption, and;
- impact of BEE on race relations in South Africa.

Growth of the black middle class

Affirmative action and BEE have had symbolic benefit in quickening the advance of black South Africans into the highest levels in business, the media, universities, and elsewhere. They have also had economic benefit in helping to stimulate the growth of a black middle class. According to the Unilever Institute at the University of Cape Town, in 2007 there were 2.6 million Africans in what it termed the 'black diamond' class, while the spending power of this class had grown to R180 billion. By November 2008 the black diamond class had grown further to three million people, while its spending power had surged to R250 billion. However, the Unilever Institute's definition of middle class status has been criticised for being too broad, for the organisation includes within the black diamond group civil servants earning in the region of some R5,000 a month. Such individuals arguably have neither the means nor the political independence to count as part of the middle class.[4]

Lawrence Schlemmer, a renowned social scientist, has adopted a different definition of the middle class. In his perspective, the 'core' or 'established' middle class is limited to individuals living in households earning at least R12,000 a month (subsequently adjusted for inflation to R16,700 a month) and falling within the two highest living standards measures (LSM categories nine and 10, as computed in annual All Media and Products Surveys (AMPS).[5]

Applying this definition, there were 185,000 adult Africans within the 'core' middle class in 2004, while Africans made up 11 per cent of the total core middle class of all races. By 2006 the number of adult Africans within the 'core' category had risen to 322,000, equal to 15 per cent of the total core middle class. By 2007 it had increased again to 454,000 (20 per cent of the total core middle class), and in 2009 it was up again at 788,000 (31 per cent of the core middle class). Notes Schlemmer:

> These figures show that the growth of the core black middle class has been phenomenal. The 2008/09 economic slowdown has brought the growth rate down from a stupendous 40 per cent+ in 2006–2007 to 32 per cent since 2008, but the growth is still setting world records for the expansion of a newly emerged middle class.[6]

A genuine middle class relies on skills, hard work, and entrepreneurial flair for its rising wealth. But BEE negates the need for such efforts, generating 'crony' capitalists whose ticket to success lies almost solely in their political connections. According to Moeletsi Mbeki (brother to former President Thabo Mbeki), BEE 'strikes a fatal blow against black entrepreneurship by creating a small class of unproductive but wealthy black crony capitalists made up of ANC politicians' (*The Citizen* 21 September 2009).

In addition, many in the 'black diamond' class are now battling to pay down debt. Says John Simpson of the Unilever Institute (*Business Day* 11 March 2011):

> After 100 golden months of undisturbed growth, the wheels came off towards the end of 2007.... Many black diamonds remain under pressure and highly vulnerable to shocks.... [In fact] many are in a worse position than they were in 1995.

The spending power of black diamonds, which had reached an estimated high of R250 billion in 2008, was thus put at R237 billion in 2010.

Direct and indirect economic costs

The limited transfer of equity ownership that has occurred thus far has involved huge amounts of capital. The value of BEE transactions has risen to some R600 billion and could rise by another R700 billion. Yet it remains unclear what advantage society is gaining from this massive diversion of scarce capital from productive investment to BEE deals. In 2005, well before the value of BEE deals was known to have risen so high, an ANC discussion document raised concerns about BEE spending, saying: 'The financing of BEE deals that do not necessarily raise productive investment levels in the domestic economy is a drain on scarce capital assets and will impact on the medium-term investment level in the country' (South African Institute of Race Relations, *2004/2005 Annual Report*: 21). The document expressed concern that this was making it more difficult to raise the growth rate, create jobs, and reduce poverty.

Such concerns are now more salient than ever. The government is finding it difficult to raise the R850 billion it plans to spend on expanding essential infrastructure over the next three years. An annual GDP growth rate of some 6 per cent a year is urgently needed to conquer unemployment and alleviate poverty, but the economy cannot grow at more than a modest 3 per cent a year without, at minimum, more efficient transport and communications and much greater security of energy supply.

Indirect costs are hard to quantify but are likely to outstrip direct costs by a significant margin. For one thing, BEE has clearly deterred direct investment in the crucial mining sector and encouraged South Africa's major mining firms to focus on expanding operations abroad. BEE has also limited the further foreign direct investment (FDI) the country might otherwise have attracted. Since businesses which decided to bypass South Africa do not advertise such decisions, neither the government nor its citizens are ever likely to know the full extent of the FDI that has been jeopardised (*Business Day* 29 June 2004). BEE thus involves a chase for the wrong numbers. In 2004, for instance, the value of BEE deals concluded was roughly R53 billion, while the FDI that year was less than R4 billion. This pattern – in which the value of BEE deals far outstrips FDI – has remained largely unchanged (2007/2008 *South Africa Survey*: 291).

The efficiency costs of BEE are also significant. Affirmative action has helped fuel the emigration of perhaps a million whites, adding to the skills shortage (Jeffery 2010 (a): 183). Given the extent of the skills deficit, the demand for rapid affirmative action in employment has also lowered average competency. In the public sector this has impeded capacity to maintain or expand essential infrastructure and services. In the local government sphere, where the skills base has always been more limited, an insistence on demographic representivity has contributed to complete dysfunctionality.

Within the private sector BEE is eroding the country's limited international competitiveness, if only by undermining productivity and adding to unit costs. South Africa – despite the many strengths of its economy – is slipping down the rankings on various global measures. It has lost significant ground on the 'ease of doing business' monitor of the International Finance Corporation, as well as on the Global Competitiveness Scoreboard of the Institute for Management Development in Switzerland (Jeffery 2010 (a): 279).

One of the greatest indirect costs of BEE is that entrepreneurship is being eroded in favour of crony capitalism, making South Africa increasingly uncompetitive. It will also encourage a victim mentality, increase dependency on the state, undermine self-reliance and promote a debilitating belief that 'Pretoria must provide'. Moreover, from crony capitalism it is but a short step to corruption – and this phenomenon is already clearly visible.

BEE and corruption

Though BEE and corruption grew in tandem, it was not until 2006 – when Jacob Zuma and his allies were mobilising to oust Thabo Mbeki from the ANC and national presidency – that media attention began to focus strongly on this issue. In 2006, as the campaign against Mbeki intensified, Zuma allies began repeatedly stressing that the 'comprador and parasitic nature of the emerging BEE elite' was diverting the ANC's attention away from the needs of its core constituency: the working class and the jobless poor (*Bua Komanisi!* 2006: 24).

In 2007 Kgalema Motlanthe, then secretary general of the ANC (and a Zuma ally), publicly acknowledged that BEE was fuelling corruption at all tiers of government. In an interview with the *Financial Mail*, Motlanthe said: 'Almost every project is conceived because it offers opportunities for certain people to make money. A great deal of the ANC's problems are occasioned by this' (*Financial Mail* 19 January 2007).

After Mbeki was ousted as ANC president and replaced by Zuma, the new ANC secretary general Gwede Mantashe said the shift in power had been 'the salvation of the ANC' and would mark a new era of rectitude and competence in governance (*Business Day* 28 August 2009). But the Zuma administration has done little to end corruption or review the role of BEE in promoting it (*Sunday Times* 1 November 2009).

Instead, the ANC has continued to draw benefit from what many people regard as corrupt empowerment deals. This is evident in BEE transactions involving Chancellor House, a company established to help fund the ruling party (*Business Day* 20 March 2007). The ANC has reportedly used its control over state tenders to award Chancellor House lucrative contracts in various spheres, including energy, engineering, logistics, and information technology. Profits from these contracts flow back to the ANC, helping it to gain a substantial financial edge over its political rivals (*Business Day* 23 March 2007).

In addition, in 2007 Chancellor House was awarded rights to mine manganese in the Kalahari that have an estimated value of some US$1 billion. This award meant that the ANC, having enacted legislation vesting custodianship of all mineral wealth in the state, was now using these new mining rules for its own financial and party-political advantage (*Business Day* 23 March 2007). Chancellor House also has a 25 per cent interest in Hitachi Power Africa, a subsidiary of

Hitachi Power Europe, which has recently secured two Eskom contracts, valued at almost R40 billion, to supply steam generators to two new coal-fired power stations. The second contract did not go out to tender (Cargill 2010: 94). The ANC stands to gain at least R1 billion from these contracts, giving it a level of funding which no opposition party can begin to match (*Business Day* 25 January 2010).

Impact on racial goodwill

The impact of affirmative action and BEE on racial goodwill is difficult to assess. Despite Afrikaner anger at being pushed out of civil service, whites have demonstrated little resentment over affirmative action or BEE. The issue came sharply to the fore in 2005 when the vice-chancellor of the University of KwaZulu-Natal, Malegapuru Makgoba, wrote that white South African males exhibited symptoms of the 'dethroned male baboon', being 'depressed, quarrelsome, and a spoiler of the new order' (South African Institute of Race Relations, *2001/02 Annual Report*: 24–5). However, the most striking thing about this statement is not so much its racial invective (for which any white vice-chancellor would have been dismissed) but rather its inaccuracy.

Contrary to Makgoba's allegation, white South Africans have proved remarkably willing to accept the new order. The former National Party, having embarked on political liberalisation in 1990, merged with the ANC a decade later. Business has not only embraced the new government but has also spent billions on transformation and BEE. Policies damaging to white interests, ranging from land reform to the expropriation of common law water and mining rights and a steady attrition in Afrikaans-medium schools and universities, have also been accepted without significant demur (*Business Day* 7 April 2005). At the same time, the existence of race-based policies such as affirmative action, with their focus on racial classification and racial inequalities, has provided a potent platform for senior figures in the government and the ruling party to condemn whites for their allegedly racist failure to transform quickly enough.

Affirmative action and BEE have also undermined black achievement by making it difficult to distinguish between people who have reached their positions on merit and those who have been put in them to fill quotas. Many black South Africans have 'made it' despite present or past racial policies, but are lumped with those who have achieved success through racial preferencing. The result has been to strengthen the racist argument that black success arises mainly from affirmative action (Botsis 2007: 3).

However, despite affirmative action and BEE with their focus on racial identity and preference, racial goodwill seems to have grown since 1994. This has been encouraged by greater social mixing, the integration of schools and suburbs, the expansion of a mixed race middle class with many common interests, and a general acceptance by whites of the need for appropriate remedial measures to help undo apartheid's legacy. In addition, the Zuma administration has not used the race card in the same way as Mbeki did. There nevertheless remains a danger of racial scapegoating, and the temptation to resort to this may increase in tandem with growing public anger over the ANC's failure to deliver 'the better life for all' that the ruling party has been promising since 1994.

Conclusion

South Africa's wide-ranging system of affirmative action and BEE has been enacted into law by a government with strong electoral support. The Commission for Employment Equity assumes this translates into strong support for affirmative action as well,[7] but this is unclear. Opinion surveys conducted by an independent institution, the Helen Suzman Foundation, before and after the Employment Equity Act took effect in 1999, show 75 per cent support for merit-based appointments among all population groups, including blacks. Among the African respondents canvassed by the Foundation, only 13 per cent endorsed the Act's view that black people should be given preferences in employment until demographic representivity at all levels had been reached (Jeffery 2010 (a): 170–1).

However, an opinion survey carried out in 2009 by the Human Sciences Research Council, a government-funded institution, puts grassroots support for affirmative action at 64 per cent: roughly the same as the ANC's parliamentary majority.[8] More independent surveys are needed to probe the true extent of public support for affirmative action and BEE, especially now that the costs and negative consequences of these policies are becoming more apparent.

Affirmative action and BEE have clearly had symbolic and economic benefit in boosting the expansion of the black middle class and increasing black spending power (at least until the recent global downturn).[9] These developments have further reduced black:white inequality, giving greater impetus to a long-term trend of diminishing racial disparities which has been evident since 1970 (Jeffery 2010 (a): 184–5).

However, the rapid advancement of the black middle class, together with a rise in unemployment among the unskilled African majority, has led to growing income inequality within the African population. Among Africans, the Gini coefficient, which measures income inequality, has increased from 0.54 in 1996 to 0.6 in 2009, an increase of 11 per cent (2009/2010 *South Africa Survey*: 251).

Surprisingly, though horizontal affirmative action programmes in other countries have stirred great animosity across ethnic lines, South Africa's pervasive system of racial preferencing has not yet had this effect. In general, white South Africans have acquiesced in affirmative action and empowerment policies. This is partly out of guilt over apartheid, partly because of the obvious need to expand and 'blacken' the middle class, partly out of hope that increased black participation in private companies will build popular support for capitalism, and partly because higher rates of economic growth since 1994 have in any event brought about a general increase in the living standards of the white minority (2009/2010 *South Africa Survey*: 258). Since 2007, however, an increasing number of white and black commentators have expressed great concern over four consequences, in particular, of affirmative action and BEE policies:

- massive loss of skills, institutional memory, and efficiency in local authorities and many national and provincial government departments;
- wasting of public revenues by inexperienced public servants and/or many of the BEE 'tenderpreneurs' to whom state contracts have been accorded;
- extent to which BEE has encouraged corruption within the new political elite, and;
- allocation of R600 billion and more to BEE ownership deals which have mostly benefited a tiny group of individuals with high political 'connectivity'.

The negative consequences of the Employment Equity Act and BEE have become increasingly apparent over the past decade. When these measures were first introduced, most commentators applauded them on the assumption that they would play a meaningful role in overcoming apartheid deficits. However, the climate of opinion has now changed. Many African journalists and other commentators now criticise these transformation laws. Cargill, formerly an ardent proponent of BEE, has doubts about its costs and the limited benefits it has generated, even for BEE investors. Moeletsi Mbeki remains scathing about the crony capitalism that BEE has spawned, while the Minister of Finance, Pravin Gordhan, said in November 2010 (*Business Report* 29 November 2010):

> South Africa's BEE policies, which were designed to improve black people's standards of living, have not worked. BEE policies did not make South Africa a fairer and more prosperous country. It led to a small elite group benefiting and that's not good enough in terms of benefiting 45m people.

In April 2010 President Zuma called for a review of BEE (*The Economist* 3 April 2010). In November 2010 Gordhan added: 'We need a very intense debate on how we create better opportunities for ordinary South Africans to participate in our economy' (*Business Report* 29 November 2010). This debate has yet to take place, while concern has not yet become strong enough to compel a rethink. Instead, the Employment Equity Act is likely to be tightened up, along with preferential procurement rules.

In the interim, the policies most urgently needed to overcome apartheid's legacies continue to be trumped by the ANC's determined pursuit of 'transformation'. Instead of embracing racial preferences for the benefit of the few, the government should be adopting race-neutral, vertical policies that have real prospects of empowering the poor and widening prosperity for all. What the poor need most are better skills, effective action against AIDS and other illnesses, better living conditions, and jobs. These gains are unlikely to be attained unless the ANC puts more emphasis on efficiency, competitiveness, improving public education and health care, and embracing the many other policy shifts required to boost economic growth.

Notes

1 See the 2000/2001 *South Africa Survey* (339, 59, 255); 2009/2010 *South Africa Survey* (375).
2 See the commentaries in *Business Report* 19 February, 29 April 2008, 27 August 2008; *FinWeek* 19 June 2008; *Business Day* 20 May 2008, 30 May 2008.
3 See Fast Facts July 2011, based on Statistics South Africa, *Statistical Release PO441*.
4 Botsis 2007: 3–11; Lawrence Schlemmer, e-mail communication to the author, 5 December 2009.
5 Schlemmer, e-mail, 5 December 2009.
6 Schlemmer, e-mail, 5 December 2009.
7 Commission for Employment Equity, *Annual Report 2008/09*: iv.
8 See 'Affirmative Action, South African Social Attitudes Survey' in *HSRC Review*, 8 (3), September 2010: 6.
9 Egan, P., UCT Unilever Institute, e-mail to the author, 29 January 2011.

References

'Affirmative Action, South African Social Attitudes Survey' in *HSRC Review*, 8 (3), September 2010.
Botsis, H., 2007, 'Drivers of and obstacles to the growth of the black middle class' in *Fast Facts*, September.
Bua Komanisi! 2006, Information bulletin of the central committee of the SACP, 5 (1), May, Special Edition.
Cargill, J., 2010, *Trick or Treat: Rethinking Black Economic Empowerment*, Johannesburg: Jacana Media.
Commission for Employment Equity, *9th CEE Annual Report* 2008/2009.
Commission for Employment Equity, *10th CEE Annual Report* 2009/2010.
Department of Labour, 1998, 'De-Mythifing the Employment Equity Bill', submission to the Portfolio Committee on Labour in the National Assembly, 21 July.
Horowitz, D.L., 1985, *Ethnic Groups in Conflict*, University of California Press, Berkeley, Los Angeles, London.
Jeffery, A., 1998, 'A wider net with mainly smaller holes' in *Fast Facts*, August.
Jeffery, A., 2008, 'Does the South African mining industry have a future?' in *Fast Facts*, February.
Jeffery, A., 2010 (a), *Chasing the Rainbow: South Africa's Move from Mandela to Zuma*, Johannesburg: South African Institute of Race Relations.
Jeffery, A., 2010 (b), 'Racial Goodwill' in *Fast Facts*, April.
Jeffery, A., 2010 (c), Scope for Free Enterprise in *Fast Facts*, May.
Jeffery, A., 2011, Employment Equity Amendment Bill, in *Fast Facts*, February.
Johnson, R.W., 2009, *South Africa's Brave New World: The Beloved Country since the End of Apartheid*, London and Johannesburg: Allen Lane
Kane-Berman, J., 1991, *South Africa's Silent Revolution*, 2nd edition, Johannesburg: South African Institute of Race Relations.
KPMG and IQuad, 2010, 'The Evolution of BEE Measurement: 2010 BEE Survey', KPMG, September.
Leon, P., 2010, 'Quo Vadis the South African mining industry?', address by Peter Leon to Miners from the Frontiers Conference, London, 1 September.
National Planning Commission, 2011, *Diagnostic Overview*, The Presidency, RSA, June.
P-E Corporate Services (SA) Pty Ltd, 2010, *P-E Human Resources Practitioners Handbook – South Africa – September 2010*.

Pienaar, D., 2000, 'South Africa's rich show their true colours' in *Fast Facts* June.
Solidarity, 2010 (a), 'The JSE and Insurance Ownership Report', *South African Transformation Monitor*.
Solidarity, 2010 (b), 'The Truth about the 10th Report from the CEE', 5 August.
South African Institute of Race Relations, 2001/02 *Annual Report*.
South African Institute of Race Relations, 2007/08 *Annual Report*.
South African Institute of Race Relations, *South Africa Survey* 2000/2001; 2002/2003; 2004/2005; 2007/2008; 2008/2009; 2009/2010.
Sowell, T., 1989, '"Affirmative Action": A Worldwide Disaster' in *Commentary*, 22.
Sowell, T., 2004, *Affirmative Action Around the World*, Yale New Haven and London: University Press.

Newspapers and magazines

Business Day
Business Report
The Citizen
Financial Mail
Finweek
Mail & Guardian
The Star
Sunday Times

6 Power-sharing, communal contestation, and equality

Affirmative action, identity, and conflict in Northern Ireland[1]

Colin Harvey

Introduction

Analysis of the conflict 'in and about Northern Ireland' tends to revolve around the complex and difficult relationships between Irish republicans/nationalists and British unionists/loyalists, the various ways in which perceptions of religious identity map onto these categories, and interactions with both the Irish and British states (Healing Through Remembering, 2006). Such a frame of reference is of necessity reductionist and limiting, when read in the context of contemporary debates on multiple and fluid identities. However, for the purposes of this chapter, the bi-national context is particularly instructive. The aim here is to use the example of Northern Ireland as a case study of the practical application of affirmative action[2] policies in the specific context of ethno-national division, and a society which has experienced – and is now emerging steadily from – the legacy of violent conflict. As the search for international and comparative lesson learning continues, this chapter probes how the development of affirmative action in the fair employment context in Northern Ireland ('contextualised equality'[3]) might be best understood, and sounds a note of caution about attempts to extrapolate more generally from this experience.

The conflict in Northern Ireland cost over 3,600 lives (in a region with a population of 1.5–1.6 million people during the period of the conflict, a figure now standing at over 1.8 million), and it has left a severe inter-communal legacy (NISRA, 2012; McGarry and O'Leary, 1996; Shirlow and Coulter, 2007). The problems of Northern Ireland are familiar ones, and it assists to frame them in international and comparative terms, but one of the arguments advanced is that this example of affirmative action must be viewed in its localised and contextual setting. The region provides a societal context where religious division (between Catholics and Protestants) maps onto broader conflicts over national and political identity (Irish and British). These are disputes between two national communities (British and Irish) that co-exist on the same territory and hold divergent national aspirations. This is a conflict where religious identification is a factor, but the principal sources of antagonism and contestation remain questions of *national* division between *two national communities*. Without being excessively narrow, there is a communal conflict sparked by contested sovereignty, societal domination and control, and rival conceptions and desires around national belonging; political mobilisation principally occurs through collective ethnonational identification. Nationalism, in multiple and diverse British and Irish guises, therefore continues to provide the basis for successful political mobilisation and formal alignment in Northern Ireland, and there is little sign that other formations are likely to emerge imminently (even if the political debate shifts significantly towards socio-economic and other 'normalised' governance agendas).[4]

This chapter will therefore sketch the context and history of Northern Ireland, with a view to offering background on the nature of the conflict, and then examine the directed and positive legal and policy measures which have been employed to address the legacy of inequality between the two main communities in substantive and institutional terms. The objective is to argue that Northern Ireland is an example of a particularised type of 'contextualised equality', and, on the basis that there may be some 'lessons' to be gleaned, probe what these might be. The tone and approach here, however, remains deliberately cautious and sceptical. The attempt to extract easily exportable models is commendably entrepreneurial and understandable, but there is good reason to tread carefully. Ultimately, it is one of the concerns of this chapter to argue that although affirmative action is underpinned by 'universal' values (tied to the presuppositions of democratic commitment intrinsic to the notion of engaged participation) the concept is a contested one, the meaning of which is contextually dependent and the source of continuing and fierce controversy. This context-focused approach is anchored in a general view of *human rights law in perspective* that is oriented towards a substantive perspective on equality.[5] If democratic dialogue is not to be distorted we need techniques to address structural inequality in a sophisticated and contextually sensitive rights-based way. That is why affirmative action in general is to be defended, but that is also why we need carefully designed models that respect underpinning values.

History and context

Reforming Northern Ireland?

The conflict 'in and about Northern Ireland' (even the name provokes disagreement[6]) is, at its core, about national identity (British-Irish), and emerged in a post-colonial context that reaches back to the politics of the seventeenth century (McGarry and O'Leary, 1996). Following the partition of Ireland in 1921, the jurisdiction of Northern Ireland remained within the United Kingdom (the full title is 'the United Kingdom of Great Britain and Northern Ireland') (Foster, 1989). Northern Ireland was consciously crafted and designed as a legal entity to create a Protestant/British/Unionist majority regime (arguably in recognition of the 'facts on the ground'), with a Catholic/Irish/Nationalist-Republican minority (Lee, 1989). The 'majority community' (Protestant/Unionist) was determined to remain within the UK, while the 'minority community' sought Irish unity

(Catholic/Nationalist).[7] The unionist community in Northern Ireland secured a position of domination and coercion in terms that are comparable to any context where partition is deployed as a tool of conflict management. Partition (and the ethno-national divisions pre-existing it and established in its wake) dominated political and social life – in Northern Ireland at least. On one reading, partition can be viewed as a 'triggering event', in the sense that the jurisdiction was designed to create a majority community aligned to Britain (Protestant/Unionist), which shared an island and a border with a neighbour viewed as hostile and expansionist (Republic of Ireland), and with a substantial 'minority community' (Catholic/Nationalist) who already felt alienated (and would increasingly be viewed as suspect and presumptively 'disloyal') (McEvoy and White, 1998). While Northern Ireland need not have taken the path it did as a direct result of this factual context, it established a structural framework that set the scene (and offered fertile ground) for future conflict and division. Partition, in the form and shape it took, was not a resolution to the complex problems that the island faced, and its history exacerbated an already challenging situation. Little was done to secure republican and nationalist integration into these new structures – and much done to lend support to persistent practices of abstentionism and disengagement. A besieged North withdrew into itself, placing stability and unionist hegemony above any other potential distractions, and as Westminster practised a policy of neglect the conditions were ripe for mistreatment and abuse.

The main actors, in the sense noted above, can then be described as the Unionist/Loyalist/Protestant community and the Nationalist/Republican/Catholic community – framed by the British-Irish intergovernmental and bi-national context. The unionist community in Northern Ireland sought to consolidate its position, viewing itself as under threat from the new regime in the south of Ireland, and constructing the Irish republican-nationalist community in the North as a real or potential 'enemy within' (McEvoy and White, 1998). Early evidence of this can be found in the removal of proportional representation in the 1920s, as well as the rapid alignment of the interests of the new Northern Ireland majority community with the 'security establishment' (McEvoy, 2011; Campbell, 1994). The hostility and suspicion engendered resulted in the creation of a system infused with discriminatory practices. This included electoral 'gerrymandering' and discrimination in the provision of, for example, social housing, as well as endemic inequality in employment. Although periods of stability varied (with periodic armed campaigns, for example the IRA campaign of 1956–1962), Northern Ireland remained in a permanent state of emergency from its inception, with a policing and security establishment created which mapped closely onto the majority unionist community (McEvoy, 2011; Farrell, 1976). The interests of the unionist community became meshed with the formation of this new entity that had failed to undergo any sustained process of constitutionalisation. Northern Ireland therefore evolved as a jurisdiction that 'viewed' itself as under external threat, and failed to gain recognition and legitimacy from a substantial section of its own population. Its formal legality simply did not map persuasively onto a binding form of legitimacy.

The 1960s witnessed the rise of the civil rights movement in Northern Ireland in direct response to these societal conditions – often linked in the literature to educational reforms of the 1940s which saw increased access to higher education from the nationalist community feed into broader political mobilisation around rights (Purdie, 1990; Prince, 2007). This movement (informed and influenced by localised knowledge, events in the US and Europe, and a global and regional reform agenda) used the language and practices of civil rights activism to demand internal reform within Northern Ireland in areas such as housing and employment. These calls for reform were met with some movement (evidenced in, for example, the spirit of the British–Irish Downing Street Declaration of 1969), but generally greeted with hostility by the unionist community, many of whom viewed the protests as part of a wider attempt to destabilise and undermine Northern Ireland. What to reformers looked like a reasonable call for civil rights and internal reform, looked to the majority unionist community like another assault on their 'state' (raising intriguing questions – and ongoing debates – about the responsibilities of both the state and human rights activists in these contexts) (Hadden, 2010). This perception was no doubt also assisted by the rise of a neo-Marxist discourse of political radicalism that did indeed wish to nurture globalised revolution from the unpromising territory of Northern Ireland (Prince, 2007).

The intensified inter-communal tensions (in a societal context primed for potential hostilities) combined with an often inept and ill-judged security response from the British Government and security forces. While many other factors were in play, these elements combined to promote the rise, re-emergence, and enhancement of paramilitarism in Northern Ireland (Campbell and Connelly, 2006). For example, the Provisional IRA was formed in 1969 – in the tradition of republican resistance to British rule in Ireland – and as a response to frustration with the left-wing political route adopted by the Official IRA to that point (English, 2003). What commenced as a campaign for civil rights was transformed in less than a decade into violent conflict, and a resurgence of republican and loyalist paramilitarism. PIRA rapidly emerged (again with the 'assistance' of both unionist reaction and the security response from the British Government) as a significant armed group with defensive ambitions (in terms of defending the Catholic population) and objectives tied to traditional Irish republican goals (Irish unity) (English, 2003). Loyalist paramilitarism (Ulster Volunteer Force and Ulster Defence Association, among others) also evolved as a communal response; and the ground was established for a violent conflict that would last for decades. The situation had deteriorated to such an extent that in 1972 the British Government prorogued the Northern Ireland Parliament and introduced direct rule from London (Hadfield, 1989). The period of British governmental neglect was coming to an end, and the long journey to a proactive peace process was to commence.

The period from 1972 onwards included several attempts to bring the conflict to an end, and to promote the return of self-government to Northern Ireland. From the earliest stage, the nature of many of the basic problems was accepted and recognised, with references to equality and non-discrimination being made by both governments, and the problems in employment and housing acknowledged.[8]

Several key themes emerged during this process. First, it became increasingly clear that an exclusively military/security response would not bring an end to the conflict. Aspects of the policy response in this field, from the use of the military to dealing with political prisoners, simply exacerbated existing problems.

Second, slowly and steadily an appreciation of what might be required to manage and resolve the conflict – in broad terms – gained wider recognition. For example, that any resolution would include a form of power-sharing government between the two main national communities, recognition of the British–Irish dimensions, as well as extensive internal reform of 'Northern Ireland' and a firm commitment to the use of exclusively peaceful and democratic means to resolve disagreement.

And third, as part of the internal reform, that fundamental change was required in areas such as equality, human rights, criminal justice, and policing. It is this element of the planned transformation of Northern Ireland that is of most significance for the purpose of this chapter; the sense that robust measures to tackle discrimination, and to advance fair employment, were viewed as part of a well-managed resolution of the violent conflict. What remains interesting here is that the need for reform (between Protestants and Catholics) was accepted early on (in, for example, the Northern Ireland Constitution Act 1973), with, for example, the enactment of the (relatively weak) Fair Employment Act 1976, and then the Fair Employment Act 1989 (more robust). Arguably, the problems were identified (and understood) even earlier than this; the difficulty was securing practical and effective measures to address them in a challenging societal context.

Long before the conflict was brought to an end it was officially acknowledged (and under a Conservative Party administration in London) that religious and political discrimination in employment needed to be challenged (by the adoption and use of measures that included affirmative action). This recognition gained ground and was acted upon by British governments (not especially attached to notions of affirmative action) through concerted and targeted political and community-based action and international influence and pressure, particularly via the US (all achieved while the conflict was ongoing). The result was that fair employment, affirmative action, and the promotion of equality (between the two main communities in particular) became part of creating the conditions for tackling some of the causes of conflict. An underpinning rationale here was that whatever political choices individuals and communities might make on constitutional status, they should do so on the secure basis of employment equality within Northern Ireland. The principle was to find a home in the 1998 Agreement.

Inter-governmental co-operation and the political parties in Northern Ireland

In formal legal and political terms, Northern Ireland remains a part of the UK; the entity created in the early 1920s may well survive to see its 100th anniversary. It is a devolved region that shares the island with the rest of Ireland (the island of Ireland). It has jurisdictional attachment to one member state of the EU, and shares territorial space with another; this EU context increasingly frames the equality debates. Both states are members of the Council of Europe and many other inter-governmental organisations, and are signatories to a significant number of international instruments on human rights and equality.

As a direct result of the divergence of *national* aspirations, both governments (British and Irish) are central to understanding the political management of conflict. These national aspirations are now regarded (following the Good Friday Agreement 1998) as being equally legitimate. Both main communities share a physical space but essentially 'owe their allegiance' to different governments and jurisdictions. The peace process only evolved once both governments were secure drivers of it and assumed the responsibility of leadership that the nature of the problem would suggest. The horizontal relationships between nationalists and unionists must also be viewed through this lens (both appeal to their national government). This frame seeks to locate ethno-national division in context and is not intended to undervalue 'from below' initiatives within and between communities.

Because Northern Ireland is currently within the UK, and has existed under long periods of direct rule from London, a particular weight of emphasis falls on the British Government to deliver reform. The Good Friday Agreement 1998 led to devolved government, which has functioned in 'stop-start' mode (although the latest period of devolution has now persisted unbroken since May 2007 – with a DUP First Minister, and a Sinn Féin Deputy First Minister sharing power together). The steady devolution of power to a Northern Ireland Assembly brings more of the focus onto the local political parties, and can be viewed as an evolving attempt by both governments to nurture cross-community democratic government and allow it to develop and flourish.

The political parties largely follow patterns of ethno-national communal division. The main unionist parties are: Democratic Unionist Party (DUP), Ulster Unionist Party (UUP), and Traditional Unionist Voice (TUV). The main nationalist parties are: Sinn Féin (SF) and the Social Democratic and Labour Party (SDLP). There is one main political party that claims to transcend the traditional approach: the Alliance Party of Northern Ireland (APNI). The May 2010 election to the UK Parliament at Westminster indicates overall levels of party support at that time: SF (25.5 per cent), DUP (25 per cent), SDLP (16.5 per cent), UCUNF (an alliance of the UUP and Conservative Party) (15.2 per cent), APNI (6.3 per cent), TUV (3.9 per cent). Contrast this with the results of the Westminster election of May 1997, before the conclusion of the Good Friday Agreement: UUP (32.7 per cent), SDLP (24.1 per cent), DUP (13.6 per cent), SF (16.1 per cent), APNI (8 per cent).

The May 2011 Assembly elections confirm the now established picture, with the two major parties of unionism and nationalism increasingly dominating: DUP (30 per cent), SF (26.9 per cent), UUP (14.2 per cent), SDLP (13.2 per cent), AP (7.7 per cent). The decade since the Agreement was marked by the replacement of the two once-dominant nationalist/unionist parties (UUP and SDLP) by their traditionally more assertive ethno-national rivals (who had to moderate their own politics in order to occupy this ground). The election results once again confirmed the ethno-national ground on which most political mobilisation in Northern Ireland continues to occur.

Framing affirmative action in the Northern Ireland context?

The argument advanced here is that affirmative action should be viewed as context sensitive. But which context is appropriate? The story told above sketches a historical picture tied to communities of primarily national allegiance; it is a tale of competing national and nationalist struggles, intertwined with a politics of coercion and domination. It is argued that this is a way of grasping what has happened in Northern Ireland in terms of the type of affirmative action that has been developed and why it has made notable advances. While the two now-dominant communal groups can be described historically in terms of majority/minority communities (and in important senses such an approach holds continuing merit), they face each other as two strong and powerful ethno-national communities governing large areas of public life in Northern Ireland together. This point could be pressed further to suggest that a form of supermajoritarianism is emerging, tied to the communal interests of the two dominant communities. While these are competing and rival national communities, often only those stories that fit neatly into strong collective narratives of communal advancement, grievance, or redress will make progress. It is not to suggest that this is the only frame of reference, or that there are not other groups and individuals who are disadvantaged, but it assists in understanding those agendas that succeed and those that fail.[9] It provides a way into a particular societal context, and the mechanisms deployed to achieve specific outcomes.

Fair employment, equality, and affirmative action in Northern Ireland

In order to address patterns of discrimination and disadvantage, laws and policies were put in place in Northern Ireland to advance 'fair participation' in employment, with a particular focus on discrimination based on religious belief or political opinion in the public and private sectors.

Edwards (1995: 95) has noted how much fair employment law was influenced by the US, rather than Britain or elsewhere, and that the approach in Northern Ireland is focused on fair representation/participation rather than explicitly targeted at a disadvantaged group. Affirmative action, depending on context, can be required for Catholics or Protestants. He cites the anxiety around the term 'affirmative action', which was often viewed as a US import with too close an association with the notion of quotas, and he observes the wise and tactical use of the notion of 'fairness' in the debates (Edwards, 1995: 26–7). This concern with terminology is evident generally in the debate in the UK. For example, in their review of anti-discrimination law, Hepple *et al.* (2000: 34) concluded: 'We have avoided using the words "affirmative action" as such, because of the connotations which this has wrongly acquired of requiring quotas or reverse discrimination.' General 'constitutional provisions' were in place for some time, but the regulatory moves have all been in the direction of the development of more precise, detailed, and focused regimes. The Northern Ireland legislation is, in many ways, innovative, and has had an impact on what was previously a highly segregated employment context (it seems to have worked for recruitment in particular).[10] An underpinning assumption remains that while anti-discrimination law is of vital significance, law and policy needed to travel well beyond traditional approaches in Britain if the objective was to promote employment equality. Thus, notions of equality of opportunity and fair participation were actively promoted to ensure employers were taking positive steps and supporting permissible affirmative action measures. It is worth outlining the measures, and also noting that several elements of fair employment law are innovative, in a UK and Irish context and more generally. As McCrudden (2004) notes, this is an attempt to achieve affirmative action in a specific context, without resort to quotas, and there is evidence that it has met many of its original objectives.

The development of fair employment law and policy

A prohibition on discrimination was included in the Government of Ireland Act 1920 s.5, but this weak 'constitutional' provision failed to make inroads into the evolving societal context, and was insufficient and ineffective in recognising the potential problems. It did not prevent the emergence of a system that was predominantly Protestant and unionist in nature, reinforced by statements like that from the Prime Minister of Northern Ireland, Lord Craigavon, in 1934, that the Northern Ireland Parliament was 'a Protestant Parliament for a Protestant People' (even if expressed in a reactive context) (Rose and Magill, 1996: 3). The build-up of a unionist-dominated system was underlined by the non-intervention of the Westminster Parliament in Northern Ireland affairs, underpinned by constitutional convention (Hadfield, 1989), and the creation of a special powers regime which led to the close alignment of the institutions of security and law and order with the interests of the emergent new government (Campbell, 1994).

The initiation of direct rule from Westminster led to a more proactive role and new legislation. The Northern Ireland Constitution Act 1973 provided for the establishment of the Standing Advisory Commission on Human Rights (SACHR), which had an anti-discrimination remit, as well as the inclusion of two anti-discrimination provisions (ss. 17 and 19) dealing with discrimination in legislation and discrimination by public authorities (Rose and Magill, 1996: 6). The difficulty was that the system was designed to operate under a devolved administration – and this proved difficult to secure in a climate of sustained violence. For example, the regime established under the Sunningdale Agreement in 1974 collapsed after a short period of time, with the re-imposition of direct rule.

The need to tackle religious discrimination was, however, gaining enhanced recognition with, for example, the van Straubenzee Report 1973 recommending the establishment of a Fair Employment Agency, and noting the role and importance of affirmative action, among other things, in overcoming discrimination in employment (Rose and Magill, 1996: 9). Many of the recommendations were implemented in the Fair Employment Act 1976. This led to the creation of a new Fair Employment Agency to address the promotion of equality of opportunity and to tackle discrimination on the basis of religious belief or political opinion. The 1976 Act was primarily a traditional anti-discrimination tool, as opposed to a regime with positive/affirmative measures. The Agency had a fairly wide-ranging remit, which included dealing with investigations and complaints and awarding appropriate remedies. However, due largely to the voluntary nature of key aspects of its work and limits to its remit and role, the Agency was not as successful as it might have been. It became clear that further reform would be needed.[11]

Several elements (top-down and bottom-up) combined to build a case for reform. First, both governments were moving closer together in their management of the conflict. The Anglo-Irish Agreement 1985 marked a significant step in a more co-ordinated and joint approach to governing Northern Ireland, and this became a major driver of reform (although official resistance to robust international mobilisation for employment equality continued).

Second, a political campaign aimed at legal reform, which emerged with assistance from the US, proved interesting (McNamara, 2007). This campaign involved a focus on those US companies and public bodies that were investing in Northern Ireland, and advanced the argument that they should adopt what were termed the 'MacBride Principles'[12] – establishing a clear commitment to anti-discrimination and the promotion of equality of opportunity in employment (McNamara, 2007). The MacBride Principles themselves (launched in 1984 and subsequently amended), and this general strategic approach to the promotion of reform, are of wider interest when considering effective transnational legal and political mobilisation around legal reform that incorporates powerful diaspora communities.

The Principles committed signatories to: make every reasonable lawful effort to increase the representation of under-represented religious groups at all levels of their operations in Northern Ireland; the protection of workers against intimidation and physical abuse in the workplace; the prevention of the display of provocative sectarian emblems; special efforts to attract applications from under-represented groups; ensure that layoff or termination policies did not impact disproportionately on one religious group; the abolition of all differential employment criteria; the development of training programmes; active recruitment of those minority employees who might advance further; and the appointment of senior managers to oversee these affirmative action efforts. These were Principles targeted expressly at employers and investors (international investors with links to Northern Ireland) with a view to the promotion of affirmative action, as part of a wider investment strategy. The campaign met with considerable official resistance from all three governments, but those leading it saw value in appealing over the heads of the political establishments and directly to the Irish-American community (McNamara, 2007). The Principles were monitored by the Investor Research Responsibility Centre, and the approach brought a form of direct economic pressure to bear (firms risked losing state or city contracts with New York City, for example, for non-implementation).

Third, further detailed work was undertaken by SACHR and others to assess how law and policy could be enhanced (SACHR, 1987). In 1987, SACHR published an authoritative and influential report that advanced several specific recommendations, including a proposal for the establishment of a new tribunal to hear complaints. The Fair Employment Act 1989 followed up on some of this work and put in place a much more proactive regime, but the Government's response also excluded many of the more significant SACHR recommendations. The FEA was replaced with a Fair Employment Commission (FEC), and complaints were then heard by a new Fair Employment Tribunal (FET). Of particular interest here were the provisions on monitoring and affirmative action contained within the new legislation. The new legislation saw the arrival of an 'affirmative action' approach as a way of addressing employment inequalities between the two main communities. The affirmative action regime introduced was, and remains, 'symmetrical', as it applies equally to both Protestants and Catholics (McCrudden *et al.*, 2009: 9). On affirmative action the Act provided for specific types of affirmative action measures, which were then supplemented by actions set out in the Code of Practice by the FEC (now ECNI).

A further review by SACHR was conducted in the 1990s, with the outcomes published in its employment equality report of 1997 (SACHR, 1997). This review, as well as other work ongoing in Northern Ireland, informed wider political developments which were to lead to the adoption of the Good Friday Agreement in 1998 (an agreement which was infused with the progressive language of rights and equality) (Harvey, 2000; Harvey and Russell, 2009; Harvey and Schwartz, 2010; Schwartz and Harvey, 2012). Of particular note here was the creation of a new single Equality Commission for Northern Ireland, which represented a merger of all the pre-existing bodies (including the Fair Employment Commission), as the institution that would take over the monitoring function in a shared institutional setting.

The Fair Employment and Treatment Order 1998 (as amended) sets out the framework of fair employment law in Northern Ireland. The order repealed and re-enacted aspects of the 1976 and 1989 legislation, with some amendments and additions (for example, extending protections beyond the employment sphere for the first time). Much of it simply follows the pre-existing system. Employers (with ten or more staff) are under a duty to conduct regular reviews of their workforce to ensure there is fair employment, and take action if it is needed. FETO requires employers to collect monitoring data each year on the community composition and gender of their workforce.[13] At least once every three years this information must be used to evaluate fair participation, and if required the employer should identify any affirmative action required. In addition to this, annual summaries of the monitoring data are supplied to the ECNI via an annual monitoring return (these are published by the ECNI, although there is no legal requirement to do so).[14] In sum, there are three key elements in the approach: ongoing employee monitoring; annual monitoring returns to the ECNI; and a triennial (Article 55) review (involving consideration of fair participation and any affirmative action required).

The law (FETO 1998, Art. 4 (1)) permits employers to undertake affirmative action

> to secure fair participation in employment by members of the Protestant, or members of the Roman Catholic, community in Northern Ireland by means including: the adoption of practices aimed at encouraging such participation; and the modification or abandonment of practices that have or may have the effect of restricting or discouraging such participation.

The definition of equality of opportunity in FETO provides a general exception for lawful affirmative action (FETO 1998, Art. 5). The affirmative action measures prohibit preferential treatment, but those measures allowed by the Order are: the encouragement of applications for employment or training for people from under-represented groups; targeting training in a particular area or at a particular class of person; the negotiation of agreed redundancy schemes to preserve fair participation; the provision of training for non-employees of a particular religious belief – following approval by the Equality Commission; and the recruitment of unemployed persons.

It is worth dwelling for a moment on the notion of 'monitoring', as it has attracted 'human rights-based criticism'. All employers who employ more than ten people are required to register with the Equality Commission (the returns of all regulated employers are published, and employers identified). As noted, all registered employers, and public authorities, must monitor the composition of their workforces by community background. The key element here is 'community background' (Protestant/Catholic), rather than a necessary focus on the actual religious beliefs of the person concerned. Detailed guidance is provided by the Equality Commission on how monitoring is to be conducted. First, an employer can ask directly (the principal method); if this does not elicit the information, the second, 'residual method' can be adopted. An employer is then permitted to use a range of sources to establish 'community background' and the employee is then informed. Monitoring returns on workforce composition must be completed annually and returned to the Commission. For those employers and public authorities who employ over 250 people, this information is required for applications for posts, as well as those who are no longer employed by the organisation. The system is not a fault-based one, as Fredman (2002: 144) notes:

> The employer is made responsible for promoting fair participation simply where disparities are apparent even though there is no proof that the employer was guilty of unlawful discrimination. It is clear from these

provisions that fair participation is to be measured in terms of groups rather than particular individuals.

The primary focus is on whether the two main communities enjoy fair participation within the workplace. If the employer concludes that this is not the case then affirmative action measures should be established – such as the setting of goals and timetables.

As is evident, much of the responsibility for gathering and monitoring data rests with employers. Enforcement of these mechanisms then falls in the first instance to the Equality Commission. Provision is in place for the Commission to reach an affirmative action agreement with employers – which can be one outcome of a formal investigation. This is a key enforcement component of the regime; the ability of the Commission to launch an investigation against an employer, and the subsequent follow-up. Directions can be made, which can then ultimately be enforced by the Fair Employment Tribunal (legally enforceable route). Most of the agreements that have been adopted relate to Catholic under-representation, but some address Protestant under-representation, and the agreements have generally been voluntary rather than legally enforceable ones (McCrudden et al., 2009).[15] What do these agreements require? Procedural requirements around human resources, advertising, promotion, and training are often included, as well as more targeted approaches to recruitment (McCrudden et al., 2009). Again, reverse discrimination and quotas are not permitted under this system (McCrudden et al., 2009). Fair participation must therefore be achieved through lawful affirmative action measures only.

The annual monitoring reports produced by the Commission are helpful evidence of trends and patterns in fair employment, based on a significant number of monitoring returns provided by employers (ECNI, 2010; ECNI 2011). Monitoring covers 70–72 per cent of all those employed in Northern Ireland (ECNI, 2010: 7). The 20th monitoring report – dealing with 2009 – was published in December 2010, and is of particular interest because for the first time it begins to capture the impact of the global and local recession (the overall monitored workforce is contracting).[16] It is worth highlighting that pre-recession, Northern Ireland had experienced a sustained 15-year period of economic growth, with the labour market performing well and a steady decline in unemployment (ECNI, 2010). The general picture in that time 'in terms of employment has been one of convergence between the two groups' (ECNI, 2010: 7).[17] In the 2010 report the early signs of the impact of the recession are evident. For the first time in a decade the total number of monitored employees fell: to 517,000. The upward trend noted in Catholic representation from 2001 continued, with another marginal increase to 45.4 per cent. The female share of the monitored workforce rose in the same period from 50.4 per cent to 52.4 per cent. While there are differences in the various sub-sectors of the economy (for example, the security-related sector), and the picture is not universally encouraging, the monitored workforce is now largely representative of societal composition in Northern Ireland (Catholics and Protestants). The 21st monitoring report was published in

December 2011, and largely confirms these established trends – with the Catholic share of the monitored workforce rising slightly again, to 45.9 per cent, compared to the figure for Protestants of 54.1 per cent (ECNI, 2011).

The impact of the fair employment regime has been subjected to analysis and comment (Edwards, 1995; McCrudden et al., 2009). A Nuffield-funded research project has reached tentative conclusions about the impact of the use of affirmative action agreements by the FEC/ECNI (McCrudden et al., 2009, 2004; Osborne and Shuttleworth, 2004, Chapter 7). While numerous caveats have been placed around the research, the improvement that has been evident in terms of fair participation and integration (there is now employment equality in relation to the overall workforce composition in Northern Ireland) can, it seems, be attributed both to the regulatory regime in place and the work of the Fair Employment Agency/Commission in reaching affirmative action agreements: 'It is likely that the work of the FEC was an integral part of the processes driving change in the Northern Ireland labour market in the 1990s' (McCrudden et al., 2009, 2004: 415).[18] One of the more striking conclusions reached in the research is the lack of evidence for any direct effect of fair employment cases (through the Tribunal), legally enforceable agreements, or the MacBride Principles. McCrudden et al., however, are keen to stress that this does not imply they were without value, and the research indicates that the mere existence of such a mechanism might help explain why the voluntary option was successful (McCrudden et al., 2009, 13). It is also worth noting that SACHR in 1997 observed that: 'Few employers considered that compliance with the legislation had adversely affected their competitiveness.'[19] This view is supported by other available evidence, including the Nuffield research. One group of leading commentators (Bamforth et al., 2008: 427) concludes: 'The Northern Irish measures have had considerable and well documented success.... [I]n fact, the emphasis on setting and meeting transparently defined targets has generated better results than virtually any other set of positive action approaches' (footnotes omitted). It would also appear that some of the most successfully 'integrated' spaces in Northern Ireland exist within the employment setting, precisely the area of life where the regulatory environment has been the most creative (and also 'robust') (Fitzpatrick in Osborne and Shuttleworth, 2004: Chapter 8). However, two points are marked in the existing literature and available research: its strength may not be the principal or only reason for its effectiveness; and employers have generally not viewed the regime as hostile to their economic effectiveness. This particularised 'success' appears connected to the regulatory creation of spaces for ongoing dialogue with employers based on evidence and targets, rather than the simple application and use of robust legal tools. However, the fact that these legal tools exist would appear to play a role in ensuring that the dialogue within the regulatory space continues.

But to what extent should other elements be factored in that go beyond this regulatory dialogue? It should also be stressed, for example, that this recent regime (since 1989) has coincided with a much more conducive (though not necessarily more integrated) societal environment and political context, created by an evolving peace process; and the approach was aided by determined and co-ordinated transnational political mobilisation on rights and equality. The objectives of fair employment evolved in a more welcoming political context, and perhaps more significantly were attuned to a powerful communal and political narrative that could generate determined and ongoing political support. Participants understood that this was a policy agenda that mattered.

The evidence that has emerged from Northern Ireland may be relevant for others considering how fair employment might be achieved in the employment sphere, in contexts where any form of preferential treatment and/or quotas is difficult.[20] However, it is also the argument of this chapter that the political and societal dynamics of Northern Ireland, combined with the nature of the regulatory regime, must be factored into any such contextualised assessment. The regulatory equality conversations could progress in a changing post-conflict climate, backed by a continuing and strong legal enforcement framework, with clear and understood targets and goals, and internal and external political mobilisation that could ensure pressure was exerted to remain focused on outcomes. This coming together of diverse elements ensured that progress was made, but also gives a sense of the type of political mobilisation around law that might be required to secure particularised outcomes and a meaningful form of 'contextualised equality'.

Mainstreaming equality

Fair employment law is not the only arena where equality, and a preventative and proactive approach, interacts with ethno-national division in Northern Ireland. Other aspects of reform are of interest when considering debates on equality, rights, and affirmative action. These elements flowed from the Good Friday Agreement 1998, but are informed by the more positive developments in fair employment on religious/political grounds throughout the 1980s and 1990s (McCrudden, 2004). In significant senses, fair employment law demonstrated what was possible, and indicated how advances might be made.

Stability first: power-sharing and equality

First, the governing democratic structures merit mention within the framework of this chapter. The Northern Ireland democratic settlement reached in 1998 is based on a consociational model of power-sharing between the two main communities (McGarry, 2001; McGarry and O'Leary 2004; McCrudden, 2007). The complex set of arrangements envisaged in the Agreement of 1998 – provided for in the Northern Ireland Act 1998 and underpinned by international agreements – give expression to the importance placed on cross-community partnership government between nationalists and unionists. The Northern Ireland Executive – formed through the use of the D'Hondt model of proportional allocation of ministries – effectively ensures that both main communities work together to make the system function (which could alternatively be described as a form of mutual veto or mandated power-sharing on a liberal model, as it retains a focus on electoral strength). While this has not always made for stable government (devolution has been stop/start, with a current period of stability), and does not permit rapid progress in policy terms (due to political disagreements within such grand coalitions), devolved government has been maintained – however insecurely – since May 2007.

The Hillsborough Agreement 2010 paved the way for the significant step of devolution of policing and justice to the Northern Ireland Assembly and, for now, devolved government continues to 'function'. Power-sharing government has therefore achieved a measure of political stability, but as one would expect in such a system, innovative legislative and policy development has thus far been largely absent. This has understandably provoked debate on the fate of the more progressive and far-reaching aspirations of the peace process, and how successful mobilisation around equality and rights might be achieved in the future. However, it was apparent for some time – and in lessons learned from comparative experience – that the dominant procedural logic was going to accord priority to inter-communal power-sharing in politics and society. Any mobilisation on rights and equality would have to figure out how to navigate this framing narrative.

Being positive about rights and equality

The Agreement envisaged a more positive and proactive approach to equality of opportunity generally (as part of a mainstreaming initiative which had evolved over decades) reflected in s. 75 of the Northern Ireland Act 1998, and the enforcement mechanism contained in Schedule 9 of the Act (McCrudden, 1999; Harvey, 2000; Dickson and Harvey, 2006; Smith and McLaughlin, 2010). This framework is the outcome of an extended and instructive campaign, and places a positive obligation on public authorities to promote equality of opportunity across nine grounds; it sets in place a detailed 'regulatory mechanism' to attempt to mainstream equality. The provision, and all the work around it, is infused with notions of examining and assessing impact, addressing inequality more proactively based on objective evidence, and the participation of affected groups in this process (McCrudden, 1999).

It became clear as the peace process progressed (and was evident from the campaigns of the 1960s onwards) that enhanced human rights protection would have to form one part of any agreement. This was explicitly recognised in the Good Friday Agreement 1998, and led to the creation of a new Northern Ireland Human Rights Commission, resulting in the abolition of SACHR. The intention was that SACHR would be replaced by stronger institutional human rights protection and promotion. One of the key tasks of this new body was to advise government on a Bill of Rights for Northern Ireland – a process that led to extensive debates around the interaction between rights protections and the equality regime noted above (McCrudden, 2006; Harvey and Schwartz, 2009). The arguments that surrounded the Bill of Rights debate, and how the Commission attempted to resolve them in its final advice to government, are instructive when reflecting on affirmative action measures in a divided society like Northern Ireland. An equality agenda dominated by inter-communal contestation between nationalists/Catholics and unionists/Protestants, had to confront an increasingly Europeanised (and internationalised) human rights discourse anchored around notions of individual rights. Some of the most controversial aspects of the Bill of Rights debate included the alleged tensions ('alleged' because international human rights law already recognises the importance of *and need for* special regimes) between these areas, and while aspects of this could be mapped onto traditional inter-communal patterns of political rivalry, it also unearthed more principled disagreements within human rights law, policy, and practice about the relationship between communal protections and individual human rights. How should human rights interact with the affirmative action regimes of Northern Ireland? How might a Bill of Rights, for example, fit into the existing equality context? The answers that have been worked out over time demonstrate that it is possible to achieve liberally inspired solutions to these dilemmas that take care to respect local contexts *and* established international human rights values and principles (Northern Ireland Human Rights Commission, 2008). The fact that, at the time of writing, the enactment of a Bill of Rights for Northern Ireland does not seem imminent highlights that even well designed proposals will struggle if they do not attach strongly enough to the logics of the communal narratives in operation locally. Even though the rhetoric of rights, and civil rights, could be traced comfortably to a story about the emergence of conflict, enacting a Bill of Rights never seemed significant enough to the political parties (even advocates) to make it subject to determined political negotiation. What does this tell us about *human rights* mobilisation in the context of a deeply divided society such as Northern Ireland?

Changing Northern Ireland? Policing reform and affirmative action

The reform of policing in Northern Ireland is highly instructive as an example of the use of robust temporary recruitment measures (introduced in November 2001) to ensure speedy progress in the promotion of a representative (Catholic–Protestant) police force, and thus to address a stark imbalance in workforce composition. Bamforth *et al.* (2008: 427) note the approach adopted 'is a dramatic use of preferential treatment based upon the detailed analysis contained in the Patten Report'. The Patten proposals were contested, but were viewed as significant enough to merit implementation.

The Royal Ulster Constabulary (RUC) never gained the acceptance of the republican and nationalist community in Northern Ireland, and was a consistent source of tension and grievance since its creation (Ellison and Smyth, 2000; O'Rawe, 2003). This police force was closely aligned with the Northern Ireland government and unionist establishment, and during its life had Catholic representation of around 7–8 per cent in a society where Catholics comprise over 40 per cent of the population (Ellison, 2007). Policing was high on the agenda of those negotiating the Good Friday Agreement 1998 (in defensive or reformist terms), and it was a source of significant disagreement during those negotiations and after (Doyle, 2010). In the final document a commitment was made to a 'new beginning to policing', and the establishment of an independent commission to make recommendations (chaired by Chris Patten, thus 'The Patten Commission'). One of the dilemmas facing this commission was how any police service – operating in the context noted above – would secure cross-community consent and be viewed as legitimate within all communities. This resulted in some of the most heated debates following the Agreement, particularly on how internal institutional and cultural reform would be achieved (Doyle, 2010). The unionist community did not largely perceive a major problem (although interestingly, policing professionals and practitioners generally did) – the RUC was viewed as a defender of 'the state', and had stood for law and order in challenging times. Any call for a radical break was met with resistance. A new system was, however, put in place, and is now generally presented as one of the more significant 'successes' of the peace process.

The name of the police service was changed from the RUC to the Police Service of Northern Ireland (PSNI); this included the adoption of new symbols and uniforms (Independent Commission on Policing, 1999). An Oversight Commissioner was appointed to monitor the practical implementation of the Patten Report, new accountability mechanisms were established, and the recruitment processes to the PSNI were reformed. The new system promoted the recruitment of Catholics and Protestants on a 50:50 basis from a 'merit pool' of suitable applicants; the overall objective was to increase Catholic representation to 30 per cent within ten years. The scheme included generous retirement packages to encourage long-serving officers to consider their future – and many availed of this opportunity. A challenge to the arrangements, on the basis of alleged incompatibility with the European Convention on Human Rights, failed,[21] and they attracted sustained hostility from unionist political parties during their period of operation.

What outcomes have been achieved by the use of these temporary recruitment initiatives as they relate to *police officers* in particular? In 2001 the newly established PSNI comprised 91.2 per cent Protestants and 8.2 per cent Catholics (in 1992, the RUC figure was 7.78 per cent Catholic in the full-time force); five years later those figures had changed to 20.1 per cent Catholic and 79.9 per cent Protestant. By 31 March 2011, the Catholic figure was 30.3 per cent (where it remains, as of July 2012), and thus above the original target of 30 per cent.[22] This reflected a rate of progress that led to calls for the scheme to be permitted to lapse in 2011 (NIO, 2010). This provoked a debate among the political parties, with the DUP – as it has done from the inception of the legislation – calling for it to be scrapped,[23] and the nationalist Sinn Féin and SDLP suggesting that the temporary measures should remain in place until the Catholic proportion reached that of the composition of the general population. Also, while figures for police officers had improved markedly, problems persisted in relation to PSNI staff, meaning that the overall picture on police personnel was less impressive (Nolan, 2012).

The Secretary of State, Owen Paterson, indicated in 2010 that he was minded to allow the scheme to end – essentially because the main objective had been achieved.[24] This set the scene for nationalist-unionist political disagreement in the run-up to the Northern Ireland Assembly elections held in May 2011. Despite criticism and ongoing concerns the Secretary of State opted to permit the scheme to lapse on 28 March 2011, and as a result it has now come to an end (the policing service does, however, remain subject to the existing fair employment and other rights, equality, and accountability regimes in Northern Ireland).[25]

This was a system deliberately designed to increase Catholic representation in the police service relatively quickly, in a targeted and direct way, as part of a process of securing nationalist/republican confidence in the new policing arrangements. It can be contrasted with the fair employment approach, which has sought to ensure fair participation of both communities in the workplace over time. Unionist political parties in Northern Ireland never accepted the new policing recruitment regime (they are generally very supportive of the policing service) and have subjected it to consistent and strong critique on the basis that they viewed it as a 'quota system' that led to reverse discrimination against the Protestant community. These are arguments that will resonate strongly with anyone familiar with global debates on the deployment of such special measures. However, judged in terms of practical outcomes, the scheme has arguably achieved several of its objectives, with Catholic representation (police officers) increasing significantly (to the target figure from 7 per cent) in a short period of time, and some evidence of more acceptance of the PSNI within the broad nationalist community (NIO, 2010).

There remains a desperate need for the new policing order to be strongly perceived as a peace process 'success'. Evidence suggests, however, that sceptical notes must be injected into the analysis above (Ellison, 2007, 2010; Ellison and O'Rawe, 2010; Nolan, 2012). Ellison (2010: 243) urges caution and questions 'whether the change process to date warrants some of the eulogies ascribed to it'. While he accepts some of the claims to success, he is less persuaded by the outcomes at the 'cross-community participative level', and questions who the 'Catholics' are in these figures (Ellison, 2010: 269; 2007: 257). A concern is that suspicion and mistrust have not been overcome in areas historically (and still profoundly) alienated from the policing regime. This caution about the more elaborate claims made is significant and necessary, and is reflective of an overall view that for all the positives the Patten Report itself was 'not perfect',[26] and implementation has not had all the intended impacts or led to the level of institutional and cultural transformation that was hoped for (Ellison, 2007: 244). The general figures mask variable practices, intriguing trends that evidence insufficient cultural transformation (such as the number of Catholic officers leaving the PSNI) and ongoing discussion about the operational effectiveness of all the accountability mechanisms. The debate is also progressing in a deteriorating security situation, with police officers once again becoming targets for armed republican attacks.[27]

With the voices of caution taken into account, and the work still to be done, this still indicates how effective targeted measures can be in securing some 'equality outcomes' over a relatively short period of time. There is also limited evidence to suggest that such reform can result in cultural changes in institutional settings that have wider equality impacts; for example the increase in the number of women police officers to 26 per cent in 2011.[28] However, it seems plain that the institutional culture of policing in Northern Ireland requires further transformation and that continuing critical assessment is required (Ellison, 2010, 2007; Nolan, 2012).

Equality, integration, and legitimacy: assessing the 'affirmative' in Northern Ireland

Changing the conversation?

Assessed in terms of general statistical outcomes, and with all necessary caveats, the conclusion from Northern Ireland seems straightforward: affirmative action arrangements dealing with ethno-national inequality have to a considerable extent 'worked' in the contexts for which they were designed (primarily employment and the workplace, but also the democratic institutions and policing regimes). This is not to overplay what has been achieved, or to promote forms of complacency – the evidence is suggestive of ongoing concerns. Northern Ireland is still, however, a deeply divided society, and levels of communal segregation (particularly in areas of socio-economic disadvantage) remain high (Shirlow and Coulter, 2007). The improvements on fair participation in employment that have taken place are impressive, and they occurred during and throughout a sustained period of economic growth, but it would not be accurate to conclude that Northern Ireland is a model of successful integrative practice, beyond the employment setting, or that the benefits of these developments are felt by everyone, including those most affected by the conflict (Shirlow and Coulter, 2007).

What flows through many of the debates in Northern Ireland is the relationship between liberal individualism and more communal approaches. The conflict took place in a liberal democratic and European context, with rights and constitutional regimes strongly aligned to notions of liberal individualism. The fair employment mechanisms adopted – although clearly 'affirmative action' in nature – could only be achieved through neutral and symmetrical provision for Protestants and Catholics, without the use of quotas or preferential treatment, and couched in the language and practice of fair participation. The policing regime is an exception, in that it was a targeted and directed scheme, time limited, and focused on one sphere of the state. However, even in a transitional justice frame this remains a liberalised affirmative action regime contextualised to the contours of ethno-national division. Great efforts were made to ensure that even the new equality regime for policing could be understood and defended in expressly liberal normative terms (and the regime survived an individualised rights-based legal challenge).

The ethno-national equality problems in Northern Ireland remain largely communal in nature, in the sense of perception of community background often being the determining factor in treatment (regardless of an individual's current position or multiple identities). It is that precise *perception of community background* that can be determinative – rendering agonised debates about self-determination of personal identity rather redundant. The mechanisms put in place navigate the tensions in ways that do not perpetuate the problems of division and separation but recognise the societal and political challenges. Criticism of the regime can still fail to understand the sophistication of the mechanisms or acknowledge properly what has been achieved (albeit in a context where further and other reforms are required). The story of fair employment is one of identifying a specific problem, mobilisation around this issue, and the steady evolution of targeted mechanisms to address it. This applies in formal terms to both the Protestant and Catholic communities and allowed for various approaches to implementation and enforcement, now undertaken by the Equality Commission for Northern Ireland. Aspects of the approach have been subjected to criticism, particularly from a liberal individualist perspective, but some of the arguments again do not display a full awareness of the nature of what has *in fact* been established. The evidence suggests that the objectives of the regime have been achieved to a significant extent. Workplaces are some of the most well integrated spaces in a society still marked by patterns of segregation and with continuing levels of socio-economic disadvantage (shared across both communities).

None of this is to make excessive claims. It all raises the straightforward question of who has gained in the reform process, how socio-economic disadvantage is tackled, and also how the conversation in Northern Ireland shifts beyond the two main national communities to address patterns of inequality for women, minority ethnic communities, and lesbian, gay, and transgender communities, among others. It is one argument of this chapter that there are clues to what has worked in Northern Ireland, that may or may not be exportable, but which should at minimum be put to use internally. If there is to be a changing conversation there is a need to learn from, and acknowledge, what has 'worked' in the past.

The politics of change: reform and communal aspiration

The policing regime is a special one, designed with the particular circumstances of Northern Ireland firmly in mind. On this, the balance of political forces succeeded in achieving a more focused and specific model that would yield demonstrable results quickly. It was an imperative of the wider inter-communal political process that it did so. Despite considerable resistance from unionist political parties the system was established and has had clear outcomes. There was a dynamic driving the agenda forward, all within a now hegemonic understanding of the wider peace process. While, for understandable reasons, nationalist parties have pressed for full implementation of the Patten Report in this respect (with calls to retain the regime until 40 per cent representation has been achieved); unionist parties always remained publicly hostile to it. If the starting point is the significance of the eventual outcome, then such an affirmative and targeted approach was required and has 'worked' (with all the notes of caution again in mind).[29] In the post-conflict context of Northern Ireland (and given its history) the legitimacy of the policing service remains vital; in achieving this, cross-community representation was essential and had to be rapidly secured.

The political dynamics are as interesting as the mechanisms. Due to the external British-Irish intergovernmental context, and the involvement of the US government among others, combined with a determined political campaign, the local political parties were not in a position to prevent this process of policing change. This raises wider questions about the reforms that are achieved in a post-conflict context, and those that are not. There is evidence that those aspects of the Agreement of 1998 that aligned closely with imperatives of stabilising inter-communal accommodation (policing reform, democratic institutions) were delivered, but those not directly tied to a strong communal narrative of 'stability first', and even a material interest in practical advancement for one community (or a specific historic grievance of one community), were not. While this generalisation requires further examination it remains instructive which reforms were viewed as vital to progress – and therefore achieved – and those that were not. It is intriguing to explore what is prioritised and what is not, and how successful mobilisation occurs. The mechanisms that are in place were created as a result of a political balance of forces that could be aligned to a campaign for internal reform. Their eventual success was the result of this wider political context, as well as the specific regulatory regime put in place. In other words, those engaged in these processes knew all too well the express political determination and will underpinning the agenda. These are regimes of transformative that were to be treated seriously, are regarded as vital to securing and stabilising inter-communal accommodation, and thus are accorded priority. They have resulted in clear representational change in ethno-national terms.

Conclusion

In sum, this chapter underlines three main points in support of the argument that the Northern Ireland experience is an instructive example of a form of 'contextualised equality'. First, systemic and structural communal inequality (between large ethno-national groups) provides fertile ground for the emergence of violent political conflict. However the conflict is presented (or perceived by protagonists and participants), entrenched horizontal inequality between groups was a key factor in perpetuating it. Embedded representational communal inequality presented a major problem, and structural inequality on socio-economic grounds offered a secure basis for violent conflict to persist. It is therefore not a coincidence that mechanisms have been designed primarily with this wider societal context in mind, or that equality and human rights are mainstreamed within the Good Friday Agreement 1998 and intended to be a central element in the new governance arrangements (McCrudden, 1999).

In examining what has happened since 1998 the communal framing has often proved decisive; it is hard to resist the conclusion that those elements of the post-1998 reform agenda which chimed most securely with the communal, material, and symbolic ambitions (of either main community) were more likely to be achieved in practice – particularly if credibly constructed as core to political stabilisation of inter-communal accommodation. This is not to endorse a narrow 'top-down' assessment. The complexity of this relational process must be grasped as a fluid interaction between the ways communities 'see themselves' and organise during and after a period of transition, and reform agendas that are advanced. Individuals and communities are here taking 'bottom up' and 'from below' subject positions in order to promote expressly political agendas – and the balance of support and alignment can shift depending on the issue and timing. This perhaps has something to tell us about the craft of successful political mobilisation on rights and equality during and after conflicts of this nature – and how the discourse is absorbed and moves around in such an environment. This is not a simple tale of the victory of the contextual over the universal, but a complex narrative about the mobilisation of communities and how rights and equality gain traction and meaning. It may also tell us something about those within communal groups who prosper during periods of transition. One of the resulting dilemmas – that stores up future problems – is whether socio-economic disadvantage and all the inequalities that fuelled conflict are tackled with sufficient vigour once inter-communal accommodation amongst elites and broad societal parity have been achieved. How far will a narrative of stabilisation reach? Who are the powerful intra-communal actors, and how can counter-hegemonic discourses be fostered *within* communities?

Second, while this may now appear self-evident, campaigns to promote forms of legal, political, and social reform were often greeted with considerable official resistance. Secure inter-governmental co-operation was significant – but issues had to be forced onto the agenda 'from below'. Many of the measures noted above were achieved only with sustained and persistent argument and international pressure; they were often not easily conceded, particularly (but not only) by unionist political parties who did not share the perception of the problems, and who have a distinct communal narrative about the formation of Northern Ireland and the conflict (as does the republican and nationalist community). The 'meta-conflict' persisted, and consistently resurfaced, as reform advanced without any shared understanding or agreement on the past (or even what the post-Agreement world was about) (Bell, 2003, 2000). It is worth underlining in this chapter that reform in these areas was achieved in the face of this continuing cross-community contestation.

Third, while the situation in Northern Ireland remains problematic, and patterns of under-representation and inequality continue (CAJ, 2006), progress was made in ensuring that overall workforce composition is reflective of employment equality between the two main communities. The fair employment regime resulted in significant change in terms of access to employment opportunities on the basis of equality. Given the incremental progress made in the composition of the PSNI

176 C. Harvey

there is one rather simple conclusion: if the objective is to challenge horizontal, systemic, and structural inequalities, then well designed (but also complex, creative, and sophisticated) affirmative/positive regulatory regimes can assist in achieving equality objectives – within a political and societal context *where effective mobilisation remains possible*. The Northern Ireland experience additionally suggests it is possible to promote fair participation and integration in employment *and* encourage and support economic growth.[30] The regimes noted above did not stand in the way of a sustained period of growth in employment in Northern Ireland up until the impact of the global recession was felt in 2008.

The significance of targeted, and robust approaches to crafting regulatory regimes – which promote fair and just outcomes for individuals, communities, and societies – should not be underestimated. This alone is, however, not enough in understanding what is happening. The Northern Ireland example provides evidence to support the claim that specific and targeted legal regulation can be useful and effective in tackling structural and systemic inequalities between ethno-national/religious communities. However, there is also evidence of what might stand behind such 'success' and the balance of political forces necessary to support such an outcome. Regulatory conversations must progress in a supportive environment where the legal tools are there to ensure progress is achieved. But the wider context of determined political mobilisation must be evident too and needs to remain in place if regulatory reform is to succeed.

Notes

1 For an earlier version of this chapter see: Colin Harvey (2012) 'Contextualised Equality and the Politics of Legal Mobilisation: Affirmative Action in Northern Ireland' in *Social and Legal Studies*, 21: 1–28.
2 According to Sabbagh (2011: 109):

> Broadly defined, *affirmative action* encompasses any measure that allocates resources – such as admission to selective universities or professional schools, jobs, promotion, public contracts, business loans, or rights to buy, sell or use land – through a process that takes into account individual membership in underrepresented groups.

3 By 'contextualised equality' I mean equality regimes that draw on international and comparative experience, but which are tied to local societal contexts and can trace their origins to empirically demonstrable structural inequality and localised participation in remedial design.
4 This picture was largely confirmed in the Northern Ireland Assembly elections 2011: Democratic Unionist Party (38 MLA), Sinn Féin (29 MLA), Ulster Unionist Party (16 MLA), Social Democratic and Labour Party (14 MLA), Alliance Party (8 MLA), Traditional Unionist Voice (1 MLA), Independents (2 MLA). Member of the Legislative Assembly (MLA).
5 Despite some of the arguments that rage around affirmative action, human rights law recognises that special measures will be needed. See, for example, UN Human Rights Committee, General Comment 18, para. 10: 'The principle of equality sometimes requires States to take affirmative action in order to diminish or eliminate conditions which cause or help to perpetuate discrimination prohibited by the Convention.' See also General Comment 4.

6 Other formulations include: the North, North of Ireland, the Province, Ulster, the Six Counties.
7 The census in Northern Ireland in 2001 recorded that of a population of 1,685,267, 43.76 per cent were Catholic and 53.13 per cent Protestant. The latest census was conducted in 2011 and at the time of writing these results are pending.
8 Tackling them effectively was to prove more of a challenge.
9 One of the main concerns with this model is precisely the voices that are silenced in such debates, but the rationale here is to examine precisely what might be achieved in these contexts *in their own terms*.
10 Christopher McCrudden *et al.*, in their article 'Affirmative Action without Quotas in Northern Ireland' (2009) say:

> Historically, Catholics and Protestants in Northern Ireland were typically highly segregated from each other in employment, with Catholics being concentrated in the Labour market, and in particular firms, and suffering unemployment rates two to three times as high as those of Protestants. But for the last twenty years, Northern Ireland's programme of affirmative action has used detailed monitoring for firms' composition plus agreed action plans, where necessary, to ensure for both groups "fair participation" in employment, avoiding the setting of quotas.

Northern Ireland did, however, have a quota-based system that applied to the Policing Service of Northern Ireland (PSNI), formerly the Royal Ulster Constabulary (RUC).
11 As the SACHR report of 1997 notes: 'In a survey by the Policy Studies Institute in 1986, most companies reported that the 1976 Act had had no impact on their personnel practices.' See SACHR Report for 1997–1998: 63.
12 The Principles were named after Seán McBride, who had founded Amnesty International, was a former Minister of Foreign Affairs in Ireland, and received the Nobel Peace Prize in 1974. He had also been the IRA Chief of Staff in the 1930s. According to McCrudden *et al.* (2009: 9–10):

> Another politically important reason for employers to engage in affirmative action in Northern Ireland was provided by the MacBride Principles. This was a campaign by US-based activists, largely from the Irish-American community, together with some human rights groups, to put pressure on the British government to act more decisively on fair employment in Northern Ireland.

13 All monitored employers are required to monitor the following: employees and apprentices; job applicants; and appointees. Registered employers with 250 or more employees (and all specified public authorities) must also monitor those promoted, and those leaving.
14 Failure to submit a return to the ECNI is a criminal offence, as is failure to submit within a defined period.
15 See p. 9: 'Ultimately these legally binding agreements are backed up by sanctions although in practice the Commission has primarily employed persuasion rather than enforcement.'
16 See also: ECNI *Employment Inequality in a Downturn* (July, 2010).
17 The major exception to this statement remains the security-related sector (PSNI, Royal Irish Regiment, Royal Naval Reserve, NI Prison Service, civilian secondees to the NICS, NI Policing Board), where the differentials are stark: 20.7 per cent Catholic (representing a slight increase from 15.6 per cent).
18 The research team have advanced four main findings: (1) There was a link between agreements and improvement (for both Protestants and Catholics), voluntary agreements worked better; (2) The agreements led to improvement in overall employment and changes at all levels (not just low-skilled jobs); (3) The Tribunal cases, and MacBride Principles, did not seem to have any lasting impact on employers; (4) The regime had a wider effect beyond regulated firms (McCrudden *et al.*, 2007: 11).

19 SACHR, Report 1997–1998 p. 81.
20 'The Northern Ireland experience shows that progress can be made towards fair employment without resorting to quotas that would probably be politically unacceptable in the rest of the UK or in Europe.' p. 14.
21 *In Re Parsons* [2003] NICA 20.
22 See: www.nipolicingboard.org.uk.
23 'DUP calls for scrapping of 50:50 PSNI recruitment', BBC News, 23 February 2010.
24 'Paterson confirms 50–50 recruitment should lapse', BBC News, 11 November 2010.
25 The ending of the 50:50 scheme was opposed by Sinn Féin, the SDLP, and the Catholic Church.
26 He cites the examples of gender balance and the failure to address truth recovery (see also, O'Rawe, 2003 and 2010).
27 PSNI Officer Ronan Kerr was murdered by dissident republicans on 2 April 2011.
28 See: www.nipolicingboard.org.uk.
29 According to McGarry and O'Leary (2004: 402–3):

> [I]ntegrationist (liberal-democratic) reforms are seldom sufficient in ethnically divided societies. It is not enough to create a professional police. A representative police is necessary. In nationally divided societies, moreover, the symbols, name, and behaviour of the police should be nationally impartial.

30 According to McCrudden *et al.* (2004: 123):

> We should note that employment growth for under-represented groups and increased workplace integration have both apparently been achieved at agreement firms.... [T]his initial analysis does suggest that there is no definitive trade-off between pursuing greater employment growth and pursuing integration as strategies for achieving fair participation.

References

The Belfast Agreement: An Agreement Reached at the Multi-Party Talks on Northern Ireland, 10 April 1998, Cm. 3883 (1998).
Bamforth, Nicholas, Maleiha Malik and Colm O'Cinneide, *Discrimination Law: Theory and Context* (2008, Thomson, Sweet and Maxwell).
Bell, Christine, *Peace Agreements and Human Rights* (2000, Oxford University Press).
Bell, Christine, 'Dealing with the Past in Northern Ireland' in *Fordham International Law Journal*, 26 (1095), 2003.
Bew, Paul, *The Making and Remaking of the Good Friday Agreement* (2007, Liffey Press).
Bew, Paul, *Ireland: The Politics of Enmity 1789–2006* (2007, Oxford University Press).
Boyle, Kevin and Tom Hadden, *Ireland: A Positive Proposal* (1985, Penguin).
Boyle, Kevin and Tom Hadden, *Northern Ireland: The Choice* (1994, Penguin).
Boyle, Kevin, Tom Hadden and Paddy Hillyard, *Law and State: The Case of Northern Ireland* (1975, Martin Robertson).
Cahn, Steven M. (ed.), *The Affirmative Action Debate* (2nd ed., 2002, Routledge).
Campbell, Colm, *Emergency Law in Ireland 1918–1925* (1994, Clarendon Press).
Campbell, Colm and Ita Connolly, 'Making War on Terror? Global Lessons from Northern Ireland' in *Modern Law Review*, 69 (935), 2006.
Campbell, Colm, Fionnula Ní Aoláin and Colin Harvey, 'The Frontiers of Legal Analysis: Reframing the Transition in Northern Ireland' in *Modern Law Review*, 68 (317), 2003.
Committee on the Administration of Justice, *Civil Liberties in Northern Ireland* (4th ed., 2004).

Committee on the Administration of Justice, *Equality in Northern Ireland: the rhetoric and the reality* (2006).
Doyle, John (ed.), *Policing the Narrow Ground: Lessons from the Transformation of Policing in Northern Ireland* (2010, Royal Irish Academy).
Doyle, John, 'The politics of the transformation of policing' in John Doyle (ed.), *Policing the Narrow Ground: Lessons from the Transformation of Policing in Northern Ireland* (2010, Royal Irish Academy), pp. 167–211.
Edwards, John, *Affirmative Action in a Sectarian Society* (1995, Avebury).
Ellison, Graham, 'A blueprint for democratic policing anywhere in the world? Police reform, political transition, and conflict resolution in Northern Ireland' in *Police Quarterly*, 10 (243), 2007.
Ellison, Graham, 'Police-community relations in Northern Ireland in the post-Patten era: towards an ecological analysis' in John Doyle (ed.), *Policing the Narrow Ground: Lessons from the Transformation of Policing in Northern Ireland* (2010, Royal Irish Academy), pp. 242–76.
Ellison, Graham and Jim Smyth, *The crowned harp: policing Northern Ireland* (2000, Pluto Press).
Ellison, Graham and Mary O'Rawe, 'Security governance in transition: the compartmentalizing, crowding out and corralling of policing and security in Northern Ireland' in *Theoretical Criminology*, 14 (31), 2010.
English, Richard, *Armed Struggle: The History of the IRA* (2003, Macmillan).
English, Richard, *Irish Freedom: The History of Nationalism in Ireland* (2006, MacMillan).
Equality Commission for Northern Ireland, *Unified Guide to Promoting Equal Opportunities in Employment* (2009, ECNI).
Equality Commission for Northern Ireland, *Monitoring Report No. 20 – A Profile of the Monitored Northern Ireland Workforce: Summary of Monitoring Returns 2009* (2010, ECNI).
Equality Commission for Northern Ireland, *Fair Employment Monitoring Report No. 20 – Research Update* (2010, ECNI).
Equality Commission for Northern Ireland, *Fair Employment Monitoring Report No. 21: Research Summary* (2011, ECNI).
Farrell, Michael, *Northern Ireland: The Orange State* (1976, Pluto Press).
Ferriter, Diarmaid, *The Transformation of Ireland 1900–2000* (2004, Profile Books).
Foster, R.F., *Modern Ireland 1600–1972* (1989, Penguin).
Foster, R.F., (ed.), *The Oxford History of Ireland* (1989, Oxford University Press).
Fredman, Sandra, *Discrimination Law* (2002, Oxford University Press).
Hadden, Tom, 'War and peace in Northern Ireland: Reflections on the contribution of academic and human rights communities' in Geoff Gilbert, Francoise Hampson and Clara Sandoval (eds.), *Strategic Visions for Human Rights: Essays in Honor of Professor Kevin Bell* (2010, Routledge).
Hadfield, Brigid, *The Constitution of Northern Ireland* (1989, SLS).
Hamilton, Jennifer, Ulf Hansson, John Bell and Sarah Toucas, *Segregated Lives: Social Division, Sectarianism and Everyday Life in Northern Ireland* (2008, Institute for Conflict Research).
Harvey, Colin, 'Governing after the Rights Revolution' in *Journal of Law and Society*, 27 (61), 2000.
Harvey, Colin, 'Implementing a Bill of Rights in Northern Ireland' in *Northern Ireland Legal Quarterly*, 51 (342), 2001.

Harvey, Colin 'The Politics of Rights and Deliberative Democracy: Drafting a Northern Irish Bill of Rights' in *European Human Rights Law Review*, 48 (2001).

Harvey, Colin 'Building Bridges? Protecting Human Rights in Northern Ireland' in *Human Rights Law* Review, 1 (132), 2001.

Harvey, Colin (ed.), *Human Rights, Equality and Democratic Renewal in Northern Ireland* (Hart, 2001).

Harvey, Colin, 'Contested Constitutionalism: Human Rights and Deliberative Democracy in Northern Ireland' in Tom Campbell, K.D. Ewing, and Adam Tomkins (eds.), *Sceptical Approaches to Human Rights* (2001, Oxford University Press), pp. 163–75.

Harvey, Colin, 'The New Beginning: Reconstructing Constitutional Law and Democracy in Northern Ireland' in Colin Harvey (ed.), *Human Rights, Equality and Democratic Renewal in Northern Ireland* (2001, Hart Publishing), pp. 10–52.

Harvey, Colin, 'Building a Human Rights Culture in a Political Democracy: The Role of the Northern Ireland Human Rights Commission' in Colin Harvey (ed.), *Human Rights, Equality and Democratic Renewal in Northern Ireland* (2001, Hart Publishing), pp. 113–31.

Harvey, Colin, 'Northern Ireland in Transition: An Introduction' in Colin Harvey (ed.), *Human Rights, Equality and Democratic Renewal in Northern Ireland* (2001, Hart Publishing), pp. 1–9.

Harvey, Colin, 'Human Rights and Equality' in R. Wilson (ed.), *Agreeing to Disagree? A Guide to the Northern Ireland Assembly* (2001, The Stationery Office), pp. 1–13.

Harvey, Colin and David Russell, 'A New Beginning for Human Rights Protection in Northern Ireland?' in *European Human Rights Law Review*, 767 (2009).

Harvey, Colin and Alex Schwartz, 'Designing a Bill of Rights for Northern Ireland' in *Northern Ireland Legal Quarterly*, 60 (181), 2009.

Healing Through Remembering, *Making Peace with the Past: Options for Truth Recovery regarding the Conflict in and about Northern Ireland* (2006, HTR, Belfast).

Hepple, Bob, Mary Coussey and Tufyal Choudhury, *Equality: A New Framework – Report of the Independent Review of the Enforcement of UK Anti-Discrimination Legislation* (2000, Hart Publishing).

Kerr, Michael, *Imposing Power-Sharing: Conflict and Coexistence in Northern Ireland and Lebanon* (2005, Irish Academic Press).

Lee, Joe, *Ireland 1912–1985 Politics & Society* (Cambridge University Press, 1989).

Lijphart, Arend, *Democracy in Plural Societies: A Comparative Exploration* (1977, Yale University Press).

Lijphart, Arend, *Patterns of Democracy: Government Forms and Performance in Thirty-Six Countries* (1999, Yale University Press).

McCrudden, Christopher, 'Rethinking Positive Action' in *Industrial Law Journal*, 15 (223), 1986.

McCrudden, Christopher, 'Affirmative Action and Fair Participation: Interpreting the Fair Employment Act 1989' in *Industrial Law Journal*, 21 (170), 1992.

McCrudden, Christopher, 'Mainstreaming Equality in the Governance of Northern Ireland' in *Fordham International Law Journal*, 22 (1696), 1999.

McCrudden, Christopher (ed.), *Anti-Discrimination Law* (2nd series, The International Library of Essays in Law and Legal Theory, 2004, Ashgate).

McCrudden, Christopher, 'Consociationalism, Equality and Minorities in the Northern Ireland Bill of Rights Debate: The Inglorious Role of the OSCE High Commissioner for National Minorities' in *Oxford Legal Studies Research Paper No. 6* (2006).

McCrudden, Christopher, 'Northern Ireland, the Belfast Agreement and the British Constitution' in Chapter 10 of Jeffrey Jowell and Dawn Oliver (eds.), *The Changing Constitution* (6th ed., Oxford University Press, 2007).

McCrudden, Christopher, Robert Ford and Anthony Heath, 'Legal Regulation of Affirmative Action in Northern Ireland' in *Oxford Journal of Legal Studies*, 363 (2004).

McCrudden, Christopher, Raya Muttarak, Heather Hamill and Anthony Heath, 'Affirmative Action without Quotas in Northern Ireland' in *The Equal Rights Review*, 4 (7), 2009.

McEvoy, Kieran, 'What Did the Lawyers Do During the "War"? Neutrality, Conflict and the Culture of Quietism' in *Modern Law Review*, 74 (350), 2011.

McEvoy, Kieran and Ciaran White, 'Loyalty, Redress and Citizenship: Security Vetting in Northern Ireland' in *Modern Law Review*, 61 (341), 1998.

McEvoy, Kieran and Lorna McGregor (eds.), *Transitional Justice from Below: Grassroots Activism and the Struggle for Change* (2008, Hart Publishing).

McGarry, John, 'Political Settlements in Northern Ireland and South Africa' in *Political Studies*, 46 (853), 1998.

McGarry, John (ed.), *Northern Ireland and the Divided World: Post-Agreement Northern Ireland in Comparative Perspective* (2001, Oxford University Press).

McGarry, John and Brendan O'Leary (eds.), *The Politics of Ethnic Conflict Regulation* (1993, Routledge).

McGarry, John, and Brendan O'Leary, *Policing Northern Ireland: Proposals for a New Start* (1999, Blackstaff Press).

McGarry, John and Brendan O'Leary, *The Northern Ireland Conflict: Consociational Engagement* (2004, Oxford University Press).

McNamara, Kevin, ' "Give us Another MacBride Campaign": An Irish-American Contribution to Peaceful Change in Northern Ireland' in Marianne Elliott (ed.), *The Long Road to Peace in Northern Ireland* (2007, Liverpool University Press), pp. 78–88.

Moloney, Ed, *A Secret History of the IRA* (2nd ed., 2007, Penguin).

Murray, Gerard, and Jonathan Tonge, *Sinn Fein and the SDLP: From Alienation to Participation* (2005, O'Brien Press).

Ní Aoláin, Fionnuala, *The Politics of Force: Conflict Management and Statement Violence in Northern Ireland* (2000, Blackstaff Press).

Nolan, Paul, *Northern Ireland Peace Monitoring Report Number One* (2012, CRC).

Northern Ireland Office, *Police (Northern Ireland) Act 2000 – Review of Temporary Recruitment Provisions: Consultation Paper* (November 2010).

Northern Ireland Statistics and Research Agency (NISRA), *Census 2011: Population and Household Estimates for Northern Ireland* (NISRA, July 2012, Belfast).

Northern Ireland Statistics and Research Agency (NISRA), *Census 2011: Historic Populations Trends (1841-2011) – Northern Ireland and Republic of Ireland* (NISRA, July 2012, Belfast).

O'Leary, Brendan and John McGarry, *The Politics of Antagonism: Understanding Northern Ireland* (2nd edn, 1996, Athlone).

O'Rawe, Mary, 'Transitional Policing Arrangements in Northern Ireland: The Can't and the Won't of the Change Dialectic' in *Fordham International Law Journal*, 26 (1015), 2003.

O'Rawe, Mary, 'The importance of gender in the transformation of policing' in John Doyle (ed.), *Policing the Narrow Ground: Lessons from the Transformation of Policing in Northern Ireland* (2010, Royal Irish Academy), pp. 212–43.

Osborne, Bob, 'Progressing the Equality Agenda in Northern Ireland' in *Journal of Social Policy*, 32 (339), 2003.

Osborne, Bob and Ian Shuttleworth (eds), *Fair Employment in Northern Ireland: a generation on* (2004, the Blackstaff Press, Belfast).

Post, Robert and Micael Rogin (eds.), *Race and Representation: Affirmative Action* (1998, Zone Books).

Prince, Simon, *Northern Ireland's '68: Civil Rights, Global Revolt and the Origins of the Troubles* (2007, Irish Academic Press).

Purdie, Bob, *Politics in the Streets: The Origins of the Civil Rights Movement in Northern Ireland* (1990, Blackstaff Press).

The Report of the Independent Commission on Policing for Northern Ireland (Patten Commission, September 1999).

Rose, Sarah and Denise Magill, 'The Development of Fair Employment Legislation in Northern Ireland' in SACHR *Fair Employment Law in Northern Ireland: Debates and Issues* (1996, SACHR).

Ruane, J. and J. Todd (eds.), *After the Good Friday Agreement: Analysing Political Change in Northern Ireland* (1999, UCD Press).

Sabbagh, Daniel, 'Affirmative Action: The US Experience in Comparative Perspective' in *Daedalus*, 140 (109), 2011.

SACHR, *Religious and Political Discrimination and Equality of Opportunity in Northern Ireland: Report on Fair Employment* (1987, HMSO).

SACHR, *Employment Equality in Northern Ireland* (1997, HMSO).

Schwartz, Alex and Colin Harvey, 'Judicial Empowerment in Divided Societies' in Colin Harvey and Alex Schwartz (eds.), *Rights in Divided Societies* (2012, Hart Publishing).

Shirlow, Peter and Brendan Murtagh, *Belfast: Segregation, Violence and the City* (2006, Pluto Press).

Shirlow, Peter and Colin Coulter, 'Enduring Problems: The Belfast Agreement and a Disagreed Belfast' in Marianne Elliott (ed.), *The Long Road to Peace in Northern Ireland* (2007, Liverpool University Press), pp. 207–20.

Smith, Anne and Eithne McLaughlin, 'Delivering equality: equality mainstreaming and constitutionalisation of socio-economic rights' in *Northern Ireland Legal Quarterly*, 61 (93), 2010.

Whyte, John, *Interpreting Northern Ireland* (1990, Clarendon Press).

Wilford, Rick (ed.), Aspects of the Belfast Agreement (2001, Oxford University Press).

Wright, Frank, *Northern Ireland: A Comparative Analysis* (1987, Gill and Macmillan).

7 Appraising affirmative action in Brazil

Joaze Bernardino-Costa and Fernando Rosa

Introduction

Brazil has historically represented a somewhat peculiar case in terms of analyses of inequality. It has been comparatively absent in discussions of horizontal inequality as the country has not been viewed as one where such inequalities are glaringly present. It has also not usually been considered a society where ethnic cleavages have had a foundational character. In this it is very different for instance from Fiji, Malaysia, South Africa and the United States. Inside Brazil, until fairly recently, the dominant view has been that inequality in the country is exclusively (or at least mainly) of a vertical nature as it is class-based. In fact, this view is still largely dominant not only inside much of academia but also, for instance, in government circles and the political domain, not to mention sectors of civil society. Therefore, in comparison to virtually all other countries under debate in this volume, Brazil is a newcomer to affirmative action in more ways than one. In fact, it is still a nation state where affirmative action is of very recent origin and where its application has been so far very circumscribed. In reality it has been confined basically to academia – public universities in particular – and some sectors of the government and public service.

Importantly too, Brazil is the only country in this study not to have been a British colony at any point in time. It was a Portuguese colony. This difference is both important and difficult to elaborate. This is because Brazil's discourses on inequality and 'race' have been heavily dependent on an appreciation of Brazil's peculiar history as a Portuguese colony, even though that peculiarity is compounded by the fact that Brazil is unlike any other former Portuguese colony. None were so vast or so varied and therefore so incredibly intricate. Besides, no other colony of Portugal was located on the American continent. Therefore, referring Brazil's specific character to its colonial history – a major heuristic device in some discourses explaining the nature of Brazilian society – is at best actually positing yet another conundrum instead of offering an ultimate explanation for ethnicity and therefore also for the origins of inequality. Unsurprisingly, history itself is here a very contentious matter as both people in favour of affirmative action in Brazil and those against it have often resorted to history – colonial and post-colonial – in order to boost their arguments. Therefore, the very act of tracing the history and development of affirmative action in Brazil places us, the authors of this study, in the middle of a warring field; there is currently virtually no consensus in the country on affirmative action let alone on the historical roots of inequality.

The historical appraisal that follows is an essential part of the debate in Brazil. Crucially, too, the notion of separate ethnic identities – say, black versus white Brazilians – has itself often been the main bone of contention. In particular, opinion makers opposed to affirmative action policies in Brazil have argued that there are not separate racial identities in the country. Instead they state that 'we are all Brazilian', without 'race' distinction. Hence the current debate over whether 'miscegenation' or 'mestizos' are sociologically important factors when talking about inequality in the country (one side says that both are important whereas the other argues they have little or even no importance). Our point here is not to debate the pros and cons of each conflicting view as it relates to the nature of ethnicity, the nation state, and the origins and current state of inequality in Brazil. There is already a fairly vast literature dealing with the subject both inside and outside the country published in both Portuguese and English.[1] Our aim here, after briefly pointing out the intricacies of the debate as it is currently unfolding in Brazil, is to provide the historical analysis of the implementation of affirmative action.

The first part of this article provides a general historical background of the issue, while the subsequent sections deal with the development of affirmative action. The final section will tackle the issue of vertical and horizontal inequalities in Brazil. In this essay, the terms 'miscegenation' and 'race' (but not racial) have been put between quotes as we regard both as historically grounded social constructs.

Brazil in historical perspective

The Portuguese supposedly arrived accidentally on Brazilian shores in 1500 on their way to the Malabar Coast in India.[2] In the middle of the sixteenth century, after finding the indigenous population unsuitable to be labourers in the sugar production industry, they initiated the traffic of slave labour from Africa to Brazil. Between the mid-sixteenth and mid-nineteenth centuries, when slavery was legal, first the Portuguese Empire and later the Empire of Brazil[3] brought about 3.6 million Africans to Brazil to work initially in sugar production (sixteenth and seventeenth centuries), mining and the raising of livestock (seventeenth and eighteenth centuries), and finally, coffee production (nineteenth century). Of the immense flow of enslaved Africans who arrived alive in the Americas (many would die during the crossing), 38 per cent came to Brazilian territory, making Brazil the largest slaveholding nation in the Americas and the modern world (Hasenbalg 1979; Karasch 2000; Mattoso 1990). It was also the last to abolish slavery in 1888.[4]

The abolition of slavery[5] did not take place all at once however, having been preceded by three other laws beginning in 1850 that began the dismantling of the slaveholding regime. The Eusébio de Queiróz Law (1850) established the end of the slave trade; the Law of Free Birth (1871) established that every child of a slave born after the enactment of the law would be free; and the Sexagenarian Law (1885) established that any slave older than 60 years would be set free. This process of transition from a slaveholding system to the formation of a free labour market coincided with a project of modernization of the country. From the perspective of that project, slavery and eventually also Africans were seen as synonymous with backwardness. Therefore, in the second half of the nineteenth century, the abolition of slavery occurred side by side with a strategy for substituting black labour with free labour of European origin. This strategy was associated with civilization, modernization, and progress.

Despite several initiatives to benefit both enslaved and manumitted black workers, such as a proposed land distribution, the principal political and economic agents in the country invested in European migration. According to the judgement of the economic and political elite of the second half of the nineteenth century, this migration was not only a solution to the labour problem but also an opportunity to whiten – and therefore 'civilize' – the country, since 'science' claimed that whites were superior to non-whites: that is blacks, Asians and indigenous peoples. Thus the Brazilian government deliberately chose to fund European immigration to the country and close the doors to Africans – until 1934, the entry of free Africans was prohibited in the country. Japanese have been allowed to enter the country only since 1908. This policy lasted until the first decades of the twentieth century (Azevedo 2004).

If during three centuries of slavery 3.6 million Africans came to Brazil, between 1850 and 1930 4.7 million European and other immigrants arrived to form the free labour market. A significant portion of these immigrants were Portuguese, Spaniards, Italians and Germans, besides Japanese, who went to states in the south and southeast, especially the state of São Paulo, the economic centre of the country at the time, and today. As mentioned above, the promotion of European immigration was based on an ideology of whitening. This ideology was rooted in the belief of academics and politicians in Brazil that the inferiority of blacks and mestizos both in what concerned 'civilization' and 'race' could be overcome only through 'miscegenation'. They therefore believed that sexual intercourse between whites and non-whites (blacks and mestizos) would result in the elimination of the non-white population and lead to an entirely white population.

João Batista Lacerda, the director of one of the leading research institutions in the country, Museu Nacional, stated at the Universal Races Congress in 1911 in London that over the course of a century of intermarriage there would be no more black or mixed 'race' people in Brazilian society (Skidmore 1976). The result of this whitening policy was not simply a demographic and ethnic shift, but also the narrowing of socio-economic prospects to former slaves, now relegated to the margins of the process leading to the country's development. They, however, made up the majority of the country's poor. There was no segregationist institution nor were there laws that mandated segregation, but blacks were made subaltern. This is the so-called 'subordinate integration' of blacks in Brazilian society.

From the 1930s onwards 'miscegenation', envisioned as an intermediate phase in the project of whitening the country, came in this way to be seen as positive and the key to nation building. This was so as it became clear that thoroughly whitening the country would not be a feasible policy. Therefore, 'miscegenation' – previously perceived as negative – began to be seen as the mark of Brazil's uniqueness among nations; it was then imagined by some in the elite that the unity of the Brazilian people was the product of a harmonious coexistence among different 'races'. The affirmation of 'miscegenation' permitted the elaboration of a conception of Brazilian society as a 'racial democracy'. Brazil came to be thought of as a society without prejudice or racial discrimination. What many now call the myth of 'racial democracy' lasted until the mid-1970s – though it had been challenged 20 years earlier in the research of sociologist Florestan Fernandes – and served to construct the nation's image both internally and abroad. The certainty of the Brazilian state of the inexistence of racial discrimination in the country was so great that the Foreign Minister stated in 1970, in the report of the Committee for Elimination of All Forms of Racial Discrimination, that 'there is no racial discrimination in Brazil; there is no need to take any sporadic measures whatsoever of a legislative, judicial or administrative nature to ensure the equality of races in Brazil' (quoted in Telles 2003: 58).

Debating racial discrimination

It is only, however, with the (re)democratization of the country,[6] beginning in the late 1970s, that the myth of 'racial democracy' actually began to weaken. Beginning with the studies of social mobility carried out by Carlos Hasenbalg (1979), it was found that social inequality was to a great degree caused by racial discrimination and prejudice. Thus, class-based arguments did not entirely explain the inequality between blacks and whites, as had been previously maintained. Together with that important academic contribution, democratization created a political space for activists from social movements, especially the black movement. In 1978 a major black organization in Brazil, the Movimento Negro Unificado (Unified Black Movement), was founded. It then pushed for public policies to combat racial inequality in labour and education, and also demanded tougher laws against racism.

As a direct result of this black militancy at the end of the 1970s, after the election of progressive parties and candidates in the municipal and state elections of 1982, several state and municipal governments established advisory councils and bodies for the black population (Santos 2006). These bodies had as objectives the defence and promotion of blacks. It was at this juncture that the first Brazilian state institutions dedicated to the promotion of public policies for the black population were created. In this regard, Brazil's Federal Constitution of 1988 was significant. That year was the centenary of the abolition of slavery. The centenary was the object of extensive mobilization on the part of the black movement. Results of that mobilization included: (1) the creation of Fundação Cultural Palmares,[7] the federal agency devoted to the promotion and preservation of African influence in Brazilian society; (2) the establishment of 20 November as Black Consciousness Day and the recognition of Zumbi dos Palmares (a maroon leader in colonial times) as a national hero; and (3) the designation of Serra da Barriga, the seventeenth century site of Quilombo dos Palmares (a colonial maroon community) as an historical landmark.

As concerns the Constitution, the following achievements are most noteworthy: the recognition of the right to land ownership of the remaining population of *quilombos*;[8] the commitment of the Federal Republic of Brazil to the promotion of not only formal but also material equality (Article 5); the commitment to combat social, racial and regional inequality (Article 3); and the commitment to promote cultural diversity (Article 242). Furthermore, in 1995, during the commemoration of the 300th anniversary of the death of Zumbi dos Palmares, more than 30,000 black activists marched in Brasília, the country's capital. At the end of this demonstration, a document was presented to then-President Fernando Henrique Cardoso, proposing policies for promoting Brazilian society's ethnic diversity and presenting a programme for the promotion of racial equality, including affirmative action measures.

In response to this important mobilization of the black population, the President established, under the Ministry of Justice, the Inter-ministerial Task Force (GTI) for the Promotion of the Black Population, charged with advancing policies to support the social and political participation of the black population (Presidential Decree of 20 November 1995). The following year, 1996, spurred by the Unified Workers' Central (CUT),[9] which had abandoned a discourse of homogeneity and universality of the working class and had established a National Commission against racial discrimination, the federal government created the Task Force for the Elimination of Discrimination in Employment and Occupation (GTDEO). The creation of GTDEO was due to a formal complaint from CUT and other unions against the Brazilian government for breach of International Labour Organization (ILO) Convention 111.[10] The GTDEO was created with the mission to combat inequalities of 'race' and gender and to promote racial equality.

In 1996 the federal government also promoted an international seminar on Multiculturalism and Racism under the auspices of the Secretariat of Human Rights in the Ministry of Justice. Two events are notable in this seminar: (1) for the first time a President of the Republic acknowledged that Brazil is a racist country; and (2) the acknowledgement by the Brazilian state that racial inequality could be addressed through affirmative action. A few days after this seminar, through Decree No. 1904 of 13 May 1996, the federal government launched the National Plan for Human Rights, anticipating affirmative action measures for the black and indigenous populations. It is noteworthy that the public admission by the main political authority that racism existed in Brazil constituted something completely new in a country whose authorities had repeatedly declared it in the past to be a nation with no problems of racial discrimination or prejudice.

Towards the end of the 1990s, concurrent with the measures contained in the plan of the executive government, black members of the legislative branch assembled a proposal for affirmative action measures for the black population. Senators Abdias Nascimento and Benedita da Silva proposed quotas for black students in public universities, in public administration and private enterprises (draft laws 14/1995 and 75/1997). Aside from these measures few concrete affirmative action steps were taken until 2001. The watershed became the Third World Conference Against Racism, Racial Discrimination, Xenophobia and Related Intolerance, held between 30 August and 7 September of that year in the South African city of Durban.

Implementing affirmative action

The Durban conference mobilized black Brazilian activists for a number of state, regional and national preparatory conferences. The discussions at the National Conference Against Racism and Intolerance, held a month before the world conference, from 6–8 July 2001, in the state of Rio de Janeiro, aided the formulation of the Brazilian document that was submitted in Durban.

In the declaration and programme of action of this third conference, the signatory countries, including Brazil, pledged to develop policies, among them affirmative action programmes, to combat racial inequality, and recognized 'race' as a social category that could explain the profound social inequalities extant in many societies. Paragraphs 99 and 100 of the Action Plan of the World Conference Against Racism state:

> Paragraph 99 – Recognizes that combating racism, racial discrimination, xenophobia and related intolerance is a primary responsibility of States. It therefore encourages States to develop and elaborate national action plans to promote diversity, equality, fairness, social justice, equal opportunity and participation for all. Through, among other things, affirmative or positive actions and strategies.... Paragraph 100 – Urges States to establish, based on statistical information, national programs, including programs of affirmative action or positive action measures to promote access for groups of individuals who are or may become victims of racial discrimination in basic social services, including basic education, primary health care and adequate housing.
> (Moura Barreto 2002: 131)

By adopting this pledge the Brazilian state abandoned the discourse that maintained the myth of 'racial democracy', and acknowledged racial inequalities. At the same time it committed itself explicitly to the adoption of racially oriented public policies with the goal of achieving racial equality.

One consequence of the Third UN Conference was legal support and strengthening of the pro-affirmative action struggle, especially in Brazilian universities. In 2001, for the first time among state universities, Universidade Estadual do Rio de Janeiro (UERJ) adopted affirmative action policies through the implementation of a quota system in undergraduate admissions for black, mixed and destitute students. In 2003 the Universidade de Brasília (UNB), for the first time among the federal universities, did the same for black, mixed and indigenous students. Since then a growing number of federal and state institutions of higher education have adopted affirmative action policies for undergraduate candidates based on colour/'race', ethnicity, social class or other characteristics. Of a total of 98 federal and state universities in Brazil, 70 have adopted some form of affirmative action. In percentage terms, 71.4 per cent of federal and state universities in Brazil have adopted such policies.

All affirmative action programmes in universities are temporary. As a general rule universities have adopted affirmative action policies lasting 10 years. At the end of this period the policies will be evaluated and may be suspended, maintained, modified or broadened or extended. Both the modality of affirmative action in each university, and the beneficiary group, would vary according to the directives regarding the implementation of the policies enacted by the university board, acting either autonomously or following state laws. The 70 universities adopted affirmative action programmes based on the following modalities: quotas, bonuses, increased number of places and a combination of these, as Table 7.1 shows.

Of these 70 universities, not all have adopted affirmative action benefiting exclusively blacks. Diverse groups have benefited from affirmative action: the number of social programmes based on quotas for low income students and those coming from public schools exceed the number of programmes for black students. For example, there are universities that have implemented affirmative action programmes only for students who attended public high schools, without taking into consideration their racial background; other universities designed their affirmative action programmes for black students who attended public high schools, and so on.

Alongside the original demands made by the black population in the country, several other social groups took advantage of the discussions about affirmative action and also benefited. Table 7.2 shows the groups that benefited in the 70 universities with affirmative action policies.

Table 7.1 Modality of affirmative action in federal and state public universities in Brazil

Modality	Number	Percentage
Quota	35	50.0
Bonus	7	10.0
Increase in number of places	3	4.3
Quota and bonus	5	7.1
Quota and increase	19	27.1
Bonus and increase	1	1.4
Total	70	100

Source: Feres Júnior, V.T. Daflon and L.A. Campos, 2010.

Table 7.2 Beneficiaries of affirmative action in federal and state public universities in Brazil

Beneficiaries	Number	Percentage
From public schools	61	87.1
Black	40	57.1
Indigenous	36	51.4
With disabilities	13	18.6
With indigenous teaching certificate	6	8.6
From *quilombos*	3	4.3
Born in the state	3	4.3
Low income	3	4.3
Public school teachers	3	4.3
From rural areas	3	4.3
Children of police or firemen killed or disabled in service	2	2.9
Women	1	1.4

Source: Feres Júnior, V.T. Daflon and L.A. Campos, 2010.

The main front for the black movement in the last decade has been the implementation of (new) affirmative action policies in universities, as well as the consolidation of existing programmes. This is due, on one hand, to the affirmation of the university as constituting the most rational means for ascent into the middle class and, on the other, the near absence of blacks in universities, especially in the more prestigious fields of study.

To get an idea of the near absence of blacks in prestigious professions in Brazil in 2000, the year preceding the adoption of affirmative action policies in Brazilian universities, of the 284,000 physicians in Brazil, 86 per cent said they were white. It was estimated, in a hypothetical way, that if all of the places in medical schools in the country were reserved for blacks – in essence, a quota of 100 per cent – it would take 25 years for the number of black physicians to equal that of white physicians (see Petruccelli 2004). Presently the Brazilian population totals 191.7 million, 48.2 per cent white and 51.1 per cent black.[11] There are 11.2 million college graduates, of whom 73.7 per cent are white and only 24.4 per cent black (*Synthesis of Social Indicators*, 2010). Apart from the groups mobilizing for and demanding the adoption of affirmative action policies in the public higher education system, the federal government adopted the programme 'University for All' (ProUni) through Law 11.096/2004. ProUni provided tax exemptions for private institutions of higher education granting full and partial scholarships to students completing secondary school in public schools or in private schools with a full scholarship. Moreover, ProUni states that a number of scholarships will be awarded to black and indigenous students proportional to their population in their respective states.[12]

Affirmative action policies have been adopted not only in higher education. The Foreign Ministry launched a fellowship programme called 'Vocation for Diplomacy' for black candidates, which also took into account gender. The

Brazilian diplomatic service has historically been seen as a space for the white population, and throughout history access has been denied to blacks, even those passing the objective stages of the selection process. One associates this with the exporting of an image of a white country, linked to the ideology of whitening. Because of this, black diplomats have been exceedingly few in number. To reverse this image the 'Affirmative Action Programme of the Rio Branco Institute – Fellowship Award for Vocation for Diplomacy' was developed, which consists of financial assistance for preparation for the public admissions examination for diplomatic careers. From the programme's launching in 2002 through till August 2010, 16 black candidates (men and women) entered the diplomatic service (see Rio Branco Institute 2010). These results may appear paltry, but they are important in the formation of role models in the fight against racist culture.

In addition to these effective affirmative action programmes implemented in universities and the Ministry of Foreign Affairs, some sporadic measures of this type of policy have been adopted by several administrative agencies over the last decade. These administrative bodies include the Ministry of Justice, the Ministry of Rural Development, and the Federal Supreme Court. Other affirmative action measures should be mentioned. In 2003, the first year of President Luis Inácio Lula da Silva's mandate, the Special Secretariat for Policies Promoting Racial Equality (SEPPIR) was created.[13] Institutionally linked to the Presidency of the Republic, and with ministerial status, the mission of SEPPIR is to promote actions to combat racial inequality and link the policies of diverse ministries and government agencies so that the racial dimension is addressed on different fronts. Through the programme 'Brazil Without Racism', SEPPIR has brought together actions involving issues related to employment and income, culture and communication, education, health, *quilombos*, black women, youth, security and international relations. Unlike the government of former President Fernando Henrique Cardoso, Lula's government has approached the 'race' issue with a systemic and integrated vision. However, not all policies developed by SEPPIR have succeeded in these seven years of operation, for a number of reasons. These include resistance from other central ministries to consider 'race' an important variable in public policy, SEPPIR's lack of a technical-bureaucratic framework and a budget limited to systemic action cutting across multiple government agencies.

In 2003 Law 10.639/03[14] was approved, which made compulsory the teaching of African history and Afro-Brazilian culture in primary and secondary[15] public and private schools. This law has been an important tool for tackling the racial imaginary in Brazilian society that discredits the black population and naturalizes racial inequality. As a corrective, this law has encouraged the development of pedagogical practices in public and private schools aimed at valuing the black population. Likewise, this law has played an important role in stimulating research and the production of educational material on the issue of 'race' in Brazil.[16]

It is necessary to emphasize the legal process in the Federal Congress of the so-called Bill of Quotas (PL 73/1999), which proposes: (1) reserving 50 per cent of the seats in public colleges and universities throughout the country for students coming from public schools; and (2) adopting percentages for black and indigenous students representative of these demographics' populations in the states in which the institutions of higher education are located. However, due to pressure from groups opposing affirmative action, this project has been stalled in Congress and is still waiting to be voted on. What is novel in this project? If approved, all 268 public institutions of higher education in Brazil – and not just the current 70 federal and state public universities – will adopt policies of affirmative action. Recall that current affirmative action measures are a result of either autonomous decisions by the universities themselves, or by mandate of the Legislative Assemblies of each state; this explains the wide variety of affirmative action programmes and policies in practice in the country.

Finally, after a lengthy debate in Congress, the Statute of Racial Equality was adopted on 20 July 2010.[17] The Statute was formulated to promote racial equality in many areas and to guarantee the right to education, employment, health, culture, sport and leisure, the media, housing and access to land. The Statute was passed after arduous negotiations with conservative parties, and subsequently has been misrepresented as a law effectively securing new rights for the black population. The chapter that deals with education, for example, includes no rights not already guaranteed by other laws, for the article mandating affirmative action in public education was excised. Similar distortion occurred in the chapter on the right to work; the article establishing affirmative action for blacks in the labour market was excised. In other words, the Statute of Racial Equality does not prohibit the adoption of affirmative action, but nor does it establish any of these policies, making it toothless in this regard. In light of these lacunae in the statute, affirmative action for black people in the Brazilian labour market is almost completely non-existent. The exceptions are a few banks and private companies adopting affirmative action for blacks and women, not because of any Brazilian law, but because their headquarters are located in another country that requires them to do so (Myers 2003).

The political debate

The affirmative action policies being enacted in the country, the laws passed and Bill 73/1999 pending in Congress, have inaugurated a new moment in Brazil's political history. This new Brazilian political context has provoked intense debate, occupying in recent years the pages of major newspapers and television news programmes (Moya and Silverio 2009).

Invariably, the debate has revolved around the following issues: (1) affirmative action is unconstitutional; (2) 'race' does not exist in Brazil; (3) we are all mestizos, there are no blacks in Brazil; (4) the problem is not racial, but one of class; (5) affirmative action compromises the quality of Brazilian universities; and (6) affirmative action will cause a racial divide within Brazilian society. These challenges have appeared not only in the mainstream media, but also in four manifestos, two in favour of and two opposed to affirmative action policies. These manifestos were delivered to the Presidents of the Senate (the upper house) and Chamber of Deputies (the lower house) in 2006, and the President of the Supreme Court in 2008. The first manifesto was delivered to the Presidents of the Chamber of Deputies and the Senate on 29 June 2006 by a group of intellectuals opposed to affirmative action. This document was entitled 'Open Letter to Congress: All Have Equal Rights in a Democratic Republic'. In reaction to this manifesto a group in favour of affirmative action delivered on 3 July 2006, to the chairmen of the Chamber of Deputies and the Senate, the 'Manifesto in Favor of the Quota Law and the Statute of Racial Equality'. Two years later new manifestos were delivered to the President of the Supreme Court. On 30 April 2008, the group opposed to affirmative action for blacks delivered the manifesto '113 Anti-Racist Citizens against Racial Laws'. In response, the group in favour of affirmative action, on 13 May 2008, delivered the document '120 Years of Struggle for Racial Equality in Brazil: Manifesto in Defense of Justice and Constitutionality of Quotas'. Below are counter-arguments to the six most common challenges made against affirmative action policies.

Affirmative action is unconstitutional

The first of these, 'affirmative actions are unconstitutional', gradually lost strength as a growing number of universities adopted affirmative policies. Moreover, from the standpoint of legal doctrine, several lawyers have defended the constitutionality of affirmative action and its compatibility as a principle of equality. The Brazilian judicial system established equality not only in the formal sense, but also in its material sense. The jurist Carmen Lúcia Antunes Rocha, currently one of 11 members of the Supreme Court,[18] wrote (1996: 85):

> The judicial, objective, and rational definition of inequality of peoples historically and culturally discriminated is conceived of as a means to promote the equality of those who were and are marginalized by prejudice embedded in society's dominant culture.... Affirmative action is, therefore, a juridical way to overcome the isolation or social diminishment to which minorities believe themselves subjected.

There are no races in Brazil

Backed by arguments of genetic biology, opponents of affirmative action assert the inexistence of 'race' and that, therefore, affirmative action for blacks is not viable. This argument against the implementation of affirmative action for blacks in Brazil is not only one of the most ideological of the debate, it is also one of the most malicious. First, none of the proponents of affirmative action has defended the existence of 'race' in the biological sense of the term. They use the concept in its social sense, that is, as a phenotypic trait – skin colour, hair type, shape of nose, etc. – present in social relations that has justified the differential treatment of blacks by whites in Brazil. In other words, the discriminator does not request a DNA marker test before discriminating against a black person, but simply acts based on the social conception of 'race'.

We are all mestizos, we do not have blacks in Brazil

Opponents of affirmative action claim that a line of separation between blacks and whites was never established in Brazil, where the idea of the mestizo has prevailed instead. The focus of this argument is the assertion that those identified as mestizo (*pardos*) – a census category referring to miscegenation – do not encounter obstacles to social mobility. Like the previous argument, this one is characterized by its ideological content, which does not stand up to social indicators. The black population, for purposes of socio-economic studies, is formed by joining those Brazilians self-classified as either black or mestizo/brown, according to the methodology of the Brazilian Institute of Geography and Statistics (IBGE). In this way, according to the latest IBGE publication (2010), 51.1 per cent of Brazilians are black (44.2 per cent *pardos* and 6.9 per cent *pretos*) and 48.2 per cent white. If we consider any social indicator (education, life expectancy, infant mortality, housing, income, etc.), it is evident that *pretos* and *pardos* are similar and clearly distinguished from those identified as white Brazilians. Therefore, it matters little to the individual whether s/he is *preto* or *pardo*, since their material living conditions are similar, incurring prejudice, discrimination and racism. It is true that poverty in Brazil is not exclusive to blacks, with whites also among the poor. Likewise, it is true that the alleged racial mixing does not occur when we examine the middle and upper strata of Brazilian society. Let's take a look at data from the IBGE's Synthesis of Social Indicators survey of 2010:

- Among the poorest 10 per cent, 25.4 per cent are white, 9.4 per cent *pretos*, and 64.8 per cent *pardos*
- Among the richest 1 per cent, 82.5 per cent are white, 1.8 per cent *pretos*, and 14.2 per cent *pardos*
- The illiteracy rate among persons 15 years or older is 9.7 per cent in the country as a whole. The rate is 5.9 per cent among whites, 13.3 per cent *pretos*, and 13.4 per cent *pardos*
- A *preto* person with 12 or more years of education earns 69.8 per cent of what a white person with the same earns, while a *pardo* person earns 73.8 per cent of what the white person earns.

In this cursory look at a few social indicators, we find that the living conditions of *pretos* and *pardos* in Brazil are, on the one hand, quite similar and, on the other, distinct from those of Brazilians self-identified as white. Therefore, the belief in miscegenation does not act as an efficient mechanism for racial integration in the various social spaces of Brazilian society.

The problem is not racial but one of class

This argument is constantly used against proposed racial quotas. It claims that nobody is excluded simply for being black, and that the lack of access by the black population to higher education stems from the unstable economic situation. It is true that social inequality in Brazil is in part explained by perverse economic inequality. Therefore, a more just distribution of income will have positive repercussions on the pattern of inequality. However, it will not solve every problem. Studies of social mobility conducted since the late 1970s show that 'race' plays a significant role in explaining the inequalities in Brazil. Controlling for variables of economic origin, education and 'race', researchers of social mobility unanimously affirm that the opportunities for upward social mobility of blacks and whites are different. However, neither 'race' nor class acts as independent or absolute variables; on the contrary, they interact in the formation of social inequalities. The latest work on social mobility finds that the chances for upward movement are very similar for poor blacks and whites, but they increasingly diminish for blacks as they ascend the social ladder (Ribeiro 2006). In other words, in the ascent to the highest strata of the Brazilian social pyramid, 'race' is a relevant variable. This justifies affirmative action policies aimed at breaking the glass ceiling.

Affirmative action compromises the quality of Brazilian universities

This was one of the arguments most used by opponents of affirmative action prior to their implementation; however, it has fallen into disuse due to data showing similar performance between students entering because of quotas and those not. Let us examine data from the University of Brasília for an example of the performance of similar students from both groups: those who entered university due to affirmative action policies, the so-called quota students, and those students who did not directly benefit from these policies. Looking at a database that gathers information from students who entered the university in the five years after the implementation of affirmative action (between 2004 and 2008), we can verify that the performance of quota students and non-quota students is fairly similar, with the latter group having a slight edge. The Academic Performance Index (ARI), ranging from 0–5 points, showed that black quota-students scored an average of 3.31 points, while non-quota students scored 3.48 points (University of Brasília 2010). The difference of 0.17 is negligible, in no way compromising the quality of the university.

Data from the various universities with affirmative action policies are similar to these figures from the University of Brasília. Some universities show a slightly favourable performance by quota-students, as is the case at Rio de Janeiro State University (UERJ) and Bahia State University (Uneb).

Affirmative action will cause a racial divide within Brazilian society

It is argued that affirmative action could cause a racial divide in Brazil like the conflict between Tutsis and Hutus in Rwanda that sparked the genocide of nearly a million Tutsis in 1994. Rwanda is not the only country brought up in this attack on affirmative action policies; segregation in the United States prior to the 1960s is also raised.[19] The title of a book by a collective of intellectuals making these terrifying predictions and assisting academically with the text of a petition for the unconstitutionality of affirmative action quotas at the University of Brasília is suggestive: "Dangerous Divisions" (Fry et al., 2007).

This same collection of authors, along with other intellectuals, politicians and trade unionists, delivered to the President of the Federal Supreme Court on 21 April 2008 (the 120th anniversary of the abolition of slavery) a manifesto against affirmative action policies in force in the country, entitled '113 Anti-racist Citizens against Racial Laws'. This eight page manifesto states:

> Racial laws do not threaten a "white elite", as the racialists roar, but erect a brutal border in the middle of the absolute majority of Brazilians. This dividing line would run through public school classrooms, the buses that take people to work, the streets and houses in poor neighborhoods.

Despite the recentness of affirmative action policies in Brazil, insofar as their effects in all dimensions can be assessed (reduction of racial inequalities, strengthening of the black identity, quality of student graduating universities, etc.), there are no recorded incidents of dangerous or racial divisions in universities. The affirmative action programmes in Brazilian universities date from the beginning of the millennium, and there is no record of racial conflicts in the classrooms or corridors of universities. Contrary to what is alleged, affirmative action has opened the possibility of inclusion of black Brazilians who, for historical and structural reasons of a Brazilian-style racism, have encountered obstacles to the occupation of the spaces of economic, political and intellectual prestige in society. More than a century after the abolition of slavery (1888) and the Proclamation of the Republic (1889), not all areas of society are open to everyone. Among the positions and occupations almost exclusively white in Brazilian society one could cite university professors, doctors, dentists, judges, diplomats, medium and large entrepreneurs and contractors.

Instead of affirmative action policies effecting "dangerous divisions" in Brazilian society, they are much more a promise of closing the chasm between whites and blacks created by Brazilian-style racism, a racism extremely effective at keeping blacks in their place. Affirmative action policies implemented and under discussion in the country are meant to overcome the issue of racial inequality. This debate about affirmative action can broadly be classified as belonging to two different camps. One group is made up of intellectuals and government administrators who advocate that only universalist policies would be adequate to reverse racial inequality in the country. The other group is made up of activists who argue that universalist policies are inadequate and have to be complemented by affirmative action policies.

Horizontal vs. vertical inequalities

Historically in Brazil the stress has been overwhelmingly on vertical inequalities rather than horizontal ones. Therefore, ethnic differences have been largely de-emphasized as sources of inequality. Østby (2005: 7), for instance, says:

> A country can have systematic income inequality between ethnic groups, despite the fact that the overall (vertical) income inequality is rather low (as is the case in Rwanda), and vice versa; a country can have a high vertical income inequality score, even though the structural differences between ethnic groups might be low.

Her argument is intriguing because in fact Hutus and Tutsis – the two main groups in Rwanda – have the same language and culture, not wholly unlike black and white Brazilians. Østby's analysis is also interesting because it highlights the complex link between horizontal inequality and civil conflict; she also points out the violence prevailing in Brazilian society. She is not the first, in fact, to suggest that urban violence in Brazil may have a root in horizontal inequality.

However, in Brazil, black movements have historically had a fairly hard time convincing people to act in terms of a racially based solidarity that recognizes their shared destiny as blacks. This makes Brazil different from Rwanda, where at least since colonial times there has been a sharp distinction between Hutus and Tutsis that has found a political expression. Stewart, for instance, points out that Hutu leaders consistently cultivated Hutu identity and fear of Tutsis before the 1994 genocide. Black and white Brazilians may live under very disparate circumstances, as the statistics discussed above make abundantly apparent. However, they do not really speak different languages or have a different religion, or even different cultures, though of course there are some differences between them in those domains. Stewart (2000: 51) points out:

> For the emergence of group conflict, a degree of similarity of circumstance among potential members is not by itself enough to bring about group mobilization. Several other conditions must be present. Leaders must see the creation or enhancement of group identity as helpful to the realization of their political ambitions and work actively to achieve this, using a variety of strategies, including education or propaganda.

The black movements in Brazil have therefore struggled to create and emphasize group identity with a measure of success. This, of course, has been linked to yet another factor Stewart has pointed out: namely inequality in economic and political control.

Stewart also points out the close link between vertical and horizontal inequalities particularly in what concerns intra-group inequality. Namely, the more unequal a group is internally, the less likely it is to engage in inter-ethnic conflict (Stewart 2000: 253), though this is not always the case (she states that Rwanda for instance is an example of a different pattern). This idea is actually important to try and understand the Brazilian situation. Blacks are not only an internally heterogeneous group, but also their ethnic identity cannot be taken as a matter of course (one of the efforts of political organizers has therefore been to encourage people to identify themselves openly as black). The potential for political mobilization therefore is lower than in other cases mentioned by Stewart: first and foremost Rwanda.

One other important factor in the emergence of conflict is whether the differentials between the groups are narrowing or widening over time – in Brazil they seem stable. It will be interesting to see in the next few years whether the current steady economic growth will eventually bring a narrowing of the gap. Stewart (2000: 260) further posits four points to measure a country's vulnerability to conflict, namely: (1) serious past conflict at some time over the previous 20 years; (2) evidence of a considerable degree of horizontal inequality; (3) low incomes, and; (4) economic stagnation. Only the last point is clearly not present in Brazil currently, whereas the first point has to be nuanced as in the case of Brazil it is a matter of urban violence rather than civil war or strife per se.

In another study, Stewart *et al.* (2007: 6) argue that Malaysia and Latin American countries are usually at the antipodes of each other as the former has carried out very extensive group-based affirmative action policies aimed at redressing horizontal inequalities whereas the latter have usually largely ignored such policies. They also point out that many countries in fact fall in-between those two extremes. We could venture that one major difference between Malaysia and Brazil is the fact that the former's ethnic-based politics do not exist in the latter; instead, black groups have somewhat successfully tried to influence broadly based political parties (particularly on the left) which in turn have pressured government to adopt some circumscribed affirmative action policies. Brazil and Malaysia, however, have in common the fact that affirmative action – which in most countries is construed to mean an increase in the representation of minority groups in different domains such as business, education and government – actually targets majorities, not minorities (since 2008 blacks are the majority of the population in Brazil though only barely so). Therefore both countries are also in the situation of either South Africa or Sri Lanka presently (Stewart *et al.*, 2007: 28).

As Stewart *et al.* (2007) point out, policies to redress horizontal inequalities can lead to resentment on the part of formerly privileged groups. It can also entrench ethnic difference. In the United States, for instance, 'race-targeting' has consistently attracted condemnation from whites (Bobo and Kluegel 1993). Bobo and Kluegel argue, however, that this does not necessarily happen provided some provisions are made or precautions taken. They prefer an indirect approach, for instance, not targeting a specific group as a whole, but only underprivileged sections of it. However, direct affirmative action can have quick benefits, but it should then have a time limit attached to it (Bobo and Kluegel 1993: 30). They prefer an integrationist approach whereby group boundaries and identities are de-emphasized, whereas in direct affirmative action policies those are usually stressed. This is currently the situation in Malaysia, for instance. In fact there are voices in Brazil claiming that affirmative action would not only entrench but also create ethnic divisions (Fry 2007).

It is, however, difficult to see Brazil falling into a situation such as that of Malaysia as the Brazilian political system is not ethnically based. Moreover, group boundaries in Brazil are not so clear cut and deeply entrenched as they seem to be in Malaysia and South Africa. There are also no major religious divisions in Brazil. Besides, the Brazilian state remains a secular state, though Catholicism as the majority religion clearly receives preferential treatment in many official circles as well as in the public sphere. Therefore, though sharp horizontal policies such as direct affirmative action can clearly be conducive to resentment and even conflict, as shown in the case of Malaysia, Sri Lanka and South Africa, it remains to be seen whether the modest scope of affirmative action in Brazil so far – modest due to fierce resistance against it from several sectors, both in civil society and government as well as the comparatively low level of black mobilization – will indeed create or deepen divisions in the long run. A more likely scenario in the case of Brazil is one where a fairly highly Creolized society, which has developed a shared culture over the centuries where racism is nonetheless still entrenched, will have to deal with its internal inequalities through a variety of different policies other than merely direct affirmative action. In this sense another important factor here is the extent to which the new economic affluence in Brazil will steer the country away from neo-liberal policies that have in the past 20 or so years seriously affected processes of social redistribution in the country. This might in fact be a very important step towards targeting horizontal inequalities as neo-liberalism has circumscribed the ability of the state to intervene in favour of socially deprived groups.

We can therefore conclude that Brazil has a good number of particular and unique features when compared to other societies. These include a very shallow and restricted history of affirmative action (though it has a much longer history of targeting); comparatively little consensus as to identity and ethnic discourses; a strong universalist discourse which is, however, not based on a large degree of discussion with broad citizen participation but is more of a vague ideological principle permeating the state and sectors of society. Neo-liberalism has been very important in Brazil. At least in the case of Brazil, as it has also been allied to a strong need to keep inflation low and the economy on track, it has certainly circumscribed the state's ability to implement more universalist policies, including ones with redistributive schemes (i.e. targeting within universalism). Besides this problem, historically slow economic growth and even slower social mobility allied to entrenched racism have compounded Brazil's predicament as one of the world's most unequal societies. Affirmative action policies may or may not be able to redress this situation, though it is doubtful that, even in the unlikely scenario that they will be much more broadly implemented than is now the case, they alone will change the current dismal picture of social inequality prevailing in Brazil.

Notes

1. See, for instance, Htun (2004) and Sheriff (2001).
2. That is, today's Kerala, in southern India. The man who 'discovered' Brazil and took Cochin was Pedro Álvares Cabral.
3. After the Portuguese royal family fled Napoleon's troops, Brazil went from a colony to a kingdom integrated within the United Kingdom of Portugal and the Algarves as between 1808 and 1822 the royal family was based in Rio de Janeiro. On 7 September 1822, Brazil came to be independent of Portugal, and the Empire of Brazil was born.
4. Luiz Felipe Alencastro, professor at the University of Paris IV, based on data from Harvard University, writes that the total number of Africans who were taken to the Americas reached 11 million, of which approximately 5 million went to Brazil, totalling 44 per cent. He includes the number of illegal slaves who entered the country until 1856. See: www.stf.jus.br/portal/cms/verTexto.asp?servico=processoAudiencia PublicaAcaoAfirmativa.
5. The year following the abolition of slavery, on 15 November 1889, Brazil ceased to be an empire and became a republic.
6. Brazil was under military rule from 1964 to 1985. In the late 1970s a process of transition from military dictatorship to civilian rule began.
7. The Palmares Cultural Foundation was the first federal institution focusing on the issue of 'race'; however, its focus has been predominantly cultural, and it has not addressed issues related to racial inequality or the promotion of racial equality.
8. Quilombos are lands occupied by the descendants of maroons and other blacks.
9. On this occasion the President of CUT, the country's largest trade union, was the current Congressman Vicente Paulo da Silva, who identifies himself as black.
10. The ILO Convention 111 (1958) was adopted by Brazil in 1964. Signatory countries to this Convention commit to promote equality of opportunity and treatment in employment, pledging to fight unequal pay and treatment on grounds of 'race' or colour.
11. The black population is composed of those who self-identify as *pretos* and *pardos* in research conducted by the Brazilian Institute of Geography and Statistics (IBGE). In the publication *Synthesis of Social Indicators* (2010) the black population totalled 51.1 per cent of Brazilians – 6.9 per cent self-identified as *pretos* and 44.2 per cent self-identified as *pardos*. *Pretos* and *pardos* have been brought together as 'black,' as it has been found that these two population groups suffer racism, and great similarity exists in their living conditions.
12. For more information about ProUni, visit http://prouniportal.mec.gov.br/index.php.
13. See www.planalto.gov.br/seppir.
14. This law was amended in 2008 by Law 11.645/08 to include the history and culture of indigenous peoples.
15. Primary school is the first eight years of schooling, while secondary school is the 9th year through to the 11th year. Only after completing high school is the student eligible to take exams to enter university.
16. With this law, the Ministry of Education implemented the programme 'Education for All', aimed at the publication of educational material focusing on inclusion and diversity. To learn more about this programme, visit www.dominiopublico.gov.br.
17. The Statute of Racial Equality came into force on 20 October 2010. See www.planalto.gov.br/ccivil_03/_Ato2007–2010/2010/Lei/L12288.htm.
18. The Supreme Court is the highest court in the country.
19. This is one of the arguments enumerated in the Allegation of Breach of Fundamental Precept, ADPF/186, presented to the Supreme Court by the right wing party, Democratas, challenging the constitutionality of the system of affirmative action policies of the University of Brasília.

References

Azevedo, Celia Marinho de. (2004) *Onda negra, medo branco* [Black Wave, White Fear]. Segunda edição. São Paulo: Annablume.
Bernardino-Costa, Joaze. (2002) Ação afirmativa e a rediscussão do mito da democracia racial [Affirmative Action and Debating Anew the Myth of Racial Democracy] in *Estudos Afro-Asiáticos*, 2, pp. 247–73.
Bernardino-Costa, Joaze. (2004) Levando a raça a sério: ação afirmativa correto reconhecimento. [Taking Race Seriously: The Correct Acknowledgement of Affirmative Action] in Bernardino-Costa, Joaze and Galdino, Daniela (eds.) *Levando a raça a sério: ação afirmativa e universidade*. Rio de Janeiro: DP&A editores.
Besley, Timothy and Ravi Kanbur. (1990) 'The Principles of Targeting', Office of the Vice-President Development Economics, The World Bank, WPS 385.
Bobo, Lawrence and Kluegel, James R. (1993) 'Opposition to race-targeting: Self-interest, stratification ideology, or racial attitudes?' in: *American Sociological Review*, August, pp. 443–64.
Costa, Haroldo. (1948) 'Queremos Estudar' [We want to Study] in: Nascimento, Abdias [1948–1950] (2003) *Quilombo: vida, problemas e aspirações do negro* [Quilombo: life, problems, and aspirations of blacks], São Paulo: Editora 34.
Du Bois, W.E.B. (1999) *As almas da gente negra* [The Soul of Black People]. Rio de Janeiro: Lacerda editores.
Feres Júnior, João, Verônica Toste Daflon and Luiz Augustos Campos. (2010a) *Ação afirmativa no ensino superior brasileiro hoje: análise institucional* [Affirmative Action in Brazilian Tertiary Education Today: An Institutional Analysis], Grupo de Estudos Multidisciplinares da Ação Afirmativa. Rio de Janeiro: Universidade Estadual do Rio de Janeiro.
Feres Júnior, João, Verônica Toste Daflon and Luiz Augustos Campos. (2010b) 'Cotas no STF: os argumentos como eles são.' [Quotas in the Federal Higher Tribunal: An Exposition of the Arguments] in *Revista Lero-Lero*, pp. 124–36.
Fernandes, Florestan. (1978) *A integração do negro na sociedade de classes* [The Integration of Blacks in Class Society], Vol. 1. São Paulo: Editora Ática.
Freyre, Gilberto. (1992) *Casa-grande & senzala* [The Masters and the Slaves]. Rio de Janeiro: Record.
Fry, Peter, Yvonne Maggie, Simone Monteiro and Ricardo Ventura Santos. (2007) *Divisões perigosas: políticas raciais no Brasil contemporâneo* [Dangerous Divide: Racial Policies in Contemporary Brazil]. Rio de Janeiro: Civilização Brasileira.
Gomes, Joaquim Barbosa. (2001) *Ação afirmativa e o princípio constitucional da igualdade: o direito como instrumento de transformação social – a experiência dos EUA*. [Affirmative Action and the Constitutional Principle of Equality: Law as an Instrument in Social Transformation – The US Experience]. Rio de Janeiro/São Paulo: Editora Renovar.
Grogan, Colleen M. and Eric M. Patashnik. (2003) 'Universalism within targeting: Nursing home care, the middle class, and the Politics of the Medicaid Program' in *The Social Service Review*, March, pp. 51–71.
Hasenbalg, Carlos. (1979) *Discriminação e desigualdades raciais no Brasil* [Discimination and Social Inequalities in Brazil]. Rio de Janeiro: Graal.
Herd, Pamela. (2005) 'Universalism Without the Targeting: Privatizing the Old-Age Welfare State' in *The Gerontologist*, 45: 3 (June), pp. 292–8.
HTUN, Mala. (2004) 'From "Racial Democracy" To Affirmative Action: Changing State Policy on Race in Brazil' in *Latin American Research Review*, 39 (1), pp. 60–89.

Imai, Katsushi. (2004) 'Targeting versus Universalism: An Evaluation of Indirect Effects of the Employment Guarantee Scheme in India', Department of Economics, Royal Holloway, University of London.

Instituto Brasileiro de Geografia e Estatística (IBGE). (2010) *Síntese dos indicadores sociais: uma análise das condições de vida da população brasileira* [A Synthesis of Social Indicators: An Analysis of the Well-Being of the Brazilian Population], available at: www.ibge.gov.br.

Instituto Rio Branco. (2010) *Programa de ação afirmativa do Instituto Rio Branco – bolsa prêmio vocação para a diplomacia* [Affirmative Action Programme of Instituto Rio Branco: A Vocation for Diplomacy Prize Scholarship], manuscript.

Karasch, Mary C. (2000) *A vida dos escravos no Rio de Janeiro (1808–1850)* [Slave Life in Rio de Janeiro (1808–1850)]. São Paulo: Companhia das Letras.

Kidal, Nanna and Stein Kuhnle. (2002) 'The Principle of Universalism: Tracing a Key Idea in the Scandinavian Welfare Model', First Conference of the European Social Policy Research Network, Social Values, Social Policies, Tilburg University, the Netherlands, 29–31 August.

Maio, Marcos Chor. (1999) 'O Projeto Unesco e a agenda das ciências sociais no Brasil dos anos 40 e 50' [The UNESCO Project and the Social Science Agenda in Brazil in the 1940s and 1950s] in *Revista Brasileira de Ciências Sociais*, 14 (41), pp. 141–58.

Mattoso, Kátia de Queiroz. (1990) *Ser escravo no Brasil* [Being a Slave in Brazil]. São Paulo: Editora Brasiliense.

Moura, Carlos and Barreto, Jônatas. (2002) *A Fundação Cultural Palmares na III Conferência Mundial de Combate ao Racismo, Discriminação racial, Xenofobia e Intolerância Correlata* [Palmares Cultural Foundation at the Third World Conference Against Racism, Race Discrmination, Xenophobia, and Related Intolerance]. Brasília: Fundação Cultural Palmares.

Moya, Thais and Valter Roberto Silvério. (2009) 'Ação afirmativa e raça no Brasil contemporâneo: um debate sobre a redefinição simbólica da nação' [Affirmative Action and Race in Contemporary Brazil: A Debate on the Symbolic Redefinition of the Nation] in *Sociedade e Cultura*, 12 (2), pp. 235–50.

Myers, Aaron. (2003) 'O valor da diversidade racial nas empresas.' [The Value of Racial Diversity in Corporations] in *Estudos afro-asiáticos*, 3 (25), Rio de Janeiro.

Østby, Gudrun. (2005) 'Horizontal Inequalities and Civil Conflict.' Department of Political Science, University of Oslo & Centre for the Study of Civil War (CSCW), International Peace Research Institute, Oslo.

Petruccelli, José Luis. (2000) *Mapa da cor no ensino superior brasileiro* [The Map of Colour in Tertiary Education in Brazil], Rio de Janeiro: Programa Políticas da Cor na Educação Brasileira. Série Ensaio & Pesquisas 1.

Ribeiro, Carlos Antônio Costa. (2006) 'Classe, raça e mobilidade social no Brasil' [Class, Race, and Social Mobility in Brazil'] in *Dados – Revista de Ciências Sociais*, 49 (4), pp. 873–883.

Rocha, Carmen Lúcia Antunes. (1996) 'Ação afirmativa: o conteúdo democrático do princípio da igualdade jurídica' [Affirmative Action: The Democratic Contents of the Principle of Legal Equality] in *Revista Trimestral de Direito Público*, 15, pp. 85–99.

Santos, Ivair Augusto Alves dos. (2006) *O movimento negro e o Estado (1983–1987): o caso do Conselho de Participação e Desenvolvimento da Comunidade Negra no Governo de São Paulo.* [The Black Movement and the State (1983–1987): The Case of the Council for Black Community Participation and Development in the Government of São Paulo]. São Paulo: Cone.

Sheriff, Robin. (2001) *Dreaming Equality: Color, Race, Racism, and Equality in Urban Brazil*, Trenton: Rutgers University Press.

Skidmore, Thomas (1976). *Preto no branco: raça e nacionalidade no pensamento brasileiro.* [Black into White: Race and Nationality in Brazilian Thinking]. Rio de Janeiro: Paz e Terra.

Souza, Jessé. (1997) *Multiculturalismo e Racismo: uma comparação entre Brasil e Estados Unidos.* [Multiculturalism and Racism: A Comparison Between Brazil and the United States], Brasília: Paralelo 15.

Stewart, Frances. (2000) 'Crisis Prevention: Tackling Horizontal Inequalities', Oxford: University of Oxford, Oxford Development Studies, 28 (3).

Stewart, Frances, Graham Brown and Arnim Langer. (2007) 'Policies towards Horizontal Inequalities', CRISE Working Paper No. 42, CRISE, University of Oxford.

Telles, Edward. (2003) *Racismo à brasileira: uma nova perspectiva sociológica* [Racism Brazilian Style: A New Sociological Perspective], Rio de Janeiro: Relume Dumará.

Theodoro, Mário. (2008) *As políticas públicas e a desigualdade no Brasil: 120 anos após a abolição* [Public Policies and Inequality in Brazil: 120 Years After Abolition], Brasília: Instituto de Pesquisa Econômica Aplicada.

Universidade de Brasília. (2010) *Avaliação do rendimento e evasão no ensino de graduação da Universidade de Brasília – relatório preliminar.* [Performance and Dropout Evaluation in Undergraduate Teaching of University of Brasília: A Preliminary Report], Brasília: Universidade de Brasília.

Walle, Dominique van de. (1998) 'Targeting revisited' in *The World Bank Research Observer*, August, pp. 231–48.

Index

Page numbers in *italics* denote tables.

Abdul Rahman Embong 82
Academic Performance Index (ARI), Brazil 195
access to affirmative action 10–11, 20; Fiji 119–20
Adinkrah, M. 104
Advani, L.K. 37
affirmative action: access to 10–11, 20 (Fiji 119–20); arguments for and against 62–6; duration of 9, 15, 18, 20, 89–90 (Fiji 120); implementation of policies 4, 10–11; key features and issues 5–8
African-Americans 10, 13, 43, 44, 46, 49, 50, 52, 58, 60–1, 61–2
African history teaching, Brazil 191
African National Congress (ANC) 127, 148, 149, 150, 151
agricultural production, Fiji 99, 100, 101, 103
Alliance Party of Northern Ireland (APNI) 159
Ambedkar, B.R. 29
Andaya, B.W. and L.Y. Andaya 67, 69
Anderson, Benedict 4, 8
Anglo-Irish Agreement (1985) 162
Anglo Zimele 140
Anwar Ibrahim 76, 87
apartheid 126
Asian Americans 44
Azevedo, Celia Marinho de 185

Bahia State University (Uneb) 195
Bailey, S.R. 5, 16
Bainimarama, Frank 116, 117
Bakke, K.M. 18
Balaji v. *Mysore* (1963) 30
Bamforth, Nicholas 169

Bangura, Yusuf 4
Bank Bumiputra 69
Banton, Michael 7
Barisan Nasional (National Front) coalition, Malaysia 67
Barreto, J. 188
Barth, Karl 3, 5
Beckwith, Francis J. 9
Bell, Christine 175
Belshaw, C. 99
Bennell, P. 5, 16
Berjaya Corporation 112
Bernardino-Costa, Joaze 15, 183–203
Bharatiya Janata Party (BJP) 37, 38
Black Economic Empowerment (BEE) *see under* South Africa
Black Power Movement 49, 53
Bobo, Lawrence 44, 45, 49, 198
Brazil 1, 2, 7, 8, 15–16, 95, 183–203; Academic Performance Index (ARI) 195; African history teaching 191; Bill of Quotas 191–2; Black Consciousness Day 187; class 195; colonial history 183; Constitution 186, 187; constitutionality of affirmative action 193; diplomatic service 190–1; discrimination 186–8, 193, 194; education 192 (higher 15–16, 188–90, 191–2, 195, 196); employment 192; Eusébio de Queiróz Law (1850) 185; Fundação Cultural Palmares 187, 200n7; historical perspective 184–6; immigration 185; Inter-ministerial Task Force (GTI) for the Promotion of the Black Population 187; international seminar on Multiculturalism and Racism 187; land ownership 187; Law of Free

Index 205

Birth (1871) 185; mestizos 185, 194; miscegenation 185, 186, 194; Movimento Neghro Unificado (Unified Black Movement) 186; National Conference Against Racism and Intolerance (2001) 188; National Plan for Human Rights 187; race debate 186–8, 193–4, 195–6; Sexagenarian Law (1885); 185; slave labour 184–5; social mobility 195; Special Secretariat for Policies Promoting Racial Equality (SEPPIR) 191; Statute of Racial Equality (2010) 192; Task Force for the Elimination of Discrimination in Employment and Occupation (GTDEO) 187; United Workers' Central (CUT) 187; University for All (ProUni) programme 190; whitening policy 185–6
Brazilian Institute of Geography and Statistics (IBGE) 194
Brown, G.K. 4
Brown, Sue 131
Brown v. The Board of Education (1954) 49
Brubaker, R. 3, 4, 5, 19
Bua Komanisi! 148
Bumiputera 67, 68, 69, 70, 113; employment 71, 72, 82, *83*, *84*, *85*; enterprise and managerial development 72, 73, 74, 75, 76, 77; equity ownership 69, 74, 85–7, 88, 89, 90, 109; higher education 71, 78, 80, 81, 87; middle class 88
Bumiputera Commercial and Industrial Community (BCIC) 72
Burns Report 99, 102
Bush, George H.W. 59
business class, Fiji 107–10, 111

Campbell, Colm 156, 161
Campbell, Tom 3
Cardoso, Fernando Henrique 187
Cargill, Jenny 134, 135, 136 136, 137, 138, 139, 140, 143, 144, 149, 151
Carnegie Commission 4
Carpenters Corporation (Fiji) 112
Carrefour 77
Carter, Jimmy 56
caste(s), India: identity 36; scheduled (SC) 12, 28, 29–30, 31, 32, 33, 34, 35, 37
Castle, J. 5, 6, 16
Castles, Stephen 4
Chancellor House 148

Chand, S. 96, 97
Chaudhry, Mahendra 106
Chetty, K. 106
Chinese population: Fiji 99, 101; Malaysia 13–14, 67, 71, 72, *74*, 78, 80, 82, *83*, *84*, *85*, 99 (equity ownership 86)
Chua Ma Yu 75
citizenship 4, 7, 64
civil rights movement: Northern Ireland 157; US 49, 50, 60
civil service *see* government employment
class 4; Brazil 195; Fiji 99–100; *see also* business class; middle class
co-operative movement, Fiji 99
Cohen, Carl 7, 9
colonialism 1, 3; Brazil 183; Fiji 97–9
conflict management/resolution 6, 97
Connor, Walker 4
Cooper, F. 4
corruption: Fiji 97, 111, 117, 119, 121; South Africa 148–9, 151
Cottrell, J. 96
Coulter, Colin 154, 172
coups, Fiji 95, 96, 97, 104–5, 115–16, 117, 120, 121, 122
Craigavon, Lord 161
credit union movement, Fiji 100–1
crony capitalism: India 41; South Africa 146, 148, 151
cultural recognition 7, 64
Curry, George E. 6, 9

Daim Zainuddin 76, 87
Davidson, Alistair 4
de Klerk, F.W. 130–1
decentralization 10, 18–19
defeatism 10
Democratic Unionist Party (DUP), Northern Ireland 159, 170
dependency 10, 46
Desai, Sonalde 35
Despres, Leo 4, 7
Deuba Accord, Fiji 104
developmental affirmative action 19–20
devolution, Northern Ireland 159, 168
difference: assertion of 3–4; recognition of 6–7, 64
Dipankar, Gupta 7
diplomatic service, Brazil 190–1
Dippenaar, Laurie 135
discrimination 1, 5, 6, 7, 8, 12, 19: Brazil 186–8, 193, 194; Fiji 105; Malaysia 82, 90; Northern Ireland 15, 156, 158, 160–1, 162, 164–5, 171; reverse 43, 56,

discrimination *continued*
  161, 165, 171; South Africa 14, 16, 126, 127, 128, 129, 136, 139; United States 43, 47, 26, 48, 49, 50, 51, 52–3, 54, 55, 56–7, 58–9, 64
Dobbin, Frank 50, 55, 56
Dubey, Amaresh 35
Dullo, Esther 39
duration of affirmative action 9, 15, 18, 20, 89–90; Fiji 120
Dworkin, Ronald 3, 7

economic development 3; Fiji 99–104, 114, 118
education 3, 6, 8, 11, 19, 20; Brazil 192; Fiji 110, 114, 120; Malaysia 11, 67–8, 87, 88, 89; primary 11, 16, 20, 35, 89; secondary 16, 35, 89; South Africa 127, 128, 13; *see also* higher (tertiary) education
Edwards, John 160, 166
Ekuinas 77, 90
electoral systems 18
Ellison, Graham 169, 170, 171, 172
employment 3, 8, 11, 19, 20; Brazil 192; Fiji 104, 105–6, *108*, 114, 115, *116*; Malaysia 69, 71–2, 80–1, 82–5, 87, 88; Northern Ireland 15, 158, 160–7, 172, 173, 175–6; South Africa 14, 130–3, 138, 142, 147; US 45, 49–53, 54, 55–6, 58–9, 61–2; *see also* government employment
Empowerdex 137, 138, 141
enterprise development 8, 11–12, 17, 20; Fiji 100, 101, 102, 104–5, 107–10, 111–13, 114, 121; Malaysia 11, 12, 17, 72–3, *79*; South Africa 11, 12, 17, 134–5, 140, 142
entrepreneurship 12, 16
equality 1, 7, 13, 44, 54, 62–3, 64; of opportunity 63, 161, 162
Equality Commission for Northern Ireland (ECNI) 15, 163, 164, 165, 166, 173
Equity Investment Management Company Limited (EIMCOL) 112
equity ownership 8, 11, 17; Fiji 108–9, 109–10, 111, 112, 120; Malaysia 69, 73–7, *79*, 85–7, 88–9, 90, 109; South Africa 136–8, 142, 143, 145, 147
Eskom 130, 131, 149
ethnic capital 11–12
ethnic identity 13, 18, 19; Brazil; Fiji 120; India 33, 35–6, 40, 41; Malaysia 91
European Convention on Human Rights 170

European Union (EU), Northern Ireland and 159

Far Eastern Economic Review 75
Farrell, Michael 156
federalism 47–8
Fenton, Steven 4
Ferguson, J. 16
Fernandes, Florestan 186
Fiji 2, 7, 8, 10, 11, 14–15, 16, 17, 95–125; access to affirmative action 119–20; agricultural production 99, 100, 101, 103; "Agriculture Scam" 116; business class 107–10, 111; Chinese population 99, 101; civil service 105–6, 114, 121–2; class structure 99–100; "clean up campaign" 116; co-operative movement 99; colonial period 97–9; commercial sector 100, 101, 102, 104–5, 107–10, 111–13, 114, 121, 122; communal system 97, 98, 99, 100, 102; Constitution 97, 105, 113, 117; corruption 97, 111, 117, 119, 121; coups 95, 96, 97, 104–5, 115–16, 117, 120, 121, 122; credit union movement 100–1; Deuba Accord 104; discrimination 105; duration of affirmative action 120; economic development 99–104, 114, 118; education 110, 114, 120; employment 104, *108*, 115, *116*; government 105–6, 114, 121–2; Equity Index 115, *116*; equity ownership 108–9, 109–10, 111, 112, 120; 50/50 plan 115–16; forestry industry 101; Great Council of Chiefs 117, 119, 122n1; incomes 101; Indo-Fijians *see* Indo-Fijians; land ownership/reform 98–9, 100, 102, 118, 122; Malaysian investment in 112–13; Methodist Church 119; middle class 104, 111, 113–14, 118–19, 120, 121; migration 106, 114; military 96, 106, 116–17; Ministry of Fijian Affairs 107, 108; Ministry of Multi-ethnic Affairs 113; Native Land Ordinance No. 14 (1905) 98; *Nine Points Plan* 107; People's Charter 97, 117, 120, 122; police force 106; poverty/poverty reduction 96, 97, 118, 120, 122; privatization 107; Public Service Commission 105, 110; Qoliqoli Bill 116; Reconciliation, Tolerance and Unity Bill 116; rent-seeking behaviour 97; rural development projects 102–3, 117, 118, 120; service sector 102; Small Business

Equity Scheme 109; structural adjustment policies (SAP) 103; sugar industry 100, 102, 103; taxi business 109, 111; Ten Point Economic Plan (TPEP) 118; *Ten Year Plan* 107; tourism industry 101–2, 112; unemployment 104, 118; Village Housing Scheme (VHS) 109
Fiji Development Bank 109, 112; Commercial Loans to Fijians Scheme (CLFS) 108, 109
Fiji Independent Commission Against Corruption 111, 117
Fiji Islands Commission Against Corruption (FICAC) 97
Fiji National Provident Fund (FNPF) 109, 112
Fiji Post and Telecom (FPTL) 109
Fiji Television Limited (FTL) 109
Fijian Affairs Board (FAB) 107, 108, 109, 110, 112
Fijian Banana Venture (FBV) 99
Fijian Development Fund (FDF) 99
Fijian Holdings Company (FHC) 107, 113
Fijian Holdings Limited (FHL) 108–9, 111, 112, 120
Fijian Initiative Group 107
financial skills 11
Fisk, E.K. 96
foreign direct investment (FDI), South Africa 147
forestry industry, Fiji 101
Foster, R.F. 155
France, P. 98
Fraser Institute, international policy potential index 144
Fredman, Sandra 164–5
Fry, Peter 196, 199
Fryer, R.G. Jr. 6, 20
Fullilove v. *Klutznick* 61
Fullinwider, Robert K. 5, 16
Fundação Cultural Palmares (Palmares Cultural Foundation) 187, 200n7

Galanter, Marc 29, 30
Gandhi, Indira 30–1
Gandhi, M.K. 29, 30
Gaunavou Investments Company Limited (GICL) 110
Geertz, Clifford 3, 4
Gellner, Ernest 3, 4
gender reservations, India 39
Ghai, Y. 96
Glazer, Nathan 5, 7, 43
Goldman, Alan 5, 6

Gomez, Edmund Terence 1–26, 67–94
Gordhan, Pravin 134, 151
Gordon, Sir Arthur 98–9
government employment: Brazil 190–1; Fiji 105–6, 114, 121–2; India 8, 28, 29–30, 33; Malaysia 69, 71–2, 82; South Africa 130–2; US 55, 56
Government of Ireland Act (1920) 161
Graham, Hugh Davis 7, 60, 61, 62
Griggs v. *Duke Power Company* (1971) 58, 59
group dimension 4–5, 43–4, 64
Grutter v. *Bollinger* 60
Grynberg, R. 111
Guinier, Lani 9
Gupta, A. 16
Gurr, T.D. 1, 3, 8
Guthrie Corporation 75

Hadden, Tom 157
Hadfield, Brigid 161
Haliza Othman 80
hard affirmative action programmes 6
Harvey, Colin 15, 154–82
Hasenbalg, Carlos 184, 186
healthcare 3; South Africa 127
Heavy Industries Corporation of Malaysia (HICOM) 73, 76
Helen Suzman Foundation 150
Hepple, Bob 161
higher (tertiary) education 8, 11, 12; Brazil 15–16, 188–90, 191–2, 195, 196; Fiji 110; India 8, 11, 12, 28, 29, 30, 33, 35, 40; Malaysia 69, 70–1, 78, 79, 80–1, 87, 88, 89; Northern Ireland 16, 157; South Africa 128; US 13, 49, 59–60
Hitachi Power Africa 148–9
Hitachi Power Europe 149
HIV/AIDS, South Africa 127
Hobsbawm, Eric 4
horizontal inequality 3–5, 17–18, 19, 20 (Brazil 183, 197–9; Fiji 95–122; Malaysia 91; Northern Ireland 174)
Horowitz, D.L. 3, 8, 18, 128
housing construction, South Africa 133
Htun, M. 5
human capital 11, 40, 41, 45
human rights protection, Northern Ireland 155, 157, 161, 163, 166, 168–9, 174
Humphrey, Hubert 51

identity 4; caste, India 36; religious, Northern Ireland 154; *see also* ethnic identity; national identity

identity politics 2, 65
im Thurn, Everard F. 98–9
immigration: Brazil 185; India 38; US 45, 60–2
implementation of policies 4, 10–11
income inequality 197; Fiji 101; Malaysia 69, 88, 89; South Africa 150
India 2, 7, 11, 12–13, 16, 27–42, 95; Ayodhya (or "mandir") strategy 37; *Balaji* v. *Mysore* (1963) 30; caste identity 36; Constitution (1950) 29; crony capitalism 41; enterprise development 17; ethnic identities 13, 33, 35–6, 40, 41; ethnic inequality 34, 39; forward/backward distinction 35, 36; government employment 8, 28, 29–30, 31, 33; higher education 8, 11, 12, 28, 29, 30, 31, 33, 35, 40; human capital development 40, 41; immigration 38; *Indira Sawhney* v. *Union of India* (1992) 31; intra-ethnic inequality 39, 40; Janata coalition 31; Kalelkar Commission 30, 36; Mandal Commission 31, 36, 37; middle class 40; Other Backward Classes (OBCs) 29, 30–1, 32, 34, 35, 37; political participation 29; political parties 37–8; political representation 8, 28, 33; political violence 36–8; Poona Act (1932) 29; poverty/poverty reduction 33, 34; rent-seeking bahaviour 21; reservation policies (outcomes and consequences of 32–9; scope and range of 28–32); scheduled castes (SC) 12, 28, 29–30, 31, 32, 33, 34, 35, 37; scheduled tribes (ST) 12, 28, 29–30, 31, 32, 33, 34, 35, 37; spatial inequality 33, 34–5
Indian Human Development Survey (2005) 35
Indian population, Malaysia 13–14, 67, 68, 72, *74*, 78, 80, 82, *83*, *84*, *85*
Indira Sawhney v. *Union of India* (1992) 31
individual effort 43, 64
Indo-Fijians 102, 121; cane farmers 99; civil service staff 105, 106; in commercial sector 96, 97, 100, 108, 109, 111, 113, 114, 122; employment 104, 105, 106; incomes 101
industrialization, Malaysia 70, 73
inequality: horizontal 3–5, 17–18, 19, 20 (Brazil 183, 197–9; Fiji 17, 95–122; Malaysia 91; Northern Ireland 174); income 197 (Fiji 101; Malaysia 69, 88, 89; South Africa 150); intra-ethnic (India 39, 40); spatial 12, 16, 33, 34–5, 89; vertical 4, 97, 197–9
infrastructure 3; South Africa 131–2, 147
Institute of Management Development (Switzerland) 148
institutional capacity 10
institutions, importance of 10, 18, 47–8
International Finance Corporation 148
International Labour Organization (ILO): Convention 111 187, 200n10; Convention on Indigenous Rights 169 96
IRA 157
Isaacs, Harold R. 8

Jaffrelot, Christophe 31, 37
Janata coalition, India 31
Jeffery, Anthea 14, 126–53
Jesudason, James V. 69
Jim Crow laws 48
Johannesburg Stock Exchange (JSE) 134, 137
Johnson, Lyndon 50, 52, 54, 55, 56
Johnson, R.W. 144
Johnson v. *Santa Clara* 58
Jomo, K.S. 5, 8, 11, 72, 86, 89
Jones, E. 9
judicial review, US 47, 48
justice 1, 13, 44, 62, 63, 64, 65

Kalelkar, Kaka (Kalelkar Commission) 30, 36
Kane-Berman, J. 129
Karasch, Mary C. 184
Kellough, J. Edward 6, 47, 57
Kelly, Erin 50, 55, 56
Kennedy, John F. 50, 51, 56
Kennedy, Paul 5
Kerner Report, US 54
Khazanah Nasional 74
Khoo, Boo Teik 67, 69
King, Martin Luther 49, 50
Kluegel, James R. 198
Knapman, B. 100
KPMG 142
Kumba Resources 144
Kumpulan Wang Amanah Pencen 74
Kuok, Robert 75
Kymlicka, Will 4, 7

Lacerda, João Batista 185
Lal, B. 95, 97
land ownership/reform: Brazil 187; Fiji 98–9, 100, 102, 118, 122

Index 209

language 8
Latinos 10, 44, 45, 49
Lawrence, Charles R. III 6, 16
Lawson, S. 97, 98
Lee Hwok Aun 13, 67–94
Lee, Joe 155
Lee Kiong Hock 70
Leete, Richard 70
Lembaga Tabung Haji 74
Leon, Peter 143, 144
Letlape, Mpho 130
Levenstein, Keith 141
Lichtenberg, Judith 9
Lijphart, A. 8, 18
Lindsay, B. 5, 16
local government, South Africa 132, 147
London Tin 75
Lonmin 144
Loo Seng Piew 71
Loury, Glen 4, 6, 7, 20
Luban, David 9
Lula da Silva, Luis Incio 191

MacBride Principles 162, 166, 177n12
McCrudden, Christopher 161, 163, 165, 166, 167, 168, 174
McEvoy, Kieran 156
McGarry, John 3, 8, 154, 155, 167
McLaughlin, Eithne 168
McNamara, Kevin 162, 163
Magill, Denise 161
Mahajan, Gurpreet 4
Mahathir Mohamad 73, 76, 87
Majority-Based Affirmative Action (MABA) 95, 96
Makgoba, Malegapuru 149
Malamud, Deborah C. 46, 47, 58
Malayan Banking 112
Malaysia 2, 7, 8, 13–14, 16, 19, 67–94, 95, 198, 199; Bumiputera *see* Bumiputera; Chinese population 13–14, 67, 71, 72, *74*, 78, 80, 82, *83*, *84*, *85*, 86; Constitution (1957) 68; discrimination 82, 90; economy 68–9, 70, 77; education 11, 67–8, 87, 88, 89 (higher 69, 70–1, 78, *79*, 80–1, 87, 88, 89); Employees Provident Fund (EPF) 74; employment 69, 71–2, 80–1, 82–5, 87, 88 (in government 69, 71–2, 82); enterprise development 11, 12, 17, 72–3, *79*; equity ownership 69, 73–7, *79*, 85–7, 88–9, 90, 109; and Fiji investment 112–13; *First Malaysia Plan* (1965–1970) 69; Global Supplier Programme (GSP) 77; government-linked companies (GLCs) 70, 73, 76, 86–7; *Government Transformation Plan* 81, 90; income inequality 69, 88, 89; Indian population 13–14, 67, 68, 72, *74*, 78, 80, 82, *83*, *84*, *85*; Industrial Coordination Act (1975) 72, 74, 75, 76, 89; Industrial Linkage Programme (ILP) 77; industrialization 70, 73; institutional capacity 10; MARA (Council of Trust for Indigenous Peoples) 69, 70; middle class 88; national car project (Proton) 77; *New Economic Model* 81, 90; New Economic Policy (NEP) 11, 68, 70, 73–4, 87, 88, 89–90, 103, 135; party system 67; patronage 90; Petroleum Development Act (1974) 73; poverty/poverty reduction 8, 70, 87, 88, 90; Private Higher Education Act (1996) 71; privatization 76, 89, 90; professional association membership 82, *85*; Promotion of Investments Act (1986) 75–6; rent-seeking behaviour 90; service sector 77; small and medium-sized companies (SMEs) 77, 82; SME-MNC ties 77; State Economic Development Corporations (SEDCs) 72; *10th Malaysia Plan* (10MP) 81, 90; unemployment 80, 81, 88; Vendor Development Programme (VDP) 77
Malaysia Airlines (MAS) 76
Malaysian Mining Corporation 75
Mamdani, Mahmood 8
Mandal, B.P. (Mandal Commission) 31, 36, 37
Mandela, Nelson 1, 126
Mantashe, Gwede 148
Manyi, Jimmy 132, 133
Mara, Ratus Sir Kamisese 107
Matsuda, Mari J. 6, 16
Mattoso, Ktia de Queiroz 184
May, Stephen 4
Mazwai, Thami 133
Mbeki, Moeletsi 146, 151
Mbeki, Thabo 148
Mehmet, Ozay 72, 78
merit 9, 64–5
Methodist Church, Fiji 119
middle class 10, 11, 13, 16; Fiji 104, 111, 113–14, 118–19, 120, 121; India 40; Malaysia 88; South Africa 145–6, 149, 150; US 49
migration 4, 19, 185; Fiji 106, 114; *see also* immigration

military, Fiji 106, 116–17
mining sector, South Africa 143–5, 147, 148–9
Minority-Based Affirmative Action (MIBA) 95
miscegenation, Brazil 185, 186, 194
Mitchell, John 55
Moghaddam, F. M. 3
Mokhzani Abdul Rahim 75
Motlanthe, Kgalema 148
Moura, Carlos 188
Movimento Neghro Unificado (Unified Black Movement) 186
Moya, Thais 192
multiculturalism 64, 97
multinational companies (MNCs) 77

Nagel, Thomas 5
Narayan, J. 100
Nascimento, Abdias 188
nation building 4
National Association for the Advancement of Colored People (NAACP), US 50
National Bank of Fiji (NBF) 111, 112, 121
National Council for Building a Better Fiji (NCBBF) 116–17
National Equity Corporation of Malaysia 109
national identity 19; Northern Ireland 154, 155–6
Native Americans 10, 55, 61
Nehru, Jawahralal 29
neo-liberalism 199
Nevitte, Neil 5
New Africa Investments Ltd (Nail) 134
Nixon, Richard 55, 56
Nolan, Paul 170, 171, 172
Northern Ireland 1, 2, 8, 15, 16, 19, 154–82; Anglo-Irish Agreement (1985) 162; Bill if Rights 168–9; civil rights movement 157; devolved government 159, 168; discrimination 15, 156, 158, 160–1, 162, 164–5, 171; and Downing Street Declaration (1969) 157; employment 15, 158, 160–7, 172, 173, 175–6 (MacBride Principles 162, 166, 177n12; monitoring 164–6); equality 172–6 (and employment 160–7, 175–6; and power-sharing 167–8; and rights protection 168–9); Equality Commission (ECNI) 15, 163, 164, 165, 166, 173; and European Union (EU) 159; Fair Employment Acts 158, 162, 163; Fair Employment Agency 162, 166; Fair Employment Commission (FEC) 163, 166; Fair Employment and Treatment Order (1998) 15, 163–4; Fair Employment Tribunal (FET) 163, 165; Good Friday Agreement (1998) 159, 163, 167, 168, 170, 174; higher education 16, 157; Hillsborough Agreement (2010) 168; history and context 155–60; Human Rights Commission 168, 169; human rights protection 155, 157, 161, 163, 166, 168–9, 174; and national/political identity 154, 155–6; paramilitarism 157; and partition 155, 156; Patten Commission/Report 169, 170, 171, 173–4; policing reform 169–72, 173–4, 175–6; political parties 158–60, 170; power-sharing government 158, 167–8; religious communities 154, 155–6 (and fair employment 160–7, 172, 173, 175–6; and policing reform 169–72, 175–6); republican-nationalist community 156; Standing Adisory Commission on Human Rights (SACHR) 161, 163, 166, 168; Sunningdale Agreement (1974) 161; unionist community 156, 157
Northern Ireland Act (1998) 167, 168
Northern Ireland Constitution Act (1973) 158, 161
Northern Ireland Executive 167–8
Nozick, Robert 3

Oberst, R. 5, 16
O'Leary, Brendan 3, 8, 154, 155, 167
opportunity, equality of 63, 161, 162, 168
O'Rawe, Mary 169, 171
Osborne, Bob 166
Ostby, G. 4, 197
outreach programmes, US 50–1

P-E Corporate Services 132
Palmares Cultural Foundation (Fundação Cultural Palmares) 187, 200n7
Palmares, Zumbi dos 187
Parikh, Sunita 5, 6, 7, 8, 12–13, 16, 18, 27–42
Paterson, Owen 171
patronage 9, 17, 45, 66, 90
Patten Commission/Report. Northern Ireland 169, 170, 171, 173–4
Permodalan National Berhad (PNB) 74, 75
Petroliam Nasional (Petronas) 74
Petruccelli, José Luis 190

Index

Phillips, Ann 3
Pienaar, D. 129
Plange, N. 100
Plessey v. *Ferguson* 48
Pojman, Louis P. 3
police force: Fiji 106; Northern Ireland 169–72, 173–4, 175–6
Police Service of Northern Ireland (PSNI) 170, 171, 175–6
policy implementation 4, 10–11
political mobilization 3
political participation 64; India 29
political parties: India 37–8; Malaysia 67; Northern Ireland 158–60, 170; US 45, 48
political representation, India 8, 28, 33
political violence, India 36–8
poverty/poverty reduction 8, 14, 27, 33, 65; Fiji 96, 97, 118, 120, 122; Malaysia 70, 87, 88, 90; South Africa 147; US 49
power-sharing government, Northern Ireland 158, 167–8
Prasad, S. 106
preferential affirmative action 17, 20, 43, 54
Premdas, Ralph 1–26, 43–66
primary education 11, 16, 20, 35, 89
Prince, Simon 157
private property 63
privatization: Fiji 107; Malaysia 76, 89, 90
procurement, South Africa 133–4, 139–40, 142
professional association membership, Malaysia 82, *85*
public sector employment *see* government employment

Qarase, Laisenia 97, 107, 109, 115, 116, 119, 121

Rabuka, Sitiveni 104, 106, 110, 111, 113
Rabuska, A. 4
Rachels, James 6
racial categorisation, South Africa 129
Rantao, Jovial 133–4
Rashid Hussain Bhd 75
Rashtriya Swayamsevak Sangh (RSS) 37
Ratuva, Steven 14, 95–125
Rawls, John 3
Reagan, Ronald 56
recognition of differences 6–7, 64
Regents of California v. *Bakke* (1978) 59–60
religion 7, 8, 19; Brazil 199; US 51, 52, 56, 63
religious communities: Northern Ireland 154, 155–6 (and fair employment 160–7, 172, 173, 175–6; and policing reform 169–72, 175–6); *see also* India, reservation policies
rent-seeking behaviour: Fiji 97; India 41; Malaysia 90; South Africa 144
reservation policies, India: outcomes and consequences of 32–9; scope and range of 28–32
responsibility 64, 65
reverse discrimination 43, 56, 161, 165, 171
Ribeiro, Carlos Antônio Costa 195
Rocha, Carmen Lúcia Antunes 193
Rosa, Fernando 15, 183–203
Rose, Sarah 161
Rosenfeld, Michel 5
Routledge, D. 99
Royal Ulster Constabulary (RUC) 169, 170
Rumney, Reg 135
rural development, Fiji 102–3, 117, 118, 120
rural enterprises 12, 17
Russell, David 163
Rwanda 195–6, 197–8

Sanlam 134
Santos, Ivair Auguto Alves dos 186
Sateras Resources Limited 112
Scarr, D. 98
Schlemmer, Lawrence 146
Schulze, D. 101
Schwartz, Alex 163, 168
secondary education 16, 35, 89
segregation, US 48–9
self-determination 65
Selvaratnam, Viswanathan 78
Sen, Amartya 3
separation of powers, US 47, 48
separatism 4
service sector: Fiji 102; Malaysia 77
Sexwale, Tokyo 133
Shabango, Susan 145
Shamsuddin Kadir 75
Shepsle, K. 4
Sher, George 6, 7
Sheth, D. 7
Shirlow, Peter 154, 172
Shuttleworth, Ian 166
SIA Cash and Carry 112
Silva, Benedita da 188
Silverio, Valter Roberto 192
Simpson, John 146
Singh, V.P. 31, 37

Sinn Féin (SF) 159, 170
Siwatibau, Savenaca 107
Skidmore, Thomas 185
Skrentny, John David 5, 6, 7, 53, 54, 55
slavery: Brazil 184–5; US 48
small and medium-sized enterprises (SMEs) 77, 82
Smith, Anne 168
Smyth, Jim 169
Social Democratic and Labour Party (SDLP), Northern Ireland 159, 160, 170
social mobility, Brazil 195
social welfare, South Africa 14
soft affirmative action programmes 6, 127
Soqosoqo Duavata Lewenivanua (SDL) 115, 116
Soqosoqo ni Vakavulewa ni Taukei (SVT) 106, 110, 113
South Africa 1, 2, 7, 8, 10, 11, 14, 16, 17, 95, 126–53, 199; African National Congress (ANC) 127, 148, 149, 150, 151; apartheid 126; Black Economic Empowerment Act (2003) 135; Black Economic Empowerment (BEE) policy 11, 14, 127, 134–50, 151 (compliance with codes 142; and corruption 148–9, 151; costs and consequences 145–50; and crony capitalism 146, 148, 151; employment equity 138, 142, 147, 150; enterprise development 140, 142; equity ownership 136–8, 142, 143, 145, 147; management control 138, 142; in mining sector 143–5, 147, 148–9; preferential procurement 139–40, 142; and racial goodwill 149–50; skills development 138–9, 142; socio-economic development 140–1, 142; verification agencies 136, 141–2); Black Economic Empowerment Commission (BEECom) 135; Commission for Employment Equity (CEE) 130, 132, 150; Constitution 127; Department of Mineral Resources (DMR) 143, 144; education 127, 128, 139; discrimination 14, 16, 126, 127, 128, 129, 136, 139; employment 138, 142, 147, 150 (government 130–2; private sector 132–3); Employment Equity Act (1998) 14, 128–30, 150, 151; Employment Equity Amendment Bill (2010) 133; enterprise development 11, 12, 17, 134–5, 140, 142; foreign direct investment (FDI) in 147; Government of National Unity 127; healthcare 127; HIV/AIDS 127; housing construction 133; Human Sciences Research Council 150; income inequality 150; infrastructure 131–2, 147; local government 132, 147; majority rule 127; management control 138; middle class 145–6, 149, 150; Mineral and Petroleum Resources Development Act (MPRDA) 2002 143, 144; National Party 149; Population Registration Act (1950); 126, 129; poverty reduction 14, 147; preferential procurement 133–4, 139–40, 142; Public Service Commission 131; racial categorisation 129; rent-seeking behaviour 144; social welfare 14; socio-economic development 140–1; transformation laws 127; transport 131–2; unemployment 127, 147, 150
South Africa Survey 130, 138, 139, 147, 150
South African Institute of Race Relations 147, 149
South African National Accreditation System (Sanas) 141
South Pacific Textile (Fiji) Ltd 112
Sowell, Thomas 5, 16, 61, 95, 128
Spate, O.H.K. 99, 102
spatial inequality 12, 16, 33, 34–5, 89
Sports Toto 76
Sri Lanka 198, 199
Staats, Elmer 55
Stanmore, Lord (Arthur Gordon) 98–9
Stavenhaegn, Rodolfo 3
Steelworkers v. *Weber* 58
Sterba, James 6, 7, 16
Stewart, Frances 4, 96, 197, 198
Strachan, B. 5, 16
structural adjustment policies (SAP), Fiji 103
Sturm, Susan 9
sugar industry, Fiji 100, 102, 103
Sukuna, Ratu Sir Lala 98
Sutherland, W. 100

Tajfel, Henry 3
targeting 17, 18
Tarling, Nicholas 5
taxi business, Fiji 109, 111
Taylor, Charles 6
Taylor, Donald M. 3
Television New Zealand (TVNZ) 109
Tesco 77
tourism industry, Fiji 101–2, 112

Traditional Unionist Voice (TUV), Northern Ireland 159
training 6; Black Economic Empowerment (BEE) policy 138–9
transport, South Africa 131–2
Twyford, I. 101

Ulster Defence Association 157
Ulster Unionist Party (UUP) 159, 160
Ulster Volunteer Force 157
unemployment: Fiji 104, 118; Malaysia 80, 81, 88; South Africa 127, 147, 150
Unified Black Movement (Movimento Neghro Unificado) 186
Unilever Institute (University of Cape Town) 145, 146
United Malays' National Organization (UMNO) 67, 69, 90
United States of America (USA) 2, 7, 8, 10, 13, 19, 43–66, 95, 196, 198; African-Americans 10, 13, 43, 44, 46, 49, 50, 52, 58, 60–1, 61–2; Asian immigrants 61; Bill of Rights 47; Black Power Movement 49, 53; *Brown v. The Board of Education* (1954) 49; Civil Rights Act (1964) 43, 49, 51, 52, 53, 54, 56–7, 59, 60; Civil Rights Act (1991) 56, 59; civil rights movement 49, 50, 60; Civil Service Reform Act (1978) 56; Congress 48; Constitution 47; discrimination 43, 46, 47, 48, 49, 50, 51, 52–3, 54, 55, 56–7, 58–9, 64; disparate impact, doctrine of 59; due process and equal protection clause 57; employment 45, 49–53, 54, 55–6, 58–9, 61–2; Equal Employment Opportunity Act (1972) 56; Equal Employment Opportunity Commission (EEOC) 52–3; federal system 47–8; *Fullilove v. Klutznick* 61; Government Accountability Office (GAO) 55; *Griggs v. Duke Power Company* (1971) 58, 59; *Grutter v. Bollinger* 60; higher education 13, 49, 59–60; immigration issues 45, 60–2; Immigration and Nationality Act (1965) 60; Jim Crow laws 48; *Johnson v. Santa Clara* 58; judicial review 47, 48; Kerner Report 54; legal and constitutional challenges to affirmative action 56–60; National Association for the Advancement of Colored people (NAACP) 50; Native Americans 10, 55, 61; Office of Federal Contract Compliance Programs (OFCCP) 50, 55; outreach programmes 50–1; Philadelphia Plan 55, 61; *Plessey v. Ferguson* 48; political parties 45, 48; poverty 49; presidential executive orders 50, 53, 55, 56; President's Committee on Equal Employment Opportunity (PCEEO) 50, 51, 52, 53; *Regents of California v. Bakke* (1978) 59–60; separate but equal doctrine 48–9; separation of powers 47, 48; slavery 48; Small Business Administration (SBA) 61; states' rights 47, 48; *Steelworkers v. Weber* 58; Supreme Court 57, 58, 60, 61; *Wards Cove Packing Co. v. Antonio* (1989) 59
Universidade de Brasilia (UNB) 189, 195
Universidade Estadual do Rio de Janeriro (UERJ) 188–9, 195
university education *see* higher (tertiary) education

van Rensburg, Nick 140
van Straubenzee Report (1973) 162
Varshney, A. 3, 19
vertical inequality 4, 97, 197–9
vertically-based policies 4
victimology, ideology of 10, 66
Vishva Hindu Parishad (VHP) 37

Walzer, Michael 3, 62
Wards Cove Packing Co. v. Antonio (1989) 59
Weisskopf, T.E. 5, 6, 7, 8, 16
Westen, Peter 3
Westmoreland, R. 3
White, Ciaran 156
Wibbels, E. 18
Wilkinson, Steven I. 37
Wirtz, Willard 55
women 43, 44, 46, 50, 53, 56; black 130, 138; police officers, Northern Ireland 172
World Bank 103
World Conference Against Racism, Racial Discrimination, Xenophobia and Related Intolerance (2001) 115
Wright, A. 101

Yacob, Shakila 13, 67–94
Yasana Holdings Limited (YHL) 109
Yasuda, Nobuyuki 76
Young, Crawford 3, 5
Young, Iris Marion 3, 6, 9, 65

Zuma, Jacob 148, 151

Taylor & Francis
eBooks
FOR LIBRARIES

ORDER YOUR FREE 30 DAY INSTITUTIONAL TRIAL TODAY!

Over 23,000 eBook titles in the Humanities, Social Sciences, STM and Law from some of the world's leading imprints.

Choose from a range of subject packages or create your own!

Benefits for **you**
- Free MARC records
- COUNTER-compliant usage statistics
- Flexible purchase and pricing options

Benefits for your **user**
- Off-site, anytime access via Athens or referring URL
- Print or copy pages or chapters
- Full content search
- Bookmark, highlight and annotate text
- Access to thousands of pages of quality research at the click of a button

For more information, pricing enquiries or to order a free trial, contact your local online sales team.

UK and Rest of World: online.sales@tandf.co.uk
US, Canada and Latin America:
e-reference@taylorandfrancis.com

www.ebooksubscriptions.com

Taylor & Francis eBooks
Taylor & Francis Group

A flexible and dynamic resource for teaching, learning and research.